john brown to james brown

THE LITTLE FARM WHERE LIBERTY BUDDED, BLOSSOMED AND BOOGIED

BY ED MALISKAS

HAMILTON RUN
PRESS

PUBLISHED BY HAMILTON RUN PRESS
11736 Patrick Road
Hagerstown, MD 21742

John Brown to James Brown
The Little Farm Where Liberty Budded, Blossomed and Boogied

To learn more about Ed Maliskas and John Brown's Farm, visit
www.johnbrownsfarm.com

Library of Congress Control Number: 2016911819
History: United States/Music

Hardcover
ISBN-10: 0-9976772-0-1
ISBN-13: 978-0-9976772-0-1

Paperback
ISBN-10: 0-9976772-1-8
ISBN-13: 978-0-9976772-1-8

First Edition
10 9 8 7 6 5 4 3 2 1

Cover illustration by Will Carpenter
Cover design by Kate Rader

Published and printed in the United States of America

DEDICATION

This book is dedicated to those nurturing communities that made John Brown's Farm the wonderland that it was: black families, churches, and fraternal organizations. May America and the world benefit, and benefit once again, from your special love for, and distinctive expressions of, liberty and community.

PREFACE

It was one of the strangest sentences I had ever heard: "You would have loved the music scene at John Brown's Farm." John Brown, the abolitionist? He had a farm? And what does that have to do with music?

The answers to those and other questions popped open a fascinating story of how one little plot of land became arguably the geographic heart of racial freedom in America. Here's how the adventure began.

My wife Judi and I had lived in Miami, Florida, for twenty years. There are basically only two seasons in Miami: summer and mid-summer. Therefore, we had only warm-weather clothing: cotton, loose-fitting, short sleeves, sandals — whatever let in a little breeze was a good thing.

We moved north to Hagerstown, Maryland, in mid-winter and thus were in lively need of a new wardrobe. We discovered L&L Classic Clothing, a women's consignment store. While Judi explored, I chatted with the owner's brother-in-law, Wendell Greene, who was minding the shop.

A radio was on in the background playing oldies. I remarked during a Temptations tune that I had been in a soul band back in the late 1960s and that that song had been in our repertoire. A few minutes later the radio station played a James Brown number. Our band, Eddie and the Sensations, had played that one, too.

That's when Mr. Greene made that strange statement: "You would have loved the music scene at John Brown's Farm." Explain, please. The John Brown in view was indeed the abolitionist. So, why was this place called his "farm"? Wendell wasn't quite sure. Where was it located? Maybe fifteen miles south of Hagerstown. Okay, and what about the music? They had rhythm and blues artists there. Then it wasn't during the Civil War? No, it was in the 1950s and 1960s.

Were these rhythm and blues artists anybody I would have heard of? I should say so. Ray Charles, James Brown, Ike and Tina Tuner, and others.

Turns out that the "others" included Chuck Berry, Little Richard, Chubby Checker, the Drifters, Aretha Franklin, Fats Domino, Marvin Gaye, the Coasters, and scores more — the giants of R&B.

I was ridiculously interested from that moment on. Apparently this John Brown's Farm was a barn, or perhaps an auditorium, where they had these big dances out in the middle of pretty much nowhere. Wendell had been there several times before he went into the United States Army in 1958. The dances were still going on when he got back, but his first-hand knowledge from that point on was limited.

Well, now I had a bunch more questions, but by then Judi was finished shopping. I was confident that I would get those questions answered when I got home and searched the Internet. Nothing. Local library? Nothing. What did the local newspaper know about it? Nothing.

I was relieved to find Wendell again at the consignment shop the next time we visited. I explained to him that I had been unable to find out anything about the (imaginary?) music scene at this (supposed?) John Brown's Farm.

His sister-in-law, Lola (Burnett) Mosby was in the store this time. She told us a charming story about the time she and her twin sister Lela (Wendell's future wife) got caught "sneaking" down to John Brown's Farm (Okay, I guess there is something to this, after all).

As my wife can amply attest, those early conversations started me on a multi-year tactic of approaching just about any African-American with even a hint of gray in his or her hair. "Um, excuse me. Would you happen to know anything about the music scene at John Brown's Farm?" Thankfully, several of the first people I approached did. Otherwise, I might have quit.

I persisted, however, and unearthed enough tidbits and followed enough leads to recognize that there was a marvelous story here — one that had lain dormant for decades. The farm property that Wendell referenced had housed John Brown in his preparation for the daring raid that touched off the Civil War. The very same site a century later had hosted the biggest stars of rhythm and blues.

Serendipitously, the 150th anniversary of John Brown's raid on the federal arsenal at Harpers Ferry was approaching. There were major observances scheduled throughout the region attendant to that history-altering event.

On a whim I visited the local newspaper, *The Herald-Mail,* to share the general outline of the story and to ask, if the story were well-written, might they be willing to print it. Chris Copley, Assistant Lifestyle Editor, assured me of that possibility, and we stayed in touch over the course of the next several months.

As a pastor, I had written about a thousand sermons and a doctoral dissertation, but this was a new challenge that included primary research, a different writing style, and a different audience. Our son Joel (a journalism major at the time) was with us for the summer, so he and I collaborated. About six weeks before the sesquicentennial date of October 16–18, 2009, I turned in our fifteen-hundred-word article and waited for notice of the publication date. And waited.

I called Chris Copley to badger him that the sesquicentennial was fast upon us and that the story would have less poignancy after that. And then I waited some more. Finally, Chris called to say that the article would be in the October 10, 2009 edition. Whew! But why the suspense?

Chris confided sheepishly that the newspaper had been disinclined to publish the story. Why? Because they didn't believe it. They had checked all their sources, formal and informal, and for a long time could find nary a shred of evidence for it.

And that is part of what makes this story so cool. It is kind of unbelievable. The biggest music stars in the world were playing virtually "down the block" and nobody had heard anything of it? Well, a lot of people had. It's just that the people who did know about it (black people) had never told the people who put stuff in the local newspapers (white people).

The positive reception of the article gave me the oomph I needed to keep going. As one thread of information led to another, I found that the story was even more engaging and extensive than I had imagined.

I soon came to the sad realization, however, that if someone had pursued this story even five years earlier, then the principal figures would still have been alive. Those half-dozen or so persons could have each filled a book with their knowledge of the music scene at John Brown's Farm. Accordingly, I have come to appreciate how quickly the history of even recent events can be lost. Letters, photographs, posters, diaries, and reminiscences that might have been preserved would have been of enormous value.

On the positive side, someone with the time and inclination would have the opportunity, and even a sense of solemn responsibility, to sniff out the increasingly faint scent of this story. And I guess that's where I realized that I was in for the long haul. Oral history, here we come!

I have marveled repeatedly that if Wendell Greene had not broached this story during that first conversation in the consignment shop, most likely I would not have heard of it to this day. Certainly no one has ever brought it up to me out of the blue.

That being said, the investigative process has been a delight. I conducted well over a hundred interviews with charitable strangers, mostly older African Americans, who graciously shared with me what they knew — and remembered. Two separate things. The interviewees have my deepest gratitude for their information and kindness.

I also have come to better appreciate God's sovereignty across the course of my life. As an undergraduate student at the University of Illinois, I was two things: a fair musician in an inter-racial soul band and a lousy history major. And a third thing: a sinner.

My acute awareness of having something inherently wrong with me at the moral core of my being eventually provoked me to call out to God for forgiveness and spiritual restoration, which he graciously provided in the person of Jesus Christ. Subsequently, I matriculated at Gordon-Conwell Theological Seminary north of Boston where I met my wonderful wife.

A few years later, we moved to South Florida where for twenty years I served as pastor at Southwest Alliance Church in Miami. There, we raised our two wonderful sons, Micah and Joel. Judi and I moved to Western Maryland in late January, 2008, to help a ministry buddy with his church in Williamsport, thus the need for cold weather clothing and the trip to the consignment shop and the story about John Brown's Farm.

The music and history components of my life put me in a fortuitous position to recognize and appreciate the hundreds of musical and historical connections embedded in this story. Plucking those yarns and knitting them together has been an utter joy. I cannot tell you how many times I have been in the midst of tracking down some murky detail or far-fetched connection when I blurted out loud, "Man, I love this stuff!"

In the course of research I quickly learned how John Brown got to the farm. But I also wanted to know how there came to be dances there. How did so many top-flight musicians appear there to perform? Who were the people who went to the dances? Where did they come from? How did they get there? Who owned the place? Who orchestrated the daily details?

The more I probed, the more thrilled I was to discover the historical connectedness and symmetry of this parcel of land which hosted John Brown in 1859, and James Brown in 1959.

Implausible as it sounds, the reason that James Brown performed on that property has everything to do with W. E. B. Du Bois, and with a black fraternal organization that valued Du Bois's perspective on surely the most polarizing figure in American history. It had to do with a black property manager ideally suited to work in the midst of a white rural hinterland, and with a Charles Town, West Virginia, entrepreneur who had connections to a segregated beach in Annapolis, Maryland.

The story also has to do with young people from a hundred black communities, with an emerging American youth culture that was tired of music that sounded like it was tired of itself, and with the Chitlin' Circuit, where an ethnic musical style was being perfected toward its fast becoming America's popular music.

I love this story in large part because of its intricacy, but if I had to boil the essence of the book down to one simple word, it would be "liberty." I hope the reader will appreciate along with me the stories of an amazing assortment of aspirations that converged to create the special experience of liberty that was the music scene at John Brown's Farm.

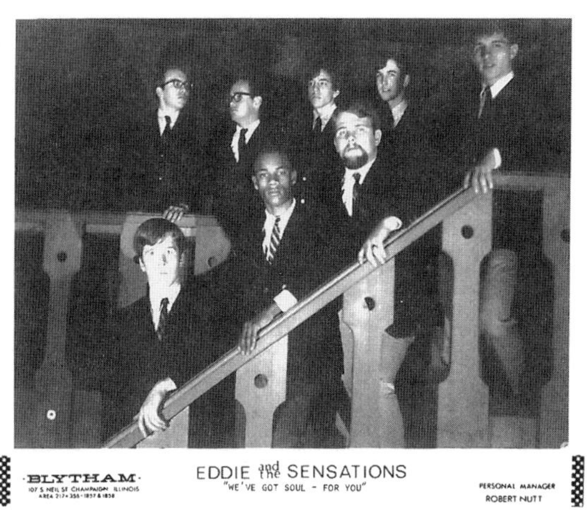

The author, upper right, was the musical leader of the soul band "Eddie and the Sensations." The group was popular in the late 1960s in and around Champaign, Illinois, and came to be managed by future music impresario Irving Azoff.

INTRODUCTION

When you think of "civil rights" in the United States, what *locations* come to mind?

The steps of the Lincoln Memorial where Dr. Martin Luther King, Jr. gave his "I Have a Dream" speech? The segregated Woolworth's lunch counter in Greensboro, North Carolina? The Edmund Pettus Bridge in Selma, Alabama? Would it be Montgomery, Alabama, where Rosa Parks refused to move to the back of the bus? Perhaps the Supreme Court Building where the 1954 Brown vs. the Board of Education decision was handed down, or the balcony of the Lorraine Motel in Memphis, Tennessee, where Dr. King was assassinated?

I have a location in mind that should be considered at least the equal of any of the above. From that place came the spark that ignited the Civil War and ended racial slavery. The same property was owned by the Improved Benevolent and Protective Order of Elks of the World (the "IBPOEW" or "Black Elks") at the height of its organizational and political power. Additionally, it was a beloved venue on the Chitlin' Circuit at the time when rhythm and blues synergized into America's popular music. That place is John Brown's Farm in southern Washington County, Maryland.

This book is about how one remote chunk of second-rate farmland became in three instances a place instrumental to racial equality in America. In these pages you will meet risk-takers, artists, a fanatic or two, and lots of everyday people pursuing happiness in both the constitutional and psychological senses of the word.

Table of Contents

PART I: THE PAST

An Unforgettable Experience 17
A Yearning for Liberty 23
A Property Destined for Significance 29
Awakening of an Abolitionist 33
Kansas, Bloody Kansas 45
Clandestine Activities 53
The Inevitable Draws Near 59
The Raid on Harpers Ferry 67
Map of John Brown's Farm 74
The Ownership of the Farm Property From 1859–1950 75
Development and Use of the John Brown Farm by the IBPOEW 89
The Neighborhood and Neighbors of John Brown's Farm 101
Maynard Henderson 105
Rumbles in the Distance 117
A New Era for John Brown's Farm 125

PART II: THE PARTICIPANTS

The Man Behind the Music at John Brown's Farm 141
Behind the Scenes 149
Getting There Was Half the Fun! 161
Experiencing John Brown's Farm 177
Map of the Auditorium/Dance Hall 178
Dancing the Night Away 193
Seeing Stars 199
The Memories Live On 205

PART III: THE PERFORMERS

The Artists Who Played at John Brown's Farm 215

Bibliography 288
Endnotes 288

{PART I}

The Past

An Unforgettable Experience

SATURDAY, JUNE 27, 1959. CHARLES TOWN, WEST VIRGINIA.

Beep-beep! Sylvia, a cute black nineteen-year-old finishes ironing her brand new blouse. Beep! Ba-beep-beeeep! She quickly buttons up, braces her palms on the window sill, and leans out from her upstairs bedroom. On the street below her cousin Bobby stands next to his newly re-painted 1951 Ford F1 pickup.

"Syl, you coming tonight or not?!"

"Of course, I'm coming. We're supposed to meet up at Fisherman's Hall at eight o'clock, right?"

"Sylvia, it's ten after eight now! Everybody else done gone!"

"Omigosh," yelps Sylvia in a panic. She scurries down the stairs, snatches her sweater off the handrail, and bolts toward the front door.

"Young lady!" booms her mother from the kitchen. Sylvia skids to a halt. "Who's driving?"

"Cousin Bobby."

"All right, then. But tell him to get you home by 11:30."

"But mama, tonight is special!"

"That's what you always say!"

Young party-goers traveled up the lane in the foreground between the renovated barn on the left and the old farmhouse on the right, then into the auditorium to dance the night away.

"But it always is!"

"Suit yourself," intervenes her father, "but I'm waking you up early for Sunday School—and breakfast before that!"

Sylvia hops into the cab of the waiting pickup and scrunches next to her cousin Mary. In the truck bed perched on orange crates are Sylvia's older brother Reginald and his pal Freddy, a handsome soldier home on leave. The two men in the back nearly topple over as Bobby steps on the gas and heads toward "the new bridge" at Harpers Ferry.

The windows are rolled down on this warm summer evening as the quintet snakes its way up little Sandy Hook Road hard by the Potomac River. Bobby had been miffed at missing the convoy of vehicles leaving Charles Town, but now can't help but lighten up as Sylvia and Mary clown and sing along with the radio.

This aerial photograph of the John Brown Farm from c. 1970 shows IBPOEW cabins in the upper left-hand corner and far right, as well as the since-demolished home of caretaker Maynard Henderson at the upper right-hand corner of the auditorium.

The IBPOEW insignia in the center of the dance floor withstood the ravages of time remarkably well.

Meanwhile, the guys in the back squint to make sense of the little map that a friend had scribbled out. The sun is about to set and finding this place is notoriously difficult in the dark. Rumor has it that the KKK is active in these backwoodsy boondocks. Sylvia is quietly getting the creeps thinking about what might happen if they get a flat tire. Her aunt Betty once had a flat tire late at night on a little road outside Sharpsburg, and just as she bent down to reach into the glove box...

Bam! Sylvia screams at the sharp rap on the back window and giggles in relief as Reginald yells over the road noise, "I think we are supposed to take this here road to the right." (Does this intersection look familiar? Does anybody recognize that barn?)

Lola and Lela Burnett

Lola (Burnett) Mosby and her twin sister, Lela (Burnett) Greene, came from a large Hagerstown family whose children shared many chores. Ironing clothes was not among them, however. Their mother always took care of that task – until one Easter Sunday night.

That was the time when the then-eighteen-year-old twins told their mom that they were going down to a local juke joint (called Kent's) for the evening. Instead, they met up with a group of young people who slipped down to John Brown's Farm for a fun night of dancing and socializing.

When they came home late past family curfew, their irritated mother ferreted out their lack of full disclosure concerning their previous whereabouts. Lola and Lela spent all of the next day and into the evening ironing mounds of clothes – with lots of crying. Their mother's unsympathetic and still-irritated reasoning was, "If you're old enough to go down there to John Brown's Farm, you're old enough to iron your own clothes!"

Hagerstown twins Lola and Lela Burnett sport matching dresses and pineapple curls. Photo courtesy of Lola Mosby.

Right then they get a major clue that they are indeed on the correct route. Gunning up behind them in a drop top Coupe de Ville is a hip cat from Baltimore with processed hair and his uptown-looking girlfriend. Mary scolds playfully, "Stop staring, cousin. They'll think we're country!"

Sylvia laughs, "Us here riding in this pickup truck? Girl, they already know we're not from Manhattan!"

Three hundreds yards up ahead, one vehicle after another is turning off the main road onto a gravel lane. "This is it! We're here!" From the north come license plates from Pennsylvania and Maryland. From the south are tags from Virginia, West Virginia, and the District of Columbia.

A gap in the white picket fence beckons the motorists to slip under and through the 14 foot high archway. Bobby brakes to a stop at a little booth halfway up the lane and is greeted pleasantly, "How many of you tonight?"

"Five," he answers.

"That'll be fifteen dollars. Have a good time."

Mary leans across Sylvia to cackle to the ticket-taker, "Oh, you know we will!"

Straight ahead the amber sun is setting behind a grove of trees silhouetted at the top of the hill. Bobby guides his cherry red F1 past the auditorium and up the rise to find a place to park. A couple of guys leaning against a gray Studebaker are checking out Bobby's paint job, but Sylvia is checking out the people and what they are wearing.

Off to the right stand three sharps from Frederick outfitted in snazzy suits, ties, and alligator shoes. Twin girls from Hagerstown are looking fine in their matching summer sheaths, and with their hair all done up! "Good thing I didn't dress down tonight!" thinks Sylvia.

As she and her group walk toward the dance hall, they tread oh-so-carefully around the plops of cow manure scattered here and there in the field. They are close enough now to hear rhythmic throbs resonating from inside the low-lying block building. A bootlegger discreetly slips open his jacket to exhibit his wares. "Maybe later," Bobby says smoothly as they pass on.

Up ahead, a black sheriff's deputy keeps things commotion-less as he patrols the grounds with his leashed German Shepherd. Reginald warns, "Girls, stay clear of that dog. He means business."

"Here, Sylvia," says handsome Freddy as he extends his elbow. "You better walk next to me."

With her free hand Sylvia gestures across the property to several girls she knows from attending Page-Jackson High School. You can just bet they're asking, "Who's that handsome guy Sylvia is with?" A nice young man from Winchester, Virginia, that Sylvia danced with last summer winks in playful recognition as they all join the line at the center door.

Once inside, Sylvia's eyes adjust to see the room filled with hipsters making the scene. A mirrored ball hangs from the ceiling directly above the Elks' insignia regnant in the center of the dance floor. The auditorium is packed with partiers doing dances she already knows like the Bop, the Hully Gully, and the Madison. And there will be some moves she has never seen before because the best dancers bring something fresh every week.

Chairs and tables ring the outside of the rectangular room where clusters of young people talk, laugh, and line up dance partners. No wallflowers here! Several bartenders man the long, ornate bar, hustling to keep pace serving beer and "set-ups" to folks eager to spend their hard-earned coin.

In the far right corner of the room, an electrifying young entertainer dominates the event. He is on stage with his vocal group, the Famous Flames. The instrumentalists, studded with pioneering rhythm and blues musicians from Little Richard's former band, are laying down a funky groove.

The singer's fancy footwork testifies that he once was an accomplished boxer. His sweat-drenched face gives credence to the claim that he is the hardest working man in show business. His rough and earnest voice squeezes out the lyrics to an up-tempo jam that he and the Flames are soon to record: "If you leave me (leave me), I'll go crazy (oh yes)."

Sylvia peers over the top of the crowded dance floor that sways in exuberant motion. The bodies part just enough for her to see James Brown twirl, drop down into the splits, and pop back up again. The crowd howls in delight. The good times are rolling tonight at John Brown's Farm!

***

On hundreds of such occasions, young people thronged to John Brown's Farm to enjoy the rich experience and liberating atmosphere. Highlight events included the Fourth of July weekend of 1954 when three thousand souls crowded onto the property for a three-day celebration. On Labor Day of 1965 more than a thousand merry-makers traveled there to relax, celebrate, and dance to James Brown and his entourage playing "Papa's Got a Brand New Bag" and "I Got You (I Feel Good)."

Summer after summer the auditorium's block walls and tiled floor reverberated with the piano riffs of Ray Charles, the shouts of the Isley Brothers, the high heels of Tina Turner, the tongue-trills of Billy Stewart, the doo-wops of the Orioles, and the shrieks of James Brown.

Then one day the music stopped. The echoes faded. And winter set in.

Within months the property was sold and later sold again. Years passed: twenty, thirty, forty. Today, that once vibrant auditorium has become a dilapidated old hulk looming behind the authentically restored farmhouse.

The former dance hall's windows have been boarded. Its doors slouch on their hinges. There has been a fire. You can barely make out the faded IBPOEW insignia on the badly chipped floor. The glass ball still hangs overhead, but badly tattered. There are holes in the roof and mold in the walls. Lots of mold.

Each passing year left behind fewer people who knew those vivacious days at John Brown's Farm. Those who once knew have forgotten some things. Some of those who once knew have forgotten everything. Somebody ought to do something before everybody forgets everything.

"Excuse me, ma'am. My name is Ed. I am researching a story."

"Pleased to meet you, Ed. My name is Sylvia. What can I do for you?"

"Well, would you happen to know anything about the music scene at John Brown's Farm?"

"John Brown's Farm? Oh, that was the place!"

The auditorium that once hosted the giants of rhythm and blues displays the low-point of its dilapidation. Recent repairs make it hopeful that the site will soon welcome fans of black history. Photo by Winston Pitman.

A Yearning for Liberty

On hundreds of occasions, I had the nervous joy of soliciting perfect strangers with my question about John Brown's Farm. Their initial reactions were often a few seconds spent scanning mental archives, then faces lighting up, as if remembering having seen a miracle, and seconds later cheerfully saying something like, "It was a hey-day!" or "John Brown's Farm was always joyful" or "It was just a great place to go."

What made this place so special? The next several hundred pages explain it more fully, but, as noted earlier, it boils down to that one word, liberty. That sense of liberty experienced by the attendees of those events at John Brown's Farm is the underpinning, fulcrum, and pinnacle of this story.

Liberty was cherished by the framers of America's Constitution as an absolute value and a gift from God—a fundamental motivation and an ultimate

This 1940 photograph of the bus station in Durham, North Carolina, by Jack Delano (public domain) gives us a glimpse into the bad old days of segregation.

purpose. The Bible declares almost tautologically, "It is for freedom that Christ set us free." In the movie *Braveheart,* William Wallace exhorts his countrymen to fight in defiance of tyranny in crying out, "They may take our lives, but they will never take our freedom!"

That universal yearning for liberty quivered in the heart of John Brown, rippled through the honor given him by the IBPOEW, and soared in the experience of those young dancers at the little farm bearing his name.

The exhilaration felt by those young people was magnified because of the contrasting oppression that they experienced all too often on a daily basis. The several authors of "African Americans of Jefferson County" noted that when young African Americans traveled outside of their nurturing local communities, it was then that "they had to deal with racism and segregation."

Those twin evils can be examined by using the geographical location of John Brown's Farm as a template for deepening our sensitivity. The farm is located in a peculiar position concerning the Civil War. Take a moment to appreciate that the property is situated in western Maryland—a slaveholding state that did not secede from the Union.

From JBF northward, it is twenty miles to Pennsylvania, a non-slaveholding Union state. It sits about four miles northwest of Virginia, a Confederate state, and it is but a mile from the farm to West Virginia. West Virginia seceded from Virginia, a Confederate state, during the Civil War, but the new state continued to harbor slavery (mostly in the southern counties) until the adoption of the Thirteenth Amendment in 1865.

What effect did that diversity of ensuing social systems continue to have on race relations continuing into the mid-twentieth century? Let's take a moment to contrast the demographic histories of the county seats of two contiguous counties in the mid-1950s—Hagerstown in Washington County, Maryland, and Charles Town in Jefferson County, West Virginia.

Perhaps you have heard the adage concerning the difference between racism in the North and in the South. It is said that, in the North, whites' traditional attitude toward blacks has been, "You can get high, but don't get too close," whereas in the South the attitude has been, "You can get close, but don't get too high." ("Close" meaning where you live and how you conduct your "personal space"; "high" connoting a supposed loftiness in attitude, attainment, or display.)

Although Maryland is technically south of the Mason-Dixon line, the prevalent white attitude toward race relations was more Northern—don't get too

Willie Mays

Willie Mays (b. 1931), a professional baseball player from the time he was barely old enough to shave, had been getting paid since age fifteen to play for the venerable Birmingham Black Barons in the Negro American League. On the day that he graduated from high school, he was signed to Major League Baseball's New York Giants by Ed Montague for a fifteen thousand dollar bonus.

Tim Kurkjian of ESPN described Willie Mays as "the greatest combination of power, speed and defense in baseball history."

Mays was assigned to the club's Trenton affiliate in the Class B Interstate League, the first black player in that league. The Giants placed him there because Trenton was geographically close to New York and because only one team in the league lay south of the Mason-Dixon line—the Hagerstown Braves.

Mays arrived by train into Hagerstown just in time to suit up for his very first game. Although he did not play that day, racist rumbles echoed through the crowd. After the game he and his white teammates got on the bus to go to the hotel. "Hotels" plural in this case. Before the rest of the team continued on to the whites-only Alexander Hotel on the town square, Mays was dropped off at the black-owned Harmon Hotel on Jonathan Street.

Mays had experienced racism in the past but never before had been separated from teammates on the road overnight. He was alone in a new circumstance in a strange town—understandably uneasy. While Mays was sleeping, he heard a thump on his upper-story window.

Three of his new teammates were on the fire escape and concerned for his well-being. Although Mays insisted that it was unnecessary, his new teammates Hank Rowland, Herb Perelto, and Bob Easterwood slept the night on the floor of his room.

The following day, June 24, 1950, the young center-fielder, barely turned nineteen, took the field as the first black professional to play in Hagerstown's Municipal Stadium. As he stepped out of the dugout, the harassment began immediately. Mays heard someone shouting, "Who's that nigger walking on the field?!" Throughout the game Mays endured merciless name-calling and booing.

Mays endured the abuse, was called up the following year to the "big club," and became the 1951 National League Rookie of the Year. He went on to a splendid career. He and Hank Aaron are the only players in history to finish their careers with over six hundred home runs, three thousand hits, and a .300 batting average.

Despite those successes, the taunts Willie Mays received in Hagerstown rang in his ears for decades. He spoke of it repeatedly. To Hagerstown's belated credit, Mays was honored there with appropriate apologies on July 17, 2005, helping to salve a fifty-five-year-old wound on the Hall-of-Famer's heart.

close. The black neighborhood in Hagerstown, for instance, was a tight rectangle outside which blacks in, say, 1955 ventured at their peril after dark (as I was told by local blacks and whites), except on cold evenings to glean coal from the nearby rail yard. Charles Town in West Virginia had more of a Southern ethos. There wasn't just one black neighborhood, but several that meandered here and there.

Another difference between Hagerstown and Charles Town in the 1950s was the ethnic ratio. Charles Town was nearly 30 percent black, while Hagerstown was less than 5 percent. Still another dissimilarity was the years in which their public schools were desegregated.

In Hagerstown, integration began soon after the Supreme Court's 1954 Brown vs. the Board of Education decision. A bi-racial committee there designated the 1955–1956 school year to be "a period of transition" in which the formerly all-white Hagerstown High and the formerly all-black North Street School were open to both races. Following that school year, North Street School was closed and the construction of a new high school was completed, which thereby created today's two integrated high schools, South Hagerstown and North Hagerstown.

In Charles Town, desegregation took longer. Ten years longer.

Thus, young people attending John Brown's Farm went there with different Monday through Friday realities concerning black-white sociology and interaction. In light of that generalization, here are some observations by JBF attendees that illustrate the diversity of backgrounds and how some of that played out at the dances.

Charles Town native Al Baylor summarized his sentiments about the importance of what went on sociologically at John Brown's Farm by saying, "No one can not be grateful about that period. It was a period of fellowship, of coming together."

Baylor expanded his reflections to provide a flavor of race relations in Charles Town during the JBF era of 1950–1965. "Outside of some work friendships, there was no socializing between blacks and whites. Separate spheres. There was no animosity; everybody 'knew their place' and it was no big deal. Restaurants were not integrated, but if you wanted a sandwich or something from a white restaurant, you could go around to the back door, and they'd serve it up to you."

Baylor on Hagerstown—"To us Hagerstown was 'the big city.' Some of the Hagerstown guys had white girlfriends. They were too big for us even to play them in football, but when they came down for a basketball game, they just tore us up."

One of those Hagerstown hoopsters was Joseph "Junior" Henderson. He was the leading scorer at North Hagerstown High School for the 1961–'62 season. During my interview with him he would occasionally gesture widely. In so doing he would display a broad wingspan extending from his six-foot-two-inch frame (well, maybe a little less now than in his playing days).

Henderson had his own cross-cultural experience just going to visit his rural kinfolk. His family has its roots just outside tiny Burkittsville, Maryland, a bit closer to Charles Town than to Hagerstown.

Junior's grandmother was his Uncle Maynard's mother, Mary Henderson. Junior described her as "so light-skinned that she could 'pass.'" She was always glad to see him and would cook ahead of time foods he especially liked so as to delight him upon his arrival. "She would fatten me up a little first, then she would take me farther up the hill to visit friends and relatives living back up there in shacks." As he put it, "They were country—barefootin' all summer."

Al Baylor's and Junior Henderson's experiences illustrate that young blacks from within even a twenty-five mile radius of JBF came from diverse circumstances. They came from small cities, large towns, villages, and rural areas. They came from integrated and segregated high schools. They came from various economic backgrounds and family situations, but they were united in their experience of John Brown's Farm.

John Brown's Farm was arguably the one place they could venture beyond their communities and not have to deal with the wearying aspects of racial prejudice, especially in contrast to the vestiges of the odious Jim Crow laws. As one anonymous interviewee put it, compared to the constricting prejudice he felt in Hagerstown, "There was no law down there." Rather, it was a place of liberty.

A VIRTUAL "SECRET GARDEN"

When I asked Hagerstown's Reginald Johnson what he would typically do at John Brown's Farm, he paused before replying wistfully about that liberty, "Whatever I felt like doing, I guess. It was just a great place to go."

Diane Puller-Williams of Charles Town ratcheted up her description, "It was an exciting atmosphere. Everybody was very loving, and just couldn't wait to just get in there to dance and just have a great time." Reginald Johnson brightened up to flip that notion around and exclaim, "We hated the place to close each Saturday night because you had to wait a whole week!"

Ruth McDaniel, an attendee from Charles Town, West Virginia, verbalized a similar sentiment in gleaming, "John Brown's Farm was such a fun place to go, a place where you felt so happy, and once you got over there you didn't want to leave. You didn't want the night to end, because everybody was just having fun."

Acquaintances from the various black communities re-engaged their existing friendships or made new ones. Gal pals Rose Williams and Edwina Mason of Millwood, Virginia, made lots of new pals from the various geographic areas. "We would look for them the next week—some remain friends to this day."

Some friendships became romantic. Ruby Turner from Upperville, Virginia, and Barry Burns from Charles Town, West Virginia, met at John Brown's Farm, fell in love, and got married.

Senator Joanne C. Benson is a Maryland State Senator representing Prince George's County, Maryland, near Washington, D.C. She is a native of Hagerstown and the daughter of Rev. William Claybon. As a young woman she attended the dances at John Brown's Farm. During our phone interview, which she so graciously granted, Senator Benson glowed recalling her time at JBF.

"Some of the most enjoyable moments I ever had were at John Brown's Farm. All of us African-Americans looked forward to going to John Brown's Farm. It was more than a dance hall; it was a gathering place. The churches often would get together to take the children down there for picnics. On the weekends, it was the only place that we could go and have a wonderful time. We would all get in the cars and find our way to John Brown's Farm."

She paused to lament, "The thing that saddens my soul in comparison to those wonderful days is the deterioration of the black community. Now there are so few eyes on the prize; so few fingers on the pulse."

She brightened as she spoke again of that halcyon era, "The thought of John Brown's Farm, even today, excites me. It was a wonderful atmosphere of camaraderie. There was a certain respect, a decorum, there. It was a village, a refuge, a family."

Reginald Johnson gave ultimate respect to JBF event-organizer John Bishop for his premier role in the near-utopian phenomenon by saying, "To do what he did in bringing those artists to a little place like John Brown's Farm was unheard of. It couldn't happen, but it happened!" Yes it did!

A Property Destined for Significance

John Brown's Farm nestles in the southern extremity of the Hagerstown Valley, which is the Maryland portion of what is known to the north as the Cumberland Valley and to the south as the Shenandoah Valley. This multi-state basin is part of an undulating twelve-hundred mile trough traversing the eastern part of the United States called the Great Appalachian Valley.

In 1727, the chiefs of the Iroquois Confederacy known as the Six Nations deeded a large swath of land on the Maryland side of the Potomac River to a frontiersman and colonial Maryland ambassador named Israel Friend. To this

The authentically renovated farmhouse appears virtually identical to when John Brown rented it in 1859. Photo by Winston Pitman.

This remnant section of the Antietam Iron Works displays the fading glory of what was once the principal employer of southern Washington County, Maryland. Photo by Winston Pitman.

parcel of indeterminate size (described as "two hundred shoots as fur as an arrow can be slung,") Friend later added other tracts of land.

A generation later, a settler named Joseph Chapline received one thousand acres of Friend's tentative holdings in reward for his efforts during the French and Indian War. Chapline then entered into an agreement in 1765 to form the Frederick Forge, which was later called "Antietam Iron Works," on an adjacent plot of land acquired by Iron Works developer John Semple from Friend. A furnace was built in 1768, and the forge became fully operational by 1775—just in time to supply pig iron to a Baltimore company producing cannonry for the Continental Army heading into the American Revolutionary War.

The ore on neighboring South Mountain and the abundant supply of nearby chestnut, hickory, and oak trees used for making charcoal enabled this startup to eventually become the largest business in the region, employing up to two hundred fifty free men and fifty slaves.

Decades later, the Financial Panic of 1837 precipitated a prolonged economic depression that adversely affected the Iron Works. The death of its then owner, John Brien, exposed the forge's enormous debts. A business re-structuring led by his son, John McPherson Brien, and grandson, John Brien, Jr., eventuated in the company becoming a successful producer of cut nails.

A change in the nation's tariff laws regarding iron provoked a change in 1842 from charcoal to coal-based coke, which contributed to the decline of the business. The demand for charcoal was diminished further by the advent of the railroad and the C&O Canal, which made shipping coal from the west even more economically feasible.

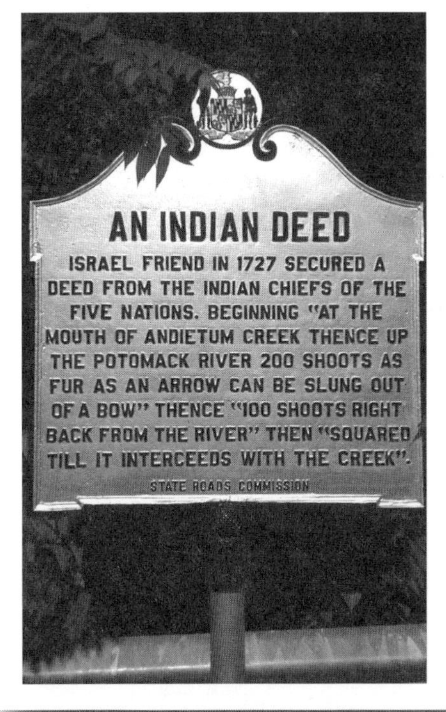

This plaque, near the hamlet of Antietam, commemorates the deeding of Iroquois land to Israel Friend. Photo by Judi Maliskas.

Upon the death of John McPherson Brien in 1849, his widow, Isabel A. Brien, attempted to keep the estate solvent by leasing the Iron Works and selling off chunks of its once-seventeen-thousand-acre woodlands holding. Local farmers purchased some of those parcels to log for firewood and fence posts.

A *Historic American Buildings Survey,* done in 1958 by the National Park Service, records the sale of one such parcel. "Isabel A. Brien (through her trustees Jonathan Meredith and John Spear Nichols) sold the property to Dr. Robert Kennedy in December of 1852."

The sale initiated the transfer of 108 acres located in what was known as Samples Manor to a Dr. R. F. Kennedy (not "Booth Kennedy" as is often and erroneously cited) for the princely sum of 706 dollars.

Dr. Kennedy soon had a story-high stone foundation built and then raised a one-room cabin onto it. He later added a larger, two-story wing to the northeast. He did not, however, receive the transfer of deed to the property until 1854, perhaps upon the completion of some terms of the contract. Kennedy apparently acquired an additional 127 acres over the next several years before dying without a will in early 1859.

In the legal aftermath following his death, Dr. Kennedy's family became embroiled in a court case with three Baltimore men who filed a bill of complaint over Kennedy's having provided surety for another man's promissory notes. While the dispute was in progress, the financially-strapped Kennedy family was approached unexpectedly by a vigorous older gentleman seeking to rent the estate for a cattle operation. "Isaac Smith" he said his name was. John Brown his name really was. THAT John Brown.

Awakening of an Abolitionist

"John Brown, the ______." In addition to "abolitionist," people have filled in that blank with a bewildering range of modifiers: hero, villain, prophet, lunatic, martyr, murderer, principled sage, and misguided fanatic.

How a person completes this sentence probably has a great deal to do with what values he or she regards as fundamental. Some believe John Brown to be, as was said of the apostle Paul in Acts 24:5, "a plague, an instigator of insurrection." Others believe John Brown to be a great man, even an instrument of God.

For the purposes of our story, however, the only opinion that ultimately will matter is that of those who consider John Brown to be a great man. That was the conclusion of Brown's biographer, black historian W. E. B. Du Bois, at the beginning of the twentieth century. Nearly a half century later, in the late 1940s, in segregated America, Du Bois's opinion inspired an

---

John Brown, here pictured in his middle-age, is almost certainly the most controversial person in U. S. history. Photos public domain.

influential black fraternal organization to resurrect the reverence for John Brown and a little farm property that would come to bear his name.

YOUNG JOHN BROWN

John Brown (1800–1859) grew up rough and tumble in frontier Ohio. He had two effectual schoolmasters. One was nature. As a pioneer youth he spent many hours exploring the capricious woods and surveying the loyal heavens.

Young John's other mentor was the Bible, which he read repeatedly and from which he committed long passages to memory. The Bible's precepts increasingly scaffolded his life paradigm. Its prophecies stoked his imagination; its poetry sculpted his emotions; its vocabulary stocked his personal lexicon.

Even as a boy, John Brown could work like a man. While still in his early teens, he once drove unaccompanied a small herd of cattle some hundred miles through the wilderness to a buyer's farm. There he encountered a slave near his age—one who was wantonly mistreated and routinely abused.

That cruelty was an unforgettable and unforgotten experience that made young Brown contemplate God's perspective on this palpable evil. He also puzzled over what effect slavery must have on the millions of persons upon whom it was cavalierly perpetrated.

After spending some time in New England on his intermittent education, he returned home at age fifteen to more hard work. He learned the tannery business, becoming a foreman and a manager. There he learned what it takes to get along with men, including how to lead them. He also used that season of life to ruminate upon his potential place in the world and how he might realize it.

A FAMILY MAN

According to Du Bois's biography, Brown became a husband at twenty and a first-time father at twenty-one. He was the undisputed leader of his home but warranted the position through provision, wise counsel, and tenderness, rather than autocratic behavior. Du Bois wrote that, "Almost before he himself knew the full meaning of life, he was trying to teach it to his children." [1]

To his children, Brown was a personified blend of law and grace. One of his daughters was impressed with how kind and solicitous her father was to his own aging father. She observed, "When any of the family were sick he did not often trust watchers to care for the sick one, but sat up himself and was like a tender mother."[2]

John Brown's biographer, W. E. B. Du Bois, was the first African American to earn a Ph. D. from Harvard University; he was also the co-founder of the NAACP in 1909. Photo public domain.

Another daughter recalled of his honorable bearing; "He had such a way of saying, 'Tut, tut!' if he ever saw the first sign of a lie in us, that he often frightened us children." [3]

In Brown's orthodox understanding of the Bible, Jesus Christ was bruised for transgressions committed by others. He incorporated this principle into his parenting. On one occasion, one of his sons had accumulated a previously agreed upon number of disciplinary lashes. Brown administered a portion. He then handed the lash to the boy who learned an unforgettable lesson as he dispensed the remaining portion upon his insistent father.

Much of John Brown's early adulthood was consumed with providing financially for his ever-growing family. His care was demonstrated also through ethical guidance and frequent bedside vigils. Nine of his twenty offspring died before reaching adulthood.

However, Brown would not allow himself to linger in the melancholia that attended the burial of every one of his beloved children. He still had a family that looked to him for hope and direction as well as material provision.

With his wife and brood in tow, he traversed America's northeast, homesteading in Ohio, Pennsylvania, New York, and Massachusetts. Of a restless and ambitious nature, Brown mastered numerous skills and engaged in various industries—land surveyor, lumber dealer, postmaster, wool-grower, and farmer. At several points he was advancing in business, employing up to fifteen men in his tannery, for instance.

A PIVOTAL YEAR

Brown's reaction to two major events in 1837, would demarcate the course of his life. The first event cemented Brown's antipathy to slavery. Upon learning of the politically-motivated murder of abolitionist Elijah P. Lovejoy, Brown vowed publicly, "Here, before God, in the presence of these witnesses, from this time, I consecrate my life to the destruction of slavery!"[4]

The second event impelled Brown to invest in his spiritual development. The Panic of 1837 was one of a series of financial recessions that skulked throughout the mid-nineteenth century, ruining many a business and many a man. Over 40 percent of the nation's roughly 850 banks failed. Brown and his businesses were among the many that were overextended and drawn into the ensuing vortex toward financial ruin.

Despite the collapses of his enterprises and the deaths of his first wife and several young children, Brown persevered in seeking after God and God's will for his life. He experienced a spiritual renewal sometime in the late 1830s or early 1840s. Years later, his abolitionist compatriot Frederick Douglass said of him, "I never felt myself in the presence of a stronger religious influence than while in this man's house."[5]

In chronicling Brown's character development as he persevered through virtually unrelenting life difficulties, Du Bois summarized,

> *"All this is evidence of a striving soul, of a man to whom the world was a terribly earnest thing... To him the world was a mighty drama. God was an actor in the play and so was John Brown."*[6]

BUSINESS ACHIEVEMENTS

Following the events of 1837, Brown returned to his early love of shepherding. He and a new business partner, Simon Perkins, prospered in it. In July 1844 they reported 560 lambs raised and a stock of 2,700 pounds of high-grade wool at fifty-six cents a pound. By 1845, their flock of Saxony sheep was worth twenty thousand dollars—a fortune.

In 1846, they moved their business headquarters to Springfield, Massachusetts, where Brown used his newfound prosperity to provide better care for his large family and to become a widely recognized expert in wool. He organized a consortium of independent wool growers against the power of the mills and manufacturers. Although the worthy project folded in 1849, he filed away the experience as a life lesson and came away with a heightened passion for the plight of the underdog.

ACTIVISM AWAKENED

Springfield was an early bastion of abolitionist sympathies which the bulk of its influential and affluent citizens supported. Brown attended services at the traditionally black Sanford Street Church. He heard abolitionist lectures by, and became acquainted with, two noble figures in the movement—Sojourner Truth and Frederick Douglass. He used the opportunity to become better informed and more appreciative of the successes of the Underground Railroad.

In 1847, Frederick Douglass courageously returned to America from the comfort and safety of a sojourn in England. Immediately, he heard whispers of "the strange determined man of Springfield who flitted silently here and there among the groups of black folk and whose life was devoted to eternal war against slavery."[7] Du Bois also notes that both men were eager to meet each other—John Brown to become acquainted with "the greatest leader of the race which he aimed to free, Frederick Douglass to know an intense foe of slavery."[8]

Douglass's account of his first meeting with Brown included astonishment at the austerity and sincerity of the latter's domicile:

> *"Everything implied stern truth, solid purpose, and rigid economy. I was not long in company with the master of this house before I discovered that he was indeed the master of it, and was likely to become mine too if I stayed long enough with him."*[9]

Before Brown would move his operations entirely from Springfield, the 1850 Fugitive Slave Act gave federal marshals authority to pursue, capture, and return runaway slaves to their masters. It also imposed fines on those who aided runaways in their escape and spawned a corrupt industry of bounty hunters. In response, John Brown founded his first militant anti-slavery organization, the League of Gileadites, named after a biblical reference from the book of Judges meaning "warriors unafraid."

This was not the first cause that Brown had assumed on behalf of slaves. As early as 1825 he had assisted runaways in Ohio. He was aware of and sympathetic to the Nat Turner Rebellion of 1831 in Virginia. In 1834, he wrote of considering to adopt a black child and to start a school for blacks. On another occasion, Brown and his family gave up their seats to blacks at a church service and encouraged others to do the same, a gesture not well-received by the establishment.

Frederick Douglass. Photo public domain.

In 1839, in sympathetic response to a black preacher, Brown announced to his wife and older children that...

"His purpose [was] to make active war on slavery, and bound his family in solemn and secret compact to labor for emancipation... And then, instead of standing to pray as was his wont, he fell upon his knees and implored God's blessing on his enterprise." [10]

According to Du Bois, this event marked a turning point in John Brown's life.

"It began to dawn on him that he had sinned in the selfish pursuit of petty ends: that he must be about his Father's business of giving the death-blow to that 'sum of all villainies'—slavery." And again, "[H]e set his face toward the goal and whithersoever the Lord led, he was ready to follow." [11]

Brown's wife, Mary Ann, acknowledged this mounting burden when writing,

"My husband always believed that he was to be an instrument in the hands of Providence, and I believed it too... many a night he had lain awake and prayed concerning it." [12]

Thenceforth, Brown began to cogitate incessantly on the evils of slavery and how it might be ended. He adjudged slaveholders to be guilty of a consummate wickedness. As a result, he concluded that it was morally justifiable for slaves to execute their masters and to escape.

Thereupon, he began to study census charts to determine the geographic distribution of Negroes, and he made maps of fugitive slave routes indicating roads, plantations, and supplies. He learned about previous insurrections and studied the history of the Abolitionist Movement. He initiated and nurtured the acquaintance of black leaders like Henry H. Garnet who years later became the first black minister to preach to the House of Representatives.

Whereas previously Brown had made the acquaintance of individual blacks, he now familiarized himself with a community of blacks in Springfield, Ohio. He collaborated with them in systematizing and improving aspects of the Underground Railroad. He also learned to appreciate their society, including its strengths and weaknesses. Many of their foibles he recognized as being slavery-induced.

THE VISION COMES INTO FOCUS

During their initial encounter, Brown sketched out his endgame to Frederick Douglass who later recounted,

> *"[His plan] had much to commend it. It did not, as some suppose, contemplate a general rising among the slaves, and a general slaughter of the slave-masters. An insurrection, he thought, would only defeat the object; but his plan did contemplate the creating of an armed force which should act in the very heart of the South. He was not averse to the shedding of blood, and thought the practice of arms would be a good one for the colored people to adopt [in order to be respected]...*
>
> *"He called my attention to a map of the United States, and pointed out to me the far-reaching Alleghenies, which stretch away from the borders of New York into the southern states. 'These mountains,' he said, 'are the basis of my plan. God has given the strength of the hills to freedom; they were placed here for the emancipation of the Negro race; they are full of natural forts, where one man for defense will be equal to a hundred for attack...'"*[13]

Then Brown went on to describe how, once established in the hills of Virginia, they might dispatch forays to induce slaves to flee to them for safety. From there, they would send those so inclined to keep going north via the Underground Railroad while those disposed to stay would do that. If perchance the proposed valley stronghold could be breached successfully by the slaveholders or their army, then Brown was prepared to die honorably.

Frederick Douglass was "almost persuaded," but he reckoned on the power and worldwide reach of the slave system and had trouble imagining its demise in practical terms. Brown, on the other hand, reckoned that system merely as a moral evil that God would empower him to end.

Douglass was typical of the black leaders of the day: they believed in John Brown but could not envision his plan being successful. If it failed, they knew that they and their loved ones would bear the terrible ensuing cost. Although Brown presumed that his military allies would come chiefly from among the blacks, he found that their tangible support was more difficult to achieve than he first imagined it might be.

Douglass and Brown parted tactical company, but remained in cordial relationship from that point forward. Although they often disagreed on specific strategy, they were united regarding the subsequently expressed sentiments of Du Bois,

> *"American slavery was the foulest and filthiest blot on nineteenth century civilization. As a school of brutality and human suffering, of female prostitution and male debauchery; as a mockery of marriage and defilement of family life; as a darkening of reason, and spiritual death, it had no parallel in its day.*
>
> *Four things make life worthy to most men: to move, to know, to love, to aspire. None of these was for Negro slaves. A white child could halt a black man on the highway and send him slinking to his kennel. No black slave could legally learn to read. And love? If a black slave loved a lass, there was not a white man from the Potomac to the Rio Grande that could not prostitute her to his lust."* [14]

One of the characteristics that made John Brown not only uniquely effective in the cause of abolition, but subsequently beloved by the black community, was his practice of being personally intimate with individual blacks.

As Du Bois observed,

> *"From his earliest interest in Negroes, John Brown sought to know individuals among them intimately and personally. He invited them to his home and he went to theirs. He talked to them, and listened to the history of their trials,*

advised them and took advice from them."[15]

Brown appreciated that the black community had amassed decades of precious wisdom in the furtherance of the cause of emancipation. Campaigns had been initiated among free blacks for literacy, vocational skills, and character development, none of which were readily available for the enslaved.

Participation in church activities had afforded blacks opportunity not only for the necessary spiritual strength, but also for exercising leadership, organizational, and oratorical skills. The Underground Railroad provided a lifeline for those fleeing for their lives and facilitated the development of prudence, networking skills, and useful knowledge of precise conditions in the South.

The National Negro Convention movement, which had begun in Philadelphia in 1830, also promoted confidence and encouragement in the black community. Integrated conferences with black and white speakers as well as attendees spurred communal momentum.

Numerous primary and secondary schools were launched. Several colleges were established for blacks prior to the Civil War, including Cheyney University of Philadelphia in 1837, the Ashmun Institute (now Lincoln University) in 1854, and Wilberforce University in Ohio, the first college to be owned and administrated by African-Americans.

The importance of the founding of Oberlin College in 1833 can hardly be overstated, as it became a hotbed of abolitionism and, in 1835, the first college in the United States regularly to admit black students.

Cooperation with whites in other areas also proved necessary and beneficial. The work of evangelical Christians in Great Britain (notably abolitionists William Wilberforce and John Newton, a reformed slave trader and the composer of "Amazing Grace") led to the abolition of Great Britain's human trafficking via the Slave Trade Act of 1807. The British Slavery Abolition Act of 1833 subsequently abolished slavery per se throughout most of the British Empire, freeing seven hundred thousand slaves in the West Indies alone.

In Canada, there was an extensive manumission following the exhibit of superlative dedication and bravery by Canada's black soldiers and sailors during the War of 1812. Not long after that mass liberation, Canadian abolitionists extended a welcoming hand to the south as some two thousand U.S. blacks promptly accepted the offer and emigrated. By the late 1850s, approximately fifty thousand freemen made up a Canadian black community that was prospering financially and culturally.

Du Bois spoke of numerous resistances by the enslaved, to show that there burned within them a yearning for liberty. As he put it, "The great mass of Southern slaves were cowed, but they were not conquered."[16]

Concerning the anxious psychology of white overlords toward their slaves, Du Bois wrote, "The fear of that great bound beast was ever there—a nameless, haunting dread that never left the South and never ceased, but ever nerved the remorseless cruelty of the master's arm."[17]

In the midst of this institutional turbulence there was one outlet, an escape valve that harbored a continual stream of fugitives along the Great Black Way. Coursing primarily up the Alleghenies, Du Bois described how fugitive slaves joined "themselves to the free Negroes of the North, and with them organizing themselves into a great black phalanx that worked and schemed and paid for and finally fought for the freedom of black men in America."[18]

John Brown well understood that he was not the lone crusader against slavery. He appreciated that he was one of many in a long line. He would prefer to act in concert, but he also had the steely integrity of "Though none go with me, still I will follow." Let another individual match him in principled commitment and Brown would lock arms. But unless and until such a person materialized to unveil a superior plan, then "the old man" would proceed with his.

Just then a new option arose. Gerrit Smith, the wealthy leader of the New York abolition group, offered to free Negroes 120,000 acres of his lands on easy terms near North Elba, New York, in the dank Adirondack Mountains. Brown wanted to support the endeavor financially but was sensitive to a request of his own long-suffering family: they had asked that they might be permitted to furnish a single room of their family residence up to neighborhood standards.

Brown polled his wife and older children: "I want you all to express your minds. I have a little money to spare; and now shall we use it to furnish the parlor, or spend it to buy clothing for the colored people who may need help in North Elba another year?"[19] They voted unanimously to allocate the money for its use in North Elba.

In further support of the project, Brown bought land near North Elba (within which today lies the village of Lake Placid). In 1849, he moved his family there so that he might utilize his farming, frontier, and shepherding skills to help the inexperienced Southern black families become established in that harsh Northern climate.

The family's homestead there has become known as "the John Brown Farm," its name creating confusion with the property in Washington County, Maryland.

The Fugitive Slave Act of 1850 had provoked abolitionist sympathies. In response, Brown urged his black compatriots to resist, to have courage, and to arm themselves. While Brown advocated a "strike hard" attitude, he also pondered the probable reactions of threatened Southerners and of horrified Northerners. He concluded that there needed to be public buy-in by whites or else an aggressive enterprise (coupled with the ongoing loss of escaped slaves by way of the Underground Railroad) would be construed as mere racial vigilantism.

John Brown spent the bulk of the early 1850s solidifying support among white abolitionists. He criss-crossed the Northeast and impressed many influential groups—not just with his innate character and charisma. Some came to regard him as an instrument of God.

Kansas, Bloody Kansas

"King Cotton" was entrenched as an all-encompassing economic, social, and political system in the American South. The end of slavery would mean the death of that system—a pugnacious system that was not about to go down without a fight. Indeed, sometimes it even seemed as if the pro-slavery interests were without a viable opponent. This mindset was not true—at least not entirely.

The encroachment of slavery beyond Missouri had given an effective goad to the abolitionists. It became unmistakable to them that slavery as an economic system was not an inherently expiring institution—not something that would simply die away in a more enlightened time.

In fact, the chances of slavery expanding were just as likely. Resolute pro-slavery interests championed an aggressive extension of the system into the American Southwest, Central America, and South America. And into Kansas.

John Brown, here pictured in his fifties, would eventually become drained of physical vigor, nevertheless he remained strong in intellectual rigor and moral resolve. Photo public domain.

In 1854, the Kansas-Nebraska Act created the effect of repealing the Missouri Compromise of 1820, whereby slavery had been limited only to newly incoming states situated entirely south of Missouri. Many Northerners were indignant at the betrayal inherent in the Act, undermining as it did the earlier understanding that the Nebraska and Kansas territories unquestionably would enter as free states.

Rather, instead of continuing to forbid slavery above the northern border of Texas (excepting Missouri), the Kansas-Nebraska Act was written so that voters in the new territories would determine the legal status of slavery. A pro-slavery vote in Kansas would tilt the balance of power in the United States Senate to the Southern states and their interests.

The North assumed that the impending contest was merely a matter of votes. As such, and somewhat naïvely, Northerners hoped to move in a sufficient number of anti-slavery settlers and then to hold the referendum. The South counter-assumed that Kansas was already by rights a slave state, and sought by violence to exact their conviction. Well-financed pro-slavery interests organized ad-hoc militias and funded "Border Ruffian" gangs of the worst sort of hooligans to bully the Northern "Jayhawkers" affiliated with the free-state cause.

Consequently, enthusiasts on both sides of the slavery issue swarmed into Kansas in order to reinforce their positions. Partisanship almost immediately broke out into manifest hostilities.

To complicate matters, there was a third faction with interest in the Kansas outcome—the Free Soil Party. The Free-Soilers were anti-slavery, but not because they loved the slave. Rather they believed slave ownership among larger farmers brought an economic disadvantage to independent farmers and cattlemen.

The situation in Kansas was akin to tying three alley cats together by their tails. Into this political maelstrom waded five of John Brown's sons, who were hoping to tilt the Kansas tally in the free state direction. In the spring of 1855, they drove cattle westward to a homestead eight miles from Osawatomie, Kansas, where they were to be joined in due course by their families. On their way there, Brown's sons experienced first-hand a number of armed Missouri roughnecks intent on "persuading" Kansas into slavery.

An early vote toward establishing the Kansas territorial legislature was commandeered with impunity by the southern ruffians. Many among the abolition-minded refused to acknowledge the resultant legislature or to obey its dictates, including one law making it illegal even to speak against the right of slaveholding.

Pro-slavery newspapers in Missouri urged the use of force upon the anti-slavery resisters. As violence began to break out against the Northerners, Brown's sons appealed to their father back in New York to send arms. Brown hesitated for a bit, occupied as he was with the experiment at Elba and with his dream of building an armed sanctuary in the Alleghenies. Presently, a new vision dawned in Brown's mind—perhaps the Lord himself had an intermediate plan: first for Kansas and then for Virginia.

Brown's "brooding masculine mind" called him, as ever, to action. He attended an abolitionist meeting in Syracuse, New York, which put him in touch for the first time with significant financial backers. These men hinted interest in funding the "dirty work," though not in performing it themselves. In fiery speeches, Brown expressed his willingness to go and join his sons, if only he had the money for supplies and armaments. That money came right in.

John Brown advanced forthwith to Kansas. Concealing weaponry beneath surveying equipment in a covered wagon, he arrived there in October, 1855. His first work was to get his sons settled before the harsh Kansas winter set in. That task soon accomplished, Brown, ever the strategist, next occupied himself with reconnoitering. He crept back and forth, here and there, visible and then veiled, a ghost in the making.

In December, a report came to the Brown family's Osawatomie homestead concerning the pro-slavers' surrounding of the free city of Lawrence some fifty miles away. Brown marched there with six companions under arms to find five hundred Lawrence men about to be beset by some sixteen hundred Missouri ruffians. Brown stirred the citizenry toward defensive action, consequently achieving a stand-off and negotiated truce. Brown, constitutionally inclined to believe the best about men and their oaths, was persuaded that the truce was genuine. It turned out to be merely a winter cease fire.

"CAPTAIN" JOHN BROWN

President Franklin Pierce had timidly (perhaps drunkenly) yielded to his Secretary of War, Jefferson Davis (the future President of the Confederacy), in placing Federal troops into the hands of the Kansas pro-slavery powers. Additionally, privately armed pro-slavery bands increasingly assembled in the hopes of terrorizing Free-Stater Kansans, who wanted to keep blacks out of Kansas, whether slave or free.

One such group from Georgia encamped on the "Swamp of the Swan," a reedy lowland marsh of eastern Kansas, not far from the Brown encampment. John Brown daringly entered their camp on the pretense of being a government surveyor, tools and all.

Because virtually all official government officers in the territory supported making Kansas a slave state, the ruffians assumed Brown to be like-minded. Thus, they freely told Brown and his sons of their plans, even naming "the Browns over yonder" to be among those they hoped to whip, drive out, or kill. As they detailed their plans, including precisely whom they intended to assault, Brown quietly wrote down virtually their every word, casually pretending to be making surveying notes into his log.

Brown removed himself thence to warn the appropriate parties, as well as several secret councils in Osawatomie, Lawrence, and other places. Previously, these councils' own actions had displayed passivity in hopes of conciliation. With this new information, however, they came to the tacit conclusion that if the ruffians made any advance of their threatened plans, then they should be met with force. They also concluded that Brown should be the man to provide it.

On May 21, 1856, the pro-slavery forces sacked and burned half of Lawrence while its inhabitants largely stood by in trembling submissiveness. That brutal attack seemed to have quashed the debate. Kansas would be a slave territory. The Free-Staters had been abandoned, even repudiated, by the U.S. government. Their wills were broken and their cause apparently doomed.

> *"Then suddenly came a flash of an awful stroke—a deed of retaliation from the free state side so bloody, relentless and cruel that it sent a shudder through all Kansas and Missouri, and aroused the nation."* [20]

Upon receiving the news of the attack on Lawrence, Brown rushed there to find the town smoldering in ashes. He smoldered correspondingly, indignant that there had been virtually no resistance from the cowed citizenry. Just then came a report that some Georgia-based ruffians had been harassing the now-unprotected women in the Brown settlement, warning them that they must leave within days or be driven out. Columns of smoke billowing from farmhouses on the horizon provided tangible proof of the marauders' seriousness.

"I will attend to those fellows," declared John Brown. He gathered his band comprised of himself, four sons, a son-in-law, and two others. They filled a borrowed wagon with sharpened cutlasses, leaving behind an initially apprehensive but subsequently cheering crowd in Lawrence.

Brown and his seven companions sought out and located the offending ruffians, who were still under their original impression that Brown was a surveyor and a Southern sympathizer. In the dark of the night at the appointed date, May 24, 1856, the individual houses of the brutes were visited. The five who were home were dragged out into a location in the woods and, at the signal of Brown, were hacked to death in what became known as the Pottawatomie Massacre. Brown disavowed that any of the ruffians had died by his direct hand, but allowed that they were killed by his order.

The deed inflamed Kansas. Some say it freed Kansas; others said it plunged Kansas back into renewed civil war. Both assessments can be considered correct, as even Brown believed. In his reckoning, such bloodshed was the cost of freedom, but less than the price of repression.

Following the incident, the Free-Staters initially shrank back, reckoning that the retaliation indubitably coming upon them would be too much to bear. However, the bold among them prevailed, and the predominant stance changed from passivity and a futile appeal to toothless law toward an active resistance. Correspondingly, the most rabid of the pro-slavery people also now came to the fore, mustering three thousand armed and vindictive men in northern Missouri.

What ensued was one of the ugliest episodes in American history. Towns were fortified, garrisons were built, vigilantes roamed, and homesteads were torched. Plumes of smoke rose across the Kansas landscape as cities burned. Hell on earth. Widows and orphans were thrust out into the open wilderness, some forced to seek refuge among the Native Americans. Lawlessness within Kansas was entire. Thievery, rape, and murder ensued until, as DuBois accounted, "the scared governor signed a truce... and fled for his life." [21]

Following the Pottawatomie Massacre, John Brown became an outlaw—iterally a wanted man with a bounty on his head. Virtually overnight, three dozen idealistic and devoted men joined Brown in a remote hideout. Their hideout was a place of covenant discipline, military readiness, and high character. A reporter wrote of the ethos of the camp, "Never before had I met such a band of men. They were not earnest but earnestness incarnate." [22]

One of Brown's troop later wrote,

> *"We were united as a band of brothers by the love and affection toward the man who with tender words and wise counsel, in the depth of the wilderness of Ottawa Creek, prepared a handful of young men for the work of laying the foundation of a free commonwealth."* [23]

Brown drilled the volunteers in individual combat skills and in military strategy. They made effective forays and strikes here and there. They gained ground and reputation to the point that resolute men began to swear by the name of John Brown.

In August of that same year, a company of more than three hundred Missourians under the command of Mexican War veteran Maj. Gen. John W. Reid sallied into Kansas. Their intent was to destroy the Free-State settlements at Osawatomie, and from there to march on Topeka and Lawrence.

Captain John Brown and his militia went out to meet them. Outnumbered nearly eight to one, Brown positioned his thirty eight men along the road. Firing from behind natural defenses, they managed to kill twenty of the marauders and wound forty more while initially losing none of their own. (Brown's son Frederick and another man had been killed earlier in the day in a separate skirmish.)

The Missourians regrouped as Brown's troop ran low on ammunition. That forced Brown to retreat across a river while losing one man to death and another four to imprisonment. Reid's ruffians then turned aside to plunder and burn Osawatomie.

Although technically a defeat for Brown, his bravery and shrewdness in battle brought him national attention. He was given by many northern abolitionists the status of hero and the nickname "Osawatomie Brown."

Intervention by the new governor, John W. Geary, created a temporary lull in the hostilities. The deteriorating conditions in Kansas became the nation's primary concern and the defining issue of the fall of 1856's presidential election. Going forward, only intermittent skirmishes occurred, and as Kansas became a free state, the situation gradually began to resolve itself—although other significant events continued to galvanize and harden both sides of the slavery debate into a nationwide stalemate. For instance, the Supreme Court's Dred Scott Decision on March 6, 1857, declared the 1820 Missouri Compromise unconstitutional, effectively legalizing slavery in all U.S. territories. No state could now bar slave owners from bringing slaves into that state. Many infuriated abolitionists concluded that the court's decision was proof that King Cotton had come to control even the Supreme Court of the United States.

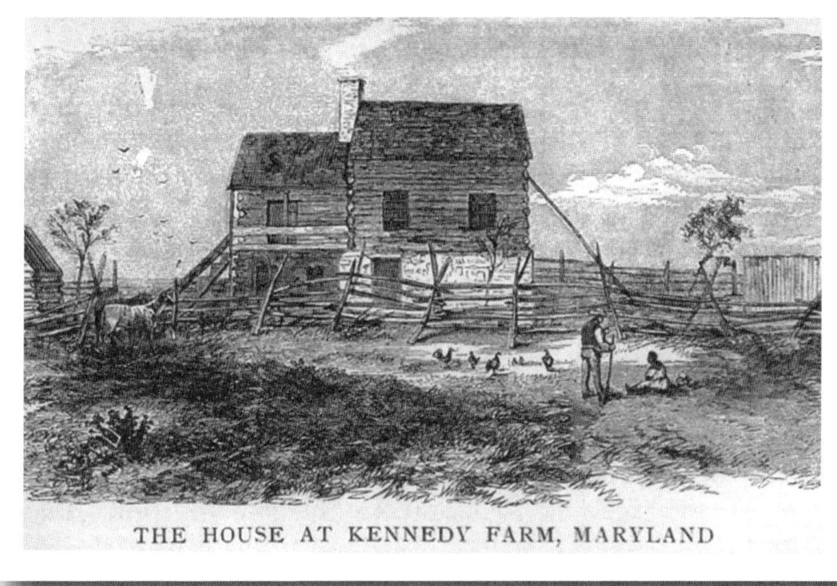
THE HOUSE AT KENNEDY FARM, MARYLAND

Clandestine Activities

"Captain Brown" used the opportunity to slip away from Kansas and to spend the next two years cultivating relationships and casting vision throughout the Northeast. There, he discovered that 'Osawatomie Brown' had become a revered name in eastern abolitionist circles.

Amidst his newfound fame, Brown met a group of wealthy abolitionists who came to be known as "The Secret Six." They agreed to fund his future activities on a "no questions asked" basis. Early in 1858, Brown arranged to purchase two hundred Sharps rifles, their ammunition, and one thousand pikes—long spears for use by unskilled defenders such as Kansas housewives and runaway slaves.

On a trip to New England, Brown met American Transcendentalists Henry David Thoreau, Ralph Waldo Emerson, and other notables. George L. Stearns wrote of that meeting, which he joined in progress:

This sketch of John Brown's rented farmhouse appeared in Frank Leslie's *Illustrated Newspaper* on November 26, 1859, and was instrumental in the building's eventual architectural restoration.

"When I entered the parlor, [Brown] was sitting near the hearth, where glowed a bright, open fire. He rose to greet me, stepping forward with such an erect, military bearing, such fine demeanor, such fine courtesy of demeanor and grave earnestness, that he seemed to my instant thought that some old Cromwellian hero suddenly dropped down before me." [24]

Brown asserted,

"Gentlemen, I consider the Golden Rule and the Declaration of Independence one and inseparable; and it is better that a whole generation of men, women, and children should be swept away than that this crime of slavery should exist one day longer." [25]

Traveling to New York City, Brown was introduced to the experienced English mercenary Hugh Forbes who was hired to serve as an associate tactician and a drill-master for Brown's volunteer militia. Brown next stopped to visit his faithful family in Hudson, Ohio, before traveling on to Tabor, Iowa, an abolitionist bastion. Arriving there, he planned strategy with Forbes until the mercenary became disgruntled with Brown over various differences and quit.

After the October 1857 elections settled the future of Kansas as a free state, Brown re-gathered his scattered militiamen to Iowa and there hinted to them of his plans for Virginia. He left those men and their ongoing military training in early 1858 and journeyed to Rochester in order to entreat Frederick Douglass once again for his support.

During an extended stay at Douglass's home, Brown finalized the Provisional Constitution that would govern the virtual state that he envisioned in the mountains of Virginia. Also on this occasion, he showed Douglass specific means by which he could defend the mountainous region as necessary.

THE CAPTAIN AND THE GENERAL

Brown developed another important relationship with an African-American when, in April, 1858, he was taken into the home and confidence of Harriet Tubman. On a subsequent occasion, Brown introduced her by saying, "I bring you one of the best and bravest persons on this continent—General Tubman, as we call her." [26] Tubman herself was equally effusive in her praise of Brown. She later told a friend: "[H]e done more in dying than 100 men would in living." [27]

In his biography of John Brown, Du Bois described Harriet Tubman as:

"A full-blooded African, born a slave on the Eastern Shore of Maryland in 1820. When a girl she was injured by having an iron weight thrown on her head by an overseer, an injury that gave her wild half-mystic ways with dreams, rhapsodies and trances. In her early womanhood she did the rudest and hardest man's work, driving, carting and plowing. Finally the slave family was broken up in 1849 when she ran away.

"Then began her wonderful career as a rescuer of fugitive slaves. Back and forth she traveled like some dark ghost until she had personally led over three hundred blacks to freedom, no one of whom was ever lost while in her charge. A reward of $10,000 for her, alive or dead, was offered, but she was never taken. A dreamer of dreams as she was, she ever 'laid great stress on a dream which she had just before she met Captain Brown in Canada.'" [28]

According to Du Bois, Tubman had a recurrent dream which included the head of "an old man with a long white beard, gazing at her." When she met Brown shortly thereafter she said, "he was the very image of the head she had seen." [29] Du Bois understood that Tubman meant to have been with Brown at Harpers Ferry, but was unable to attend due to an illness.

THE CHATHAM CONVENTION

Because Brown coveted the legitimization of an endorsement by a convention, in the spring of 1858, he and a dozen of his followers traveled to Chatham, Ontario. Among Chatham's six thousand residents were some two thousand runaway slaves, many of whom had been aided by Harriet Tubman.

The man responsible for helping Brown organize the Chatham Convention was Martin R. Delany. Delany was a free-born American black birthed in Charles Town, Virginia (now West Virginia, which became a state in 1863) and raised in Chambersburg, Pennsylvania.

In addition to his having been a business partner of Frederick Douglass, Delany was one of the first three black men admitted to Harvard Medical School. He also wrote the first novel by a black man to be published in the United States. Furthermore, as a result of a personal audience with Abraham Lincoln, Delany became the first African-American field officer in the United

States Army during the Civil War.

The abolitionist event in Chatham convened on May 8, 1858, with dozens of influential black men from Canada and the United States attending. To avoid unwanted scrutiny, the convention was conducted under the pretense that it was an assembly to organize a Masonic Lodge for colored people.

The convention's primary and first order of business was the passing of Brown's drafted Provisional Constitution for the proposed fugitive slave Republic. This was accomplished with unanimous consent.

Discussion then shifted to John Brown's strategy of making an armed foray into the South. Doubt was expressed that slaves would indeed rally to Brown. Others pressed the opinion that Brown's band was too small and that white men of his stripe in the cause could not be spared for a plan so utterly hopeless.

Brown paced for a long moment before halting suddenly, slamming his hand down, and resolutely declaiming, "Did not my Master Jesus Christ come down from Heaven and sacrifice Himself upon the altar for the salvation of the race, and should I, a worm, not worthy to crawl under His feet, refuse to sacrifice myself?" [30]

One attendee, Mr. James M. Jones, observed,

> *"He seemed to think such sacrifice necessary to awaken the people from the deep sleep that had settled upon the minds of the whites of the North. He well knew that the sacrifice of any number of Negroes would have no effect."* [31]

As the convention adjourned, Brown fully realized that he did not have to personally generate the finances for this operation. Others were willing to carry the financial burden if he were willing to carry out the work itself. Perhaps Brown's tardiness in coming to this realization explains why he did not try to work his plan several years earlier.

A SERIOUS COMPLICATION

Almost as soon as the convention concluded, a security crisis occurred that sidetracked Brown's progress, probably for a year or more. The disgruntled and frustrated mercenary, Hugh Forbes, threatened serious mischief, including the blabbing of the general outline of Brown's Virginia plan to key people, among them a U.S. Senator from Massachusetts, Henry Wilson.

Brown's "Secret Six" became fearful that their names would be revealed.

Taking Forbes's threat seriously, it was determined by Brown's leading supporters that he ought to do something to throw Forbes off his scent, which would also give others the necessary time and freedom to raise additional funds. As a result, Brown squirreled away his growing stash of weapons, scattered his men throughout the country, and laid low for the better part of a year—first in Kansas and then in various places throughout the northeast.

While some immediate strategic good came from this tack, his abrupt absence had the short-term effect of partially undermining his credibility, raising questions about his wisdom and commitment, and thus making it more difficult to recruit future allies.

Trying to make the best of the situation, Brown, now in nearly unrelenting poor health, returned in June to Kansas. There he contributed variously to the abolitionist cause over the next six months. On one occasion in December, 1858, he led an armed raid into Missouri during which he liberated eleven slaves.

The following month, he escorted those eleven northward. During the course of that trip, Kansas entered the Union as a free state on January 29, 1859. Upon arriving in Chicago, Brown stopped to meet with the abolitionist and renowned detective Allan Pinkerton. Pinkerton financed the remainder of the fugitives' trip—first to Detroit by rail, and then by ferry to Canada.

During the remainder of winter and the early spring of 1859, Brown traveled throughout Ohio and on to New England to engage additional support for his cause. In May he delivered a lecture in Concord, Massachusetts, to sympathetic men including Bronson Alcott, Emerson, and Thoreau. Alcott wrote a detailed physical description of Brown and added, ""I think him about the manliest man I have ever seen—the type and synonym of the Just." [32]

While in New England, Brown also engaged the "Secret Six" in discussing matters of strategy and supply. Then, in early June, Brown left Boston for a brief and final visit to see his wife and other family members in North Elba, New York.

The Inevitable Draws Near

On June 20, 1859, John Brown, Lieutenant Jeremiah Anderson, John Kagi, Brown's secretary of war, and two of his sons started southward on a five hundred mile trek. Toward the end of their long journey, they spent several days in Chambersburg, Pennsylvania. From there, they traveled another twenty-five miles to the south.

On June 30, Brown and his company stayed overnight in Hagerstown, Maryland. Using the assumed names of "I. Smith and Sons," they stayed in room six at the four-story Washington House near the city square, which years earlier had been the site of the Globe Tavern, whose guests included George Washington. The Washington House hotel was destroyed by fire in 1879 and was replaced the following year by a five-story hotel, the majestic Baldwin House. That building is now part of the University System of Maryland complex on West Washington Street.

This view of the lower level of the John Brown farmhouse facing eastward displays the autumnal beauty of the Hagerstown Valley. Photo by Winston Pitman.

As Brown and his band exited Hagerstown, they were now but thirty miles from their penultimate goal of Harpers Ferry, a site key to taking strategic locations in the Blue Ridge.

As did Thomas Jefferson a half century earlier, John Brown loved the beauty of the Harpers Ferry area. He also was enamored of the idea that a successful raid on its Federal Arsenal would bring added drama to their endeavor.

Ultimately, Brown chose Harpers Ferry because it stood at the safest natural entrance to the "Great Black Way," along which three million of America's four million slaves either lived or had easy access. As Du Bois put it, "Along that path were fastnesses and hiding-places easily capable of becoming permanent fortified refuges for organized bands of determined armed men." [33]

It is imperative to appreciate what Du Bois understood John Brown's ultimate goal to be,

> *"A glance at the map shows clearly that John Brown intended to operate in the Blue Ridge mountains rising east of the Shenandoah and known at Harpers Ferry as Loudon Heights. The Loudon Heights rise boldly five hundred to seven hundred feet above the village of Harpers Ferry...*
>
> *"They run due south and then southwest, dipping down a little the first three miles, then rising to 1,500 feet, which level is practically maintained until twenty-five miles below Harpers Ferry where the mountains broaden to a dense and labyrinthical wilderness, and rise to a height of 2,000 or more feet.*
>
> *"Right at this high point and in sight of High Knob [a peak of 2,400 feet] began, in Fauquier County, the Great Black Way. In this county in 1850 were over 10,000 slaves and 650 free Negroes, as compared with 9,875 whites. From this county to the southern boundary of Virginia were a series of black counties with a majority of slaves, containing in 1850 at least 260,000 Negroes. From there the Great Black Way went south, which John Brown indicated in his diary and undoubtedly in the marked maps, which [the state of] Virginia afterward hastily destroyed.*
>
> *"The easiest way to get to these heights was from Harpers Ferry. An hour's climb from the arsenal grounds would easily have hidden a hundred men in inaccessible fastnesses, provided they were not overburdened; and even with*

arms, ammunition and supplies, they could have repelled, without difficulty, attacks on the retreat."[34]

Du Bois's summary leaves no question of what he believed to be Brown's intent:

"The plan without doubt was, first, to collect men and arms on the Maryland side of the Potomac; second, to attack the arsenal suddenly and capture it; third, to bring up the arms and ammunition and, together with those captured, to cross the Shenandoah to Loudon Heights and hide in the mountain wilderness; fourth, thence to descend at intervals to release slaves and get food, and so retreat southward.

"This then was the great plan which John Brown had been slowly elaborating and formulating for twenty years—since the day when kneeling beside a Negro minister he had sworn his sons to blood feud with slavery."[35]

Harpers Ferry National Historical Park's chief historian Dennis Frye is of the conviction that Brown's grand strategy and the intended upshot of his plan was the undermining of slavery as an economic system. If so, then it is founded on a brilliant and potentially non-violent tactic. Here is how it would work.

In 1859 the value of a healthy young male slave was equivalent to roughly three years' income for the average farmer. The cost of one such slave equaled the value of hundreds of acres of land. Thus, the loss of even one high-priced slave would plunge the typical slaveholder into financial ruin.

If Brown could precipitate the running away of hundreds of slaves, then the economic tranquility of an entire region could be destabilized. The running away of thousands arguably could undermine the slave system entirely by making the purchase and maintenance of slaves a prohibitive risk.

Concerning Brown's specific tactic, Du Bois went on to assert,

"Most writers have apparently supposed that Brown intended to retreat from the arsenal (northward) across the Potomac. A moment's thought will show the utter absurdity of this plan. Brown knew guerilla warfare, and the failure of the Harpers Ferry raid does not prove it a blunder from the start. The raid was not a foray from the mountains, which failed because its retreat

> *was cut off; but it was a foray to the mountains with the village and arsenal on the way, which was defeated apparently because the arms and ammunition train failed to join the advance-guard."* [36]

"Osawatomie Brown" and his advance team first appeared at Harpers Ferry on July 3. There they met their old comrade from Kansas days, John Cook, who had been living there under cover for more than a year. During that year, Cook, in addition to sending out helpful information regularly to Brown, had been occupying himself with selling maps and keeping the canal lock nearest the arsenal.

While in town that day, Brown met an amiable farmer. Brown first tendered the cover story that he and his entourage were cattlemen looking for a place to fatten up their cattle before shipping them back north for sale. Through that same farmer he learned of a farm for rent—the Kennedy Farm—which Brown promptly secured for nine months at thirty-five dollars under the assumed name of Isaac Smith.

BROWN SETTLES AT THE KENNEDY FARM

Per Du Bois' account,

> *"[The farm] was on the main road between Harpers Ferry, Chambersburg, and the North, about five miles from the Ferry and in a quiet secluded place. The house stood about three hundred yards back from the Boonesborough pike, in plain sight... Here Brown settled and gradually collected his men and material."* [37]

Brown's core troop of men had been scattered throughout the country, and perhaps were not in any haste to congregate because of the unspecified time of the raid. Armaments, too, were slow in coming. By August, most of the guns had arrived to Chambersburg where John Kagi sorted and prioritized their uses, but the one thousand pikes from Connecticut were another month in arriving.

Brown conducted frequent trips to Chambersburg, chiefly at night. One of his remaining goals was to convince Frederick Douglass to go all in, because Douglass was esteemed by other blacks as a pivotal leader. At a Chambersburg meeting with Douglass on August 19, Brown revealed to him the fullness of his plan. Douglass ultimately could not bring himself to accede to it, feeling it would overly arouse the nation.

Toward the end of the several days of earnest discussion, Douglass described Brown's final plea:

"In parting he put his arms around me in a manner more than friendly, and said: 'Come with me, Douglass; I will defend you with my life. I want you for a special purpose. When I strike, the bees will begin to swarm, and I shall want you to help hive them.' But my discretion or my cowardice made me proof against the dear old man's eloquence—perhaps it was something of both which determined my course....

"When about to leave, I asked [Shields] Green [a former slave] what he had decided to do, and was surprised by his coolly saying, in his broken way, 'I b'lieve I'll go wid de old man.' Here we separated; they to go to Harpers Ferry; I to Rochester."[38]

Several more men arrived on August 6, joining Cook and the rest of the advance party, who were already in Harpers Ferry. The remaining raiders dribbled in between early August and mid-October. Among their eventual twenty-one members were six or seven blacks (depending on the parentage of one), several of whom had members of their immediate families still in the bondage of slavery at the time of the raid. Of the remainder, three were John Brown's sons, Oliver, Watson, and Owen.

Even after they arrived at the rented farm, Brown's faithful compatriots of long-standing were still in the dark as to the specifics of his strategy. As Richard Realf, Brown's "Secretary of State," later expressed:

"John Brown was a man who would never state more than it was absolutely necessary for him to do. No one of his most intimate associates, and I was one of the most intimate, was possessed of more than barely sufficient information to enable Brown to attach such companion to him."[39]

Du Bois said of Brown's band,

"Their broadest common ground of sympathy lay in the personality of John Brown—him they revered and loved. Through him they had come to hate

slavery, and for him and for what he believed, they were willing to risk their lives. They themselves had convictions on slavery and other matters, but John Brown narrowed down their dreaming to one intense deed." [40]

Osborne Anderson, one of Brown's black followers who survived the raid recalled in his memoir written less than two years after the Raid,

"In John Brown's house, and in John Brown's presence, men from widely different parts of the continent met and united into one company, wherein no hateful prejudice dared intrude its ugly self—no ghost of distinction found space to enter..." [41]

Daily devotions were led by Brown who read from his Bible, and, in Anderson's words,

"...offered to God most fervent and touching supplications for all flesh; and especially pathetic were his petitions in behalf of the oppressed. I never heard John Brown pray, that he did not make strong appeals to God for the deliverance of the slave." [42]

Du Bois added,

"The men discussed religion and slavery freely, read Paine's "Age of Reason," and The Baltimore Sun.*"* [43]

During the time the men were sequestered at the Kennedy Farm, they were generally confined to quarters—the upstairs largely, which was described by Anderson as a "...spacious chamber, attic, storeroom, prison, drilling-room, comprised in the loft above..." [44]

The men occupied the daylight hours in readying themselves for the eventual raid, taking care of daily necessaries, and taking care not to be seen in large numbers by curious neighbors.

Anderson recollected,

"The principal employment of the prisoners, as we severally were when compelled to stay in the loft, was to study Forbes's Manual, and to go through

a quiet, though rigid drill, under the training of Captain Stevens, at some times. At other times we applied a preparation for bronzing our gun barrels..." [45]

In order to allay suspicion in the neighborhood, John Brown solicited assistance from two female members of his own family. Daughter Annie and daughter-in-law Martha, the wife of Oliver, arrived in the latter part of July. They remained until September 30, cooking and cleaning for the growing number of men stationed at the farm.

Brown himself cultivated the good will of the neighbors, attending with skill the sick among animals and men. A little Dunker chapel was nearby; there John Brown often worshiped and even preached. "Yet with all this caution and care, suspicion lurked about them and discovery was always imminent," [46] Du Bois noted.

Brown's daughter Annie spoke of one impoverished neighbor and her four children who frequently came to make use of the little garden that they were renting behind the farmhouse. She said,

"This made it very troublesome for us, compelling the men, when she came in sight at meal-times, to gather up the victuals and table cloth and quietly disappear up-stairs." [47]

Inauspiciously, a man known to Brown from his days in Kansas had been invited to join the operation. He not only declined the invitation, but divulged Brown's plans to a newspaperman who in turn wrote rather accurately of them to the U.S. Secretary of War, John B. Floyd. As it so happened, Floyd was disinclined to be bothered with such a far-fetched scenario, especially as he was enjoying his summer vacation.

When Captain Brown's plans were finally disclosed in August, his associates were initially dissatisfied, hoping that the raid on the government works need not be part of it. Several of them became heated over the matter, and Brown actually resigned over the incident before being "re-elected" to leadership.

All of these variables pressed on Brown to hurry up the operation. He made a hasty trip to Philadelphia in early October. There he gained some valuable additional funding, though not procuring the additional manpower he had still hoped for from abolitionist leaders of the eastern metropolises.

Brown quickly returned to the farm, only to find that other conditions were deteriorating. Neighbors and some officials were getting increasingly inquisitive. A report surfaced from Harpers Ferry that certain weapons were scheduled to be removed from the arsenal and sent south. What was more, the men in the house had carelessly exposed their full number to some prying neighbors.

The last few of the eventual number of raiders had barely arrived to the farm when, as DuBois described it, "Suddenly Brown fixed on October 17th as the date of the raid." [48] As a result, only the nearest of the willing slaves round about could be communicated with, and several already on the way would not make it in time.

The Raid on Harpers Ferry

The plan, target, and ultimate destination were now in place. Brown's men awaited his signal. In his memoir, Osborne Anderson recalled,

> *"On Sunday morning, October 16, Captain Brown arose earlier than usual, and called his men down to worship. He read a chapter from the Bible, applicable to the condition of the slaves, and our duty as their brethren, and then offered up a fervent prayer to God to assist in the liberation of the bondmen in that slaveholding land."* [49]

The time had arrived. On the evening of the raid, before they departed the farm, Brown remarked to his men of potential opponents in Harpers Ferry,

John Brown's Fort in Harpers Ferry where Brown made his last stand and was captured. Photo by Winston Pitman.

"Consider that the lives of others are as dear to them as yours are to you. Do not, therefore, take the life of any one, if you can possibly avoid it; but if it is necessary to take life in order to save your own, then make sure work of it." [50]

Anderson continued,

"At eight o'clock on Sunday evening, Captain Brown said: 'Men, get on your arms; we will proceed to the Ferry.' His horse and wagon were brought out before the door, and some pikes, a sledge-hammer and crowbar were placed in it. The captain then put on his old Kansas cap, and said, 'Come, boys!' when we marched out of the camp behind him, into the lane leading down the hill to the main road." [51]

The first order of business was to take the federal arsenal at Harpers Ferry. Drawing upon his Kansas experience in military tactics, Captain Brown gave specific assignments to each of his men. Three of them were to stay at the farmhouse and watch over the two wagonloads of arms until they were to be brought forward to the river crossing upon the successful conclusion of the raid.

He dispatched others to perform such critical tasks as cutting telephone lines, guarding bridges and natural crossings over the Potomac and Shenandoah Rivers, capturing and standing guard over the various sentinels as they were captured, seizing the rifle factory, and taking possession of the armory.

The rest of the troop and those who had completed their earlier duties were to fan out and lock down the town; still others were to go into the countryside and take hostage specified slaveholders and slaves.

The initial phase of Brown's plan went off without a hitch. According to Osborne Anderson, all of the initial assignments were accomplished "without the snap of a gun, or any violence whatever." [52]

The objectives in Harpers Ferry having been secured, some of Brown's party went out into the surrounding countryside. There they enlisted some "colored men" sympathetic to their cause to alert yet others, resulting in perhaps another score of men rallying to the cause.

At this point, about one o'clock in the morning, the eastbound Baltimore and Ohio train arrived, was detained, and "the local colored porter shot dead." [53] After sunrise, the train was allowed to proceed, with John Brown himself giving personal assurances to the conductor. After the departure of the train, the occupation continued to solidify. The bulk of the raiders gathered up the newly-captured armaments and looked toward executing their escape plan.

Du Bois wrote,

> *"Up to this point everything in John Brown's plan had worked like clockwork, and there had been but one death. The armory was captured, from twenty-five to fifty slaves had been armed, several masters were in custody and the next move was to get the arms and ammunition from the farm."* [54]

With things secured by mid-morning, all that remained was for two wagons, filled with some 2,500 pounds of arms and supplies, to arrive from the Kennedy Farm to the rendezvous and staging point—a schoolhouse on the Maryland side of the Potomac River.

From there, John Brown's band of now several dozen would head southward across the shallow ford and into the safety of the highlands of Virginia. There they would set up shop under the "Provisional Constitution" Brown had drawn up a year and a half earlier while sequestered at Frederick Douglass's home in Rochester, New York.

Inexplicably, the wagons arrived not in early morning as they should have, but rather, the three-mile trip took eleven hours! By early afternoon, Brown's party had been engaged by the townspeople, initially to little effect.

Meanwhile, the passengers of the train that had been released earlier began to alert the various nearby communities by transmitting hand-written leaflets as the train rumbled on eastbound, eventually alerting the authorities in Washington, D.C.

Even then, there was still time for Brown to retreat or, instead, to successfully negotiate. Perhaps he surmised that the delay of the wagons must mean that its advance had been slowed by a great success in recruiting others to the cause and thus to the ultimate triumph of his original plan.

Whatever his assumption, he lingered too long in town. The tide turned as experienced militia men from the greater Harpers Ferry environs began to amass and take more effective action.

Brown's band retreated to an engine house now known as "John Brown's Fort." From that last bastion, they would not escape. Throughout the ensuing decline of his band's prospects, Brown demonstrated an agile mind during various negotiations.

On the morning of October 18, a company of United States Marines under the command of then Col. Robert E. Lee arrived in Harpers Ferry. Lee selected the young Army Lieutenant J. E. B. Stuart to extend to Brown terms of surrender. When Stuart offered Brown the clemency of the government, Brown presciently recognized the offer as an artful metaphor for "a rope around your neck." Brown's negatory response concluded with the noble resignation, "I prefer to die just here."[55]

JOHN BROWN'S CAPTURE AND TRIAL

After a grisly storming of the engine house, the affair was concluded. Ultimately, six of Brown's men escaped. Ten had been killed in the fight. John Brown and six others were captured.

Stabbed, clubbed, and bleeding, the inveterate abolitionist lay on the cold floor of the engine house. The governor of Virginia, Henry Wise, bent over him and asked, "Who are you?" Brown's response provides a summary of his perspective concerning the course of the some thirty-six hour event:

> *"My name is John Brown; I have been well known as old John Brown of Kansas. Two of my sons were killed here today, and I am dying too. I came here to liberate slaves, and was to receive no reward. I have acted from a sense of duty, and am content to await my fate; but I think the crowd have treated me badly. I am an old man. Yesterday I could have killed whom I chose, but had no desire to kill any person, and would not have killed a man had they not tried to kill me and my men. I could have sacked and burned the town, but did not; I have treated the persons whom I took as hostages kindly, and I appeal to them for the truth of what I say."*[56]

Among the hostages taken were Col. Lewis Washington, a great-grand-nephew of President George Washington. During Brown's trial, Washington would testify as a witness for the prosecution. During cross-examination, he stated under oath that Brown treated his hostages well and gave orders not to harm civilians.

As he lay bleeding, Brown concluded his account to his captors,

> *"If I had succeeded in running off slaves this time, I could have raised twenty times as many men as I have now, for a similar expedition. But I have failed."*[57]

A subsequent interview that day with the wounded abolitionist was recorded by a reporter from the New York Herald. It was later published, and contributed mightily toward convincing the nation that John Brown was hardly a lunatic, but entirely lucid, well-spoken, and principled in his opinions.

During the course of the interview, an unnamed officer asked of him, "Brown, suppose you had every nigger in the United States, what would you do with them?" To which Brown responded, "Set them free." [58]

Also during that interview Brown said,

> *"I wish to say furthermore, that you had better—all you people at the South—prepare yourselves, for a settlement of that question must come up for settlement sooner than you are prepared for it. The sooner you are prepared, the better. You may dispose of me very easily; I am nearly disposed of now; but this question is still to be settled—this negro question I mean—the end of that is not yet."* [59]

As the news of the failed raid stormed throughout the land, it is fair to say that the nation was convulsed. Because of the compassion-driven, reasoned, and nearly successful plan of John Brown, the necessity of a resolution of this centuries-old political, economic, moral question of race-based slavery took on an unprecedented urgency.

Prior to October 18, 1859, the continuation of slavery could masquerade before many Americans as a highly nuanced subject whose merits and demerits were worthy of serious and prolonged moral and practical reflection.

The attendant urbane sophistry included such intellectual dodges as, "Is not slavery a natural, ubiquitous, and proven institution for the good of civilization?" "Is the Negro truly and fully a 'person'?" "Is the Negro capable of taking care of himself; would he not be happier as a slave?" "Does not the Bible support the idea of slavery?" "Is this not a question for the individual states to address?" "Would it not be better to allow this controversy to resolve itself through a series of small steps in the course of societal evolution?"

John Brown, with all the simplicity inherent in truth, cut though the sophistical hogwash. He denounced slavery as simply an indefensible evil that should be terminated immediately. As Du Bois would put it in the early twentieth century, "John Brown was right." [60] That conclusion was far from being accepted in mid-nineteenth century America. Rather, John Brown's convictions and his actions arising from those convictions were utterly polarizing.

AMERICA ON TRIAL

Brown's subsequent trial became a matter of international attention. It was held some seven miles west of Harpers Ferry in the Jefferson County seat of Charles Town. Brown was indicted on three counts: murder of five persons, conspiring with slaves to rebel, and treason against the state of Virginia.

Brown's defense attorneys argued incisively and persuasively that all three charges were unfounded and unproven, but to no avail. Following the week-long trial, on November 2 the jury deliberated for forty-five minutes before finding Brown guilty on all three counts. He was sentenced to a public hanging a month hence, on December 2.

Following his conviction Brown addressed the court as follows in part:

> *"Now, if it is deemed necessary that I should forfeit my life for the furtherance of the ends of justice, and mingle my blood further with the blood of my children and with the blood of millions in this slave country whose rights are disregarded by wicked, cruel, and unjust enactments, I submit; so let it be done!"* [61]

Although the guilty verdict was cheered in many quarters, the outcry against it was equally fervent and widespread. Literary luminaries in America and Europe pled for Brown's life, steadfast in their opinion that he was more a righteous crusader than a rogue or criminal.

Henry David Thoreau composed a lengthy essay, "A Plea for Captain John Brown." The eloquent French author Victor Hugo warned that the hanging of John Brown would be an act of murder by an otherwise great nation against one of its great citizens. Ralph Waldo Emerson predicted that Brown's death would "make the gallows glorious like the Cross." [62]

All of these supplications proved to be of no avail. The hanging moved forward as scheduled, with a nationwide commotion attending its approach. Angry abolitionists employed Brown's impending execution as a rallying point. Fearful pro-slavery states exploited the occasion as impetus to reorganize and update their state militias.

Brown utilized his remaining time on earth to comfort and encourage his family. He also composed transcendent letters filled with conviction and spiritual exhortation that were published by northern newspapers. Those letters simultaneously inspired many in the North and infuriated many in the South.

In his diary, Thoreau describes Brown's last six weeks on earth as "meteor-like, flashing through the darkness in which we live. I know of nothing so miraculous in our history."

As the appointed day arrived, among the crowd of more than two thousand onlookers were future Confederate General Thomas "Stonewall" Jackson, the poet Walt Whitman, and future presidential assassin John Wilkes Booth.

On his final day on earth, the old abolitionist penned these words:

> *"I, John Brown, am now quite certain that the crimes of this guilty land will never be purged away but with blood. I had, as I now think, vainly flattered myself that without very much bloodshed it might be done."* [63]

Brown's words proved prophetic. At the beginning of the end, on December 2, 1859, Brown shed his lifeblood.

Four months after Brown's hanging, author Victor Hugo made this perceptive observation: "The American Union must be considered dissolved. Between the North and South stands the gallows of John Brown. Union is no longer possible. Such a crime cannot be shared." [64]

A year later, the tragic American Civil War was underway with Union troops singing, "John Brown's body lies a-moldering in the grave, His soul's marching on."

At the conclusion of the war in 1865, some 350,000 soldiers lay dead and three million slaves had been freed. In December of that same year, the Thirteenth Amendment took effect, deeming slavery illegal everywhere in the United States. John Brown's soul was marching on, and would continue to do so.

The old farm property from which he led that historic raid, however, would fade into obscurity.

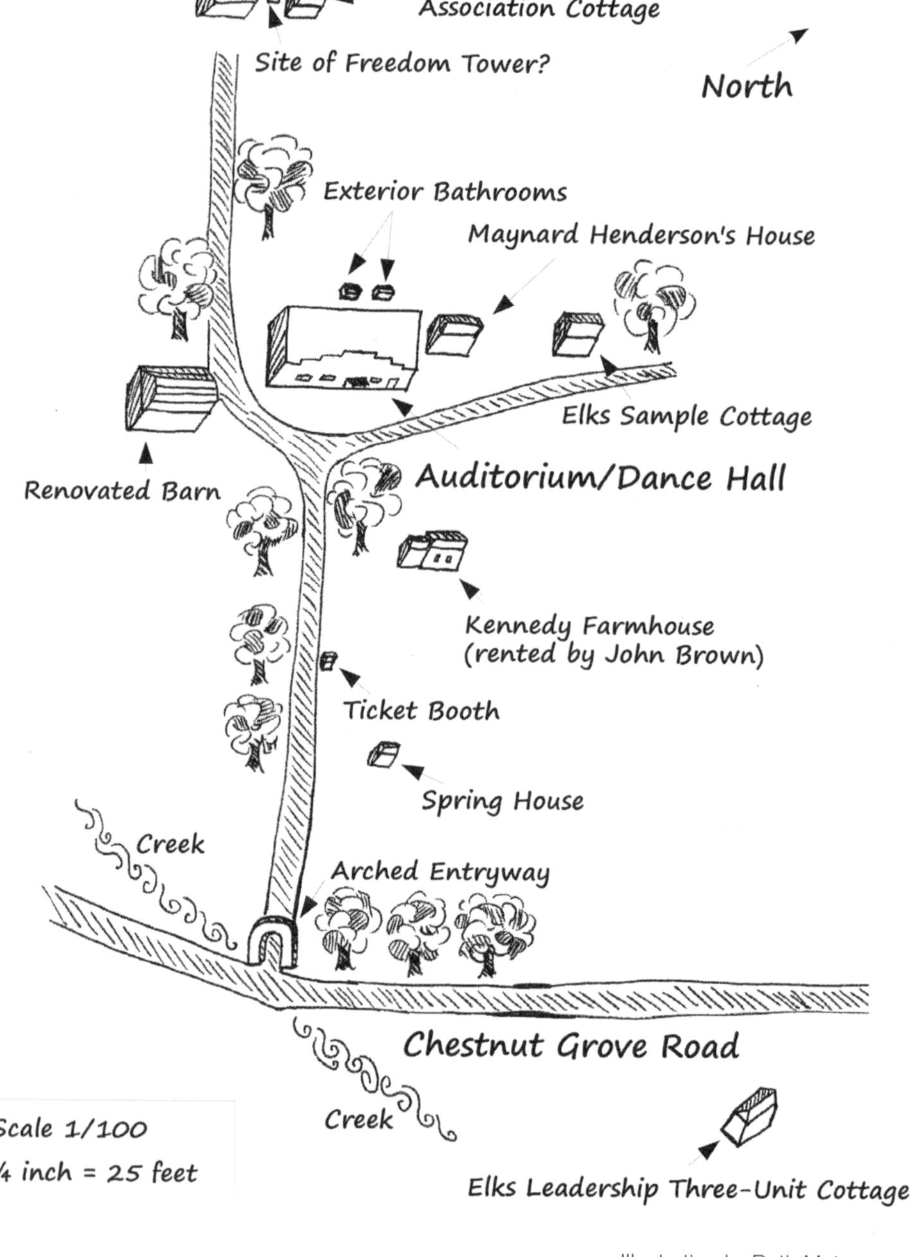

Illustration by Beth Meier

The Ownership of the Farm Property From 1859–1950

Between the time of Brown's arrest and his hanging, the circuit court appointed Judge Jacob Fiery as trustee of the Robert F. Kennedy estate. Fiery oversaw the selling of the property to Thomas Crampton in 1860. Crampton, however, proved unable to meet the terms of the contract, and so the property reverted to the care of Fiery as trustee. Eight years later in 1868, Fiery finally was able to sell the farm on behalf of the court to James W. Grove.

The John Brown farmhouse as it appeared during the time of its ownership by the IBPOEW from 1950–1965.

Over the next seventy-five years, the property passed through a succession of hands:

1869 James W. Grove to Mary A. Crampton

1890 Crampton to three brothers: Daniel W., John R., and Dr. V. Milton Reichard

1910 Daniel Reichard (alone) to Samuel M. H. Cook

1911 Cook to L. Edward Calvert

1932 Calvert to Alfred A. Ankeney

1946 Florence V. Ankeney estate auction to D. Earl and Margaret E. Neikirk for $3,300

A Close Call for the Old Farmhouse

Interestingly, early in the Reichard brothers' ownership of the farm, in preparation for an exhibit at the 1893 World's Columbian Exposition (also known as the Chicago World's Fair), the "fort" in which John Brown had been captured at Harpers Ferry had been, in 1891, bought, dismantled, and transported to Chicago. An account in Hagerstown's *Evening Globe* on November 21, 1891, reported the following concerning the nearby John Brown farmhouse:

John Brown's Residence
A Chicago Syndicate Purchases it from Reichard Brothers for $5,000

On Saturday morning Messrs. D. W. Reichard, of this city, Dr. V. M. Reichard, of Fairplay, and John Reichard, of this county, went to their farm, situated about five miles from Harper's Ferry, to superintend the setting out of additional peach trees on the place owned by them…

Before the sun had risen, a carriage drawn by a pair of beautiful horses, driven by a liveried coachmen, drew up at this residence. Two gentlemen dismounted. They inquired if the building was for sale. They received a reply that if enough money was offered it was.

The strangers proved to be members of the Chicago syndicate which purchased John Brown's Fort at Harper's Ferry. The syndicate took an option for $5,000 on the house, paying $10 spot cash to bind the agreement… It is the purpose of the syndicate to remove the building to Chicago and exhibit it at the World's Fair by the side of the fort recently removed from Harper's Ferry.

Apparently, and thankfully, the purchase and thus the dismantling of the old farmhouse was never consummated. South T. Lynn, the current owner speculated: "I guess they must have felt to move it would be too expensive or impractical at the time and let it [die]."

THE IMPROVED BENEVOLENT AND PROTECTIVE ORDER OF ELKS OF THE WORLD

During the Neikirks' tenure in the late 1940s, the farmhouse and its property came to the attention of the leaders of an influential black fraternal organization that was interested in creating a shrine to the memory of John Brown.

The closing years of the nineteenth century were harsh ones for black people in the United States. In the wake of the Reconstruction Era that ended in 1877, racism was alive and exacerbated due to discriminatory and demeaning Jim Crow laws. The 1896 *Plessy v. Ferguson* decision by the Supreme Court institutionalized the "separate but equal" fallacy by upholding the constitutionality of state laws mandating racial segregation in public facilities.

Blacks suffered along with other Americans as the financial Panic of 1893 plunged the nation into a long and grim economic depression that spawned six straight years of an unemployment rate over ten percent. As the financial discomfort at last began to ease, more and more American families joined a rising middle class. Conveniences such as pianos and bicycles, as well as new inventions like telephones, phonographs, and other electrical appliances made their way into millions of households.

Harsh poverty remained a daily reality for most blacks, though, especially in the South where sharecropping tied workers to subsistence living. Finally, by 1898 the rising general prosperity began to filter down to working class people, white and black. During this time, one of history's greatest periods of wealth creation, economic osmosis reached to the swelling black communities of the great Northern cities of Chicago, Detroit, Cleveland, Philadelphia, New York, and others.

At the turn of the century, blacks ventured out by day into the urban working world to labor in the factories, in private homes as domestics, and in many other occupations, but their hard-earned dollars were not welcomed in many white-dominated retail establishments. As a result, black people began to open parallel businesses in their own neighborhoods—grocery markets, funeral parlors, clothing stores, bars, newspapers, baseball teams, and banks, to mention just a few.

The need for salesmen to service these emergent markets set many black men traveling from city to city via the railroad. As they did so, the universal human drive to connect with like-minded others led to the formation of a nation-wide acquaintance of men and women interested in charity, justice, brotherly love and fidelity, the IBPOEW.

Having been excluded from the then all-white "Benevolent and Protective Order of Elks," black businessmen B. F. Howard and Arthur J. Riggs adopted the Elks' name and some rituals. They then formed their own organization, which they named the Improved Benevolent and Protective Order of Elks of the World—also known as the IBPOEW or "Black Elks" for short.

The IBPOEW became the largest black fraternal society in the world. The organization and its membership, including its women's organization, the Daughters of the IBPOEW, were strong participants during the height of the Civil Rights Movement in 1955–1968. Today the IBPOEW boasts an international following of some five hundred thousand members organized into more than a thousand lodges and temples.

During the first half of the twentieth century, fraternal organizations such as the IBPOEW provided vital opportunities for black leadership development. The Elks benefitted greatly from the established leadership prowess of two men in particular.

J. FINLEY WILSON

James Finley Wilson (1881–1952) served as Grand Exalted Ruler of the IBPOEW from 1922–1952. During his tenure, membership in the organization mushroomed from thirty thousand to five hundred thousand as roughly nine hundred new lodges were created.

At age thirteen Wilson had obtained a coveted position as a bellhop at the opulent and prestigious Palmer House in downtown Chicago. He subsequently worked for four years as a porter on the Missouri Pacific. Heading farther west he became a cowboy in Wyoming, a gold miner in Alaska, part-owner of a dance hall in Coalfields, Nevada, "and for a while worked with Buffalo Bill [Cody]."[65]

Wilson also worked at a small, black-run newspaper in Salt Lake City, the *Utah Plain Dealer* (probably as an assistant to Editor William W. Taylor or to his widow). Making his way back east, Wilson helped establish several black newspapers including *The Baltimore Times* and *The Washington Sun* where he functioned as editor. He also served for a season as president of the prestigious and influential National Negro Press Association.

When Democrat Franklin Delano Roosevelt was elected to the United States presidency in 1932, he acknowledged the support he had received from the IBPOEW and other black fraternal organizations. A lifelong Republican, Wilson was among the leaders Roosevelt invited to the White House in 1935, in the hope that they might back him during the next election campaign.

By the time of his convivial meeting with Roosevelt, J. Finley Wilson was the publisher of the *Washington Eagle* and the owner of real estate in six states—a wealthy and influential man.

WILLIAM C. HUESTON

Wilson's right-hand man in the IBPOEW was William C. Hueston (1880–1961). A graduate of the University of Kansas, Hueston also served in 1907 as the president of the Negro-Republican League of Missouri. He was an influential churchman and gave an address at the 1912 General Conference of the African Methodist Episcopal (A.M.E.) Church in Kansas City. He became (almost certainly) the first African-American judge in Kansas.

In 1927, Hueston assumed the presidency of the National Negro Baseball League, one of the two black "big leagues." He helped to establish and served as the president of Central State Bank in Gary, Indiana, where he also functioned as a magistrate judge.

Hueston was tapped by President Herbert Hoover to serve as a commission member toward the building of the National Museum of African American History and Culture in Washington, D.C. After nearly a century of delays, the museum is now scheduled to open on September 24, 2016.

Hueston moved from Indiana to Washington, D.C., to become assistant solicitor with the United States Post Office in 1930. There, he was active in setting up its law library, as he would do also at Howard University, near which he opened his own law office.

Judge Hueston was the grand Commissioner of Education of the IBPOEW from 1925 through the time of the purchase of John Brown's Farm. He also served at least twice as the Grand Lodge Secretary in addition to functioning as the editor of the *Washington Eagle,* the well-circulated newspaper published by the Black Elks.

HOW DID THE ELKS GET TO JOHN BROWN'S FARM?

The IBPOEW consists of a number of both state and regional entities. For instance, Pennsylvania has its own state association, while Maryland, Delaware, and Washington, D. C., are grouped together as the "Tri-State Association."

In the 1940s influential members of the Tri-State Association included its president, Leonard Curlin of Hagerstown, and his successor, the esteemed physician, Dr. Bernard Harris of Baltimore. Curlin and Harris were among those aware of the historical significance of the farm property from which John Brown had staged his historic raid on Harpers Ferry.

Let us here note that the property is sometimes referred to in the environs of Washington County, Maryland, as "the Kennedy Farm." The IBPOEW documents refer to it as "The John Brown Farm," while the attendees of the dances called it "John Brown's Farm."

The Tri-State Association officers learned that the historic property might be available for purchase, but was itself financially unable to proceed, perhaps in part because the nearby Hagerstown lodge had just concluded a large capital campaign to complete the purchase of its own building.

The Association did, however, become instrumental in the acquisition of John Brown's Farm. Its officers were quick to tout the historical importance of the property to the national Elks leadership and received authorization to make exploratory contact with its owners. A story reported by Gloria Dahlhamer in the February 24, 1975, edition of the Hagerstown *Daily Mail* corroborates: "Leonard Curlin of Hagerstown… negotiated the purchase of the farm."

For the IBPOEW to make that purchase, however, there first would have to be a vote of its membership at the succeeding annual convention, followed by a period of substantial fundraising. J. Finley Wilson and W. C. Hueston, men of means and action, evidently determined that they should not hazard the possibility of the property slipping away.

Wilson and Hueston thus set out to purchase the property in their own names. In so doing they might have been left holding the bag if (1) the IBPOEW failed to approve the purchase or (2) the IBPOEW was unable to come up with the necessary funding. Wilson and Hueston accepted that risk and made a bid

on the property. And then a funny thing happened on the way to the closing.

The deed shows that on December 28, 1948, the Neikirks conveyed the property to Leo and Ina Henson. That same day the Hensons apparently turned around and sold it to J. Finley Wilson, his wife, Leah Wilson, W. C. Hueston, and his wife, Jennie R. Hueston. Why were there two conveyances of the property performed on the same day?

Was somebody trying to hide something? Is it possible that the Neikirks were reluctant to have it be known to their white neighbors in this notoriously racist bailiwick of Western Maryland that they had sold their property to blacks? Could it have been that the Neikirks themselves did not want to sell their land to blacks? If so, then were the Hensons sympathetic go-betweens? That is, were the Hensons part of a pre-arranged pretense that they were the buyers in order to facilitate the ultimate sale to Wilson and Hueston?

It turns out that the real story was far less sensational. After much head-scratching on my part, I discovered that long-time Hagerstown attorney

The three-unit leaders' cabin stood on the opposite side of Chestnut Grove Road from the rest of the IBPOEW properties. In the foreground (from left) are Chief District Deputy Alton Lloyd, Judge William C. Hueston, and an unknown Antlered Guard member.

Leonard W. Curlin

Leonard W. Curlin (1900–1993) was an influential businessman, politician, and IBPOEW leader in Hagerstown from the early 1940s into the 1970s. He came to own several rental properties on and around Jonathan Street. His wife, the former Dorothy Hopewell, owned and operated "Dorothy's Beauty Shop" on nearby North Street.

A Jamaican by birth, Leonard Curlin retained a detectable island accent throughout his life. The son of a railroader, his early education was in the public schools in Jamaica. He later studied for a time in London, England, where his two older brothers served as barristers. He moved to the United States at age seventeen and settled in New Jersey where another brother was an optometrist. Hoping to study dentistry, Curlin took what he assumed was to be just a short-term, tuition-raising job, but got side-tracked into the insurance business.

Following a lengthy career as a supervisor with an Atlanta-based insurance agency, Curlin arrived in Hagerstown during the infamous Palm Sunday snowstorm of 1942 in order to take a war-time position as a sheet metal inspector for Fairchild Aircraft.

In the spring of 1945, Curlin opened his "Elite (pronounced EE-light) Rendezvous" at 322 Jonathan Street. Before long he upgraded the initial beer license to include wine and other alcohol. The establishment was described by Greg (Bruce) Johnson as "a classy bar. People who didn't live up to a certain minimum in looks and dress would be 'asked' to leave."

Curlin also at one time owned a "beer garden" on Bloom's Alley (now part of Murph Avenue).

Leonard Curlin near the entrance to the farmhouse, photo c. 1972.
Opposite: Leonard Curlin, right, and unidentified friend on the balcony of the farmhouse, c. 1972.

There one unfortunate fellow, soon to become known as "One-armed Slim," allegedly lost his appendage following a gunshot wound incurred over a nickel dispute during a craps game.

Curlin enjoyed "betting on the ponies," according to Reginald Johnson, Jr. who remembered fondly, "As a youngster I would approach him and say, 'Mr. Leonard, I'd like to go to the races.' Then at five-thirty, quarter to six, he'd pick me up and we'd be hittin' the road to Charles Town!"

Curlin's involvement in politics was regarded by two interviewees as initially "self-appointed." His persistence in "going downtown" to represent black causes eventually reinforced that perception to the state of reality. Curlin ran, albeit unsuccessfully, as a Republican for Hagerstown City Council three times in the 1960s. He also served as the first president of the local NAACP.

According to an article in the January 25, 1947, edition of the Richmond *Afro-American* by Ollie Stewart, Curlin became the Exalted Ruler of the Pride of Hagerstown Elks Lodge #278 in 1941, but that is too early a date, given that Curlin placed his arrival in Hagerstown in the spring of 1942. Be that as it may, under his leadership the membership ballooned from five in 1944 to one hundred in 1947.

In November, 1936, in the throes of the Great Depression, the Hagerstown Elks had forfeited the ownership of their property located at 326 North Jonathan Street to Washington County. Ten years later, Curlin made repeated appearances before the County Commissioners and eventually persuaded them to set a sale price on the former lodge.

According to the August 11, 1964, edition of Hagerstown's *Daily Mail,* Curlin next had "privately sought out one of the commissioners and asked to borrow the money to meet the purchase price." A loan (perhaps privately financed) for $4,500 was secured, and the Elks regained control of the property. Curlin orchestrated the necessary fund-raising, and the loan plus interest was paid off within a mere eleven months.

Bernard Brown, Exalted Ruler of Mountain City Lodge #382 in Frederick, Maryland, explained that Curlin also undertook assignments as "a Special Deputy for the Grand Lodge." In addition to becoming president of the Tri-State Association in 1948 (Delaware, Maryland, and Washington, D.C.), Brown related that at times Curlin was also the "head of the Blue Ridge Council that included regional lodges from parts of Maryland, West Virginia, and Virginia."

That combination of responsibilities put Curlin in a prime position to have influence concerning John Brown's Farm. Rev. Curlin is cited by several sources as having persuaded the IBPOEW of the historical worth of the John Brown's Farm property. In the recollection of South T. Lynn, a co-owner of the property since 1972, "Rev. Curlin was the man who talked the Elks into buying the Farm."

Curlin seems also to have been the person who acted on behalf of the Elks to interview and hire Maynard Henderson as the property's on-site caretaker. Curlin certainly became the supervisor of that relationship. Irma Branch, Henderson's niece, said of Curlin that "he was in charge of everything" and "paid Maynard."

Reverend Curlin remained emotionally attached to the Farm long after its sale by the IBPOEW. He maintained good relations first with Bo Morgan who bought the property from the Elks, and subsequently with South T. Lynn.

Bo Morgan evoked of Curlin, "He was well-liked. He was a mainstay up on Jonathan Street." As Curlin's personal maturation continued, he became first a deacon and later an associate pastor at Ebenezer A.M.E.—thus becoming "the Reverend Leonard Curlin."

George W. "Bill" Knight, Jr. was able to proffer an informed opinion about what probably happened at the closing. Knight was in a perfect position—professionally and personally—to solve this mystery. He grew up near John Brown's Farm and even worked on the property as a boy for the tenant. Knight is also the earliest visitor (I've been able to authenticate) to attend a dance at the property.

Speaking as a lawyer, Knight recalled that "back in the day" it was common for the sales agent to have his name recorded on the deed. Apparently, then, Leo Henson was merely the professional facilitating the sale from the Neikirks to Wilson and Hueston. Why then the presence of Henson's wife's name on the document? Her inclusion seemingly was a legal safeguard against the hypothetical occurrence of Leo Henson dying in the very process of the title transfer. Alternately, perhaps Mr. and Mrs. Henson operated some lost and forgotten co-agency. Either way, the Hensons were never true owners.

The John Brown Reader (p. 21) corroborates that the farm was "purchased for Elkdom by J. Finley Wilson and Judge W. C. Hueston." The two new owners thus also became almost nine thousand dollars lighter in their wallets at a time when, according to the *Federal Reserve Bulletin,* the average annual household income was $3,120.

In the spring of 1949, Wilson and Hueston traveled with committee members from the IBPOEW and its women's organization, the "Daughter Elks," to inspect the farm. There the joint delegation concurred to recommend its purchase to the impending Grand Lodge (that is, the membership as assembled at the Annual Meeting).

That recommendation seems to have been sufficient for Mr. Wilson and Judge Hueston to move forward with improving their newly acquired John Brown Farm. The two eventually would put another twenty thousand dollars of their own money into improving the property—to have the land surveyed, and for the costs of excavation, draining of marshy areas, intra-site road construction, and landscaping. At the time of their purchase, however, there still was no guarantee that the IBPOEW would actually buy the farm from Wilson and Hueston. Some substantial and skillful politicking remained.

THE SUMMER OF 1949

The IBPOEW's formidable administrative gears turned rapidly and efficiently to leverage a sizable event just a few months hence. Newspaper reports from the *Daily Mail* and *Morning Herald* chronicled the occasion. Although some of the particulars are at variance with one another and with other records, the general outline would seem to be as follows:

A dedicatory event at John Brown's Farm was set for the weekend of July 4, which in 1949 fell on a Monday. Housing was secured in advance in order to accommodate an expected gathering of some fifteen hundred Elks from throughout the Eastern Seaboard and as far west as Chicago. Many of the attendees spent the night of July 3 in the surrounding areas of Frederick, at the Harmon Hotel in Hagerstown, at Payne's Hotel in Charles Town, and at the campus dormitories of nearby Storer College in Harpers Ferry, West Virginia.

According to the July 2 edition of *The Daily Mail,* Sunday's program began at noon "with the breaking of ground for the Freedom Tower, a memorial to the abolitionist John Brown." Two attendant newspaper articles elucidated, "The tower will be a long shaft upon which will be an ever-burning light" and it "will bear a constantly burning light." Additional events on Sunday included "a social get together in the newly renovated barn on the property and a dance."

The following day, July 4, various orators urged an end to racial prejudice. Pennsylvania Governor James Duff was the main speaker "at the dedication of the John Brown Memorial Farm." I. Keller Shank, chairman of the Washington County Commissioners, also gave a speech in which he "stressed the history of the great anti-slavery leader and the role he played in the events that led up to the emancipation."

During the ceremony, various facts about the farm and its future use were detailed. The July 2 *Daily Mail* article reported, "When completed, the farm will contain two dormitories for children and a home for aged Negro Elks. A baseball diamond, swimming pool, riding academy, and other recreational facilities will be provided, and part of the property will be used to teach the children farming." The July 6 *Morning Herald* noted, "The Colored Elks hope to begin full-scale work soon on the property."

Curiously, various articles repeatedly cited the Tri-State Association as owners of the 254-acre farm. The Washington County land records reveal that the Tri-State Association never owned the farm and that the farm was 235 acres. There was, however, a parcel of land on the opposite side of Chestnut Grove Road upon which was built a three-unit cabin. Could it have been that that parcel was nineteen acres and was, in fact, owned for a time by the Tri-State Association?

That appears unlikely. Bonnard (Bo) Morgan bought the parcel across the road from the main property directly from the IBPOEW. Additionally, he told me that it consisted of "forty or fifty acres—maybe more like seventy." All these data points lead to the conclusion that the various assertions of the Tri-State Association's ownership are simply mistaken.

Upon the conclusion of the fabulous Fourth of July weekend, the attention of the IBPOEW leadership turned to the impending Grand Lodge, which was to be held in late August in San Francisco, California. Attendant to that event, the leadership published a fund-raising booklet.

The John Brown Reader, compiled by Judge Hueston, detailed what it described as "the salient facts of the life of John Brown and endeavored to show the high rank which he held among American immortals." In addition to a segment on the life and work of John Brown, there was an opening chapter on the "Grand Lodge History of the IBPOEW," a chapter titled "Grand Temple, Daughters of the IBPOEW," and a concluding essay by J. Finley Wilson on the "Meaning of Freedom."

The minutes of the 1949 Grand Lodge record that Hueston "described the John Brown Elks Memorial Farm, the action which had been taken toward its purchase, and the recommendation that the Lodge make its decision at this convention."

Hobson R. Reynolds, the Grand Director of Civil Liberties (and future Grand Exalted Ruler of the IBPOEW) presented his report. His remarks included that he "regarded the John Brown Farm project as a symbol of the objectives of the Civil Liberties Department and urged that Elks should support this great movement."

The minutes also noted that it "seemed to be a great event for the Elks to acquire this farm and turn it into a Shrine of historical significance so that it would serve as an inspiration to youth as they recalled the life of John Brown."

They concluded, "A major portion of the convention period was taken up with the discussion of the acquirement of the John Brown Farm. The property was valued at approximately $30,000 which would include all fees and expenses incident to the transfer... Brother Truly Hatchett moved that immediate steps be taken to negotiate for the purchase of the approximately two hundred and thirty-five acres known as the John Brown Farm by the Grand Lodge. The motion was... carried unanimously by a standing vote."

The next bit of historical insight comes from the September 7, 1949, edition of the *Morning Herald*. An article describes the condition of the farm: "Now that the national organization has granted its approval, local members of the Colored Elks Association are making plans to go to work at the John Brown Farm… No construction work has been done since the July Fourth dedication, pending the approval from the National Elks that was granted at the convention in San Francisco late last month. Local officials said yesterday that they hope to do some cleaning up of the site this month, and actually begin the improvements next month... A cabin that was on the site then has been destroyed, but the original farmhouse remains. It currently is a tenant farmer's house, and will become a museum under the organization's plans."

Several months of fundraising followed in the wake of the 1949 Grand Lodge. Then on April 28, 1950, the property was conveyed by the Wilsons and Huestons to the IBPOEW proper. Construction of several new buildings and the remodeling of the house and barn began soon after—prior to the gathering of the 1950 Grand Lodge.

Development and Use of the John Brown Farm by the IBPOEW

The minutes of the August, 1950, IBPOEW Grand Lodge in Chicago referenced the John Brown Farm, noting "its progress and the developments there as a farm and the proposal for it as a shrine." Mention was made also of "a program of education there" and "a summer camp for underprivileged youth." (The educational program soon expanded into a literacy program in conjunction with historically black Storer College some five miles away in Harpers Ferry, West Virginia.)

The Grand Lodge's promotional brochures urged the 1,105 delegates to attend the following year's convention "with the John Brown Memorial theme ranking high in their minds." Additional enticement included an artist's rendering of the proposed auditorium (that would later function as the dance hall) and

These masonry pillars topped by the identifying sign welcome visitors onto the John Brown Farm property. Photograph c. 1950.

(L–R) Remnant of barn foundation wall destroyed by fire in early 1970s; remnants of columns for JBF entryway arch. Photos by Winston Pitman.

photos of the upgraded, but not restored, farmhouse, a new front gateway, and a photograph labeled "John Brown as an old man" (though just 59 years old).

The 1951 Grand Lodge convened in late August in Buffalo, New York. In his principal address, Grand Exalted Ruler Wilson said, "We have come here to revive the throbbing heart of Old John Brown of Ossawatomie, while liberty still is cherished, and we still have time to pledge our undying love to the memory of that great soul who gave his all that we might be free."

The event's *Souvenir Journal* described the John Brown Farm property as "not only beautiful, but very productive, while a part of it has been under cultivation for more than one hundred years. Much of it is still in virgin timber. Other tracts of the farm are recognized as some of the best orchard soil in this great hearty fruit-producing region. The farm is well watered, it has five living springs."

The booklet went on to describe;

> *"A bandstand has been constructed, along with a natural auditorium. Sanitary toilets, running water, and complete electric power have been installed in the administration building."*

The above description muddies the investigative waters a bit in that a remarkable aerial photograph, probably from early summer of 1951, seems to reflect a different reality. In that photograph the two free-standing bathrooms (still in place as of this book's publication) sit immediately behind the footings for the yet-to-be-built dance hall, which would seem to be the one described as "the administration building."

Additionally, the "bandstand" that was said to have been constructed shows up in neither the aerial photo nor any subsequent references. And finally, the identity and location of the "natural auditorium" would also seem to be a mystery, unless it was a euphemism for the renovated barn.

Be all that as it may, the Elks delegates thrilled to the reminder that in a month hence, the extensively upgraded John Brown Farm would be ready to welcome them for its grand opening.

The grand opening of the "John Brown Shrine," as it was often referred to by the IBPOEW, was held on the weekend of September 22–23, 1951. Newspaper articles by the Hagerstown *Morning Herald,* Frederick's *News,* and Baltimore's *Afro-American* detailed the event, as did Charles H. Wesley's book "History of the Improved Benevolent and Protective Order of the Elks of the World, (1898–1954)."

On pages 381–383, Wesley's book recorded the events of September 22:

"...more than 2,000 Grand Lodge officers, brothers, daughters and friends from lodges and temples throughout the country assembled at the historic John Brown Farm near Harpers Ferry, West Virginia to dedicate this national shrine in a two day celebration. The purpose of this meeting was to proclaim the fact that Negroes had not forgotten and were now on the march to bring in the fulfillment of what was termed as the 'Holy Mission of John Brown, that of human equality of all men.'"

"Outstanding personages were present and participated in the program with the assembled brothers and daughters coming in more than 500 private cars and 20 buses. They saw the John Brown Home completely renovated, a renovated barn with a veranda running its entire length and seating about 200 persons, a new large auditorium fully equipped for meetings, and a sample cottage with bath. At the entrance of the National Shrine a 14 foot arch had been erected and a new picket fence had been constructed. The lawn was graded and picnic tables placed in the shady orchard."

The above-mentioned barn's veranda was created by opening up the second story of the side facing Chestnut Grove Road. It featured dozens of tables, each topped with an umbrella providing welcome summertime shade for members and guests. On multiple occasions, acoustic music combos played on the veranda for the listening and dancing pleasure of the patrons.

The "new large auditorium" that Wesley mentioned was the building in which hundreds of dances would be held with live entertainment provided by the giants of rhythm and blues.

The September 24, 1951, edition of the *Morning Herald* corroborates this:

> *"The dedication was for a concrete block building which will be used for recreational purposes... About 250* [actually 124] *feet long, this structure contains a dance hall, refreshment facilities, and other recreational equipment.*

Could this be the concrete footing for the mysterious Freedom Tower?
Photo by Winston Pitman.

The Freedom Tower Mystery

Over the course of my first five or so years of investigating this story, I found several vague references to plans by the IBPOEW to build a "Freedom Tower" on the property. Apparently it was to have been some kind of special memorial to John Brown. Several interviewees variously understood it to be something intended either to rise from the roof of the auditorium or to be built as a free-standing structure.

No one, including Bo Morgan, the man who eventually bought the property from the Elks, was aware of its exact nature or whereabouts. In hopes of discovering some clue, I held a magnifying glass to old photographs and tromped around the grounds near the farmhouse and auditorium looking for some evidence of that tower. Eventually I came to assume that the structure was merely a proposal that never came to fruition.

Very late in the discovery process, Morgan found on his own nearby property a stash of documents concerning John Brown's Farm. Among the memorabilia was a picture of a groundbreaking

"Next in line of construction on the property will be a freedom tower, a tall structure which will bear on its top a light which will keep burning at all times. This will symbolize the light that John Brown helped to bring to the slaves nearly a century ago... Groundbreaking for this tower is scheduled before the end of the year."

On September 22, *The News* contained several bits of important information that were unregistered in the other reports. "Saturday's program included contests for drill teams and drum and bugle corps. The crowd was so great the

ceremony with a well-dressed man in a summer suit wielding a shovel. In the background behind the participants was a banner heralding "Freedom Tower."

Well now, what was this! Surely the Elks did not go so far as to have a formal ground-breaking ceremony and then not follow through with the tower itself. Whatever it was, it must have been constructed.

Within days I came across an old newspaper article indicating that the "Freedom Tower" was to be a pole-like structure with an electric lamp on top. It was to be perpetually lit to symbolize the light that John Brown's anti-slavery campaign brought into the world.

Serendipitously, Mr. Morgan called me the very next day to say that he had found yet another document. The "Souvenir Journal" of the 1951 Grand Lodge Annual Convention mentioned that the Freedom Tower was to be built on the highest elevation on the property—"on its highest knoll."

Enter Google Earth, the popular satellite imaging program available on the Internet. One of its features is that you can run your cursor across the monitor and the display will indicate elevation above sea level.

I knew that two of the Elks' cabins were up on a ridge, so I started there and soon ascertained that they were both at the property's highest elevation—640 feet. So, where's the tower, then? As I zoomed in, it became apparent that there had been some kind of right-angled structure in the space between the two cabins—a rectangle perhaps 15 foot X 20 foot. Oh, baby! I think we're onto something!

I phoned South Lynn, Jr. (current co-owner of the property) to share my hypothesis that this might have been the site of the Freedom Tower. He mentioned having found a batch of discarded concrete blocks strewn about on one corner of the property, several of which had large bolts attached. Perhaps, and I would bet good money on it, they were the masonry remnants of the Freedom Tower's base.

On a subsequent trip to the Farm, I was able to inspect the rectangle spotted via Google Earth. It was indeed a concrete footing seemingly capable of supporting a substantial structure. Sadly, and to the best of my knowledge, the tower itself was never built. No wonder it was so hard to find!

A Hint of Scandal

In late 1954, a ruckus erupted attendant to the IBPOEW's 1950 purchase of the John Brown Farm from its leading officers, J. Finley Wilson and William C. Hueston. Trezzvant W. Anderson, a member Elk and unsuccessful candidate for Grand Secretary at the Grand Lodge just months earlier, brought suit in the United States District Court for the District of Columbia against Judge William C. Hueston and the estate of the recently deceased Wilson.

In the complaint, Anderson alleged that the two officers had bought the farm for only $9,000, but then represented to the Grand Lodge of 1949 that they had paid, rather, $28,000, prior to conveying the property to the Grand Lodge for $30,000.

According to an article in the December 31, 1954, edition of the *Memphis World,* Anderson complained of a "breach of trust, fraud, and misrepresentation" and a "secret profit" of $21,000 accrued to Wilson and Hueston. The article continued, "On behalf of himself and other Elks similarly situated, Mr. Anderson asks the court to award a judgment of $10,500 against Mr. Wilson's estate and Mr. Hueston each, plus court costs."

I can find no record of the case proceeding to trial. Perhaps Anderson became persuaded that Wilson and Hueston had indeed incurred some twenty thousand dollars in legitimate expenses for upgrades made to the property during their twenty months of sole ownership.

An article in the July 16, 1955, edition of *New York Age* that spoke of the Fourth of July event at John Brown's Farm is worth quoting in its entirety. Note that it seems to vindicate Wilson and Hueston in the portion underlined by this author in the second paragraph below.

> Elkdom's day was celebrated at their Shrine, John Brown Farm, where thousands came in every type of conveyance, at the invitation of the Grand Exalted Ruler, Dr. Robert H. Johnson, who with his charming wife, "Cookie," as she is familiarly known, celebrated with hot speeches and clear Elk's milk (whiskey) the temperature too hot for anything milder.
>
> The John Brown Farm, recently the center of much debate, can be appreciated more than ever since its cost and maintenance have been brought out into the open, as purchased in 1948, without a name; simply an idea. Since that time it has grown in stature and during the past seven years has become considerably important to Elkdom. It is regrettable that its use as a resort is limited due to its location. Yet it is of great significance to all as we are constantly reminded of the great sacrifice made by John Brown at Harper's Ferry to aid the cause of freedom for Negro slaves. To this end the I. B. P. O. E. of W. has given its all, in monies and labor, to develop this shrine as one of the future showplaces in American history."

Harpers Ferry school was opened to provide overnight quarters. Others found lodgings in trailers and at Hagerstown.

A few weeks later, the October 6 edition of the Baltimore *Afro-American* added yet more detail to the previous accounts, although some of it was clearly mistaken or fanciful. For instance, its head count of five thousand was two and a half times the estimates of the Elks and of the other newspapers. Additionally, the stated seating capacity of 1,800 for the new auditorium's usable floor space of 5,400 square feet (not including the kitchen and dressing room) is double what is practicable.

IBPOEW Pennsylvania State College Association Cottage. Photo by Winston Pitman.

Aside from those quirks, however, several inclusions added helpful details to the scene. Among them were, "A dance on Saturday and a cabaret party on Sunday were parts of the program" and "Each Elks' State association is pledged to build a cabin in honor of its state." The article also noted that Grand Exalted Ruler J. Finley Wilson (despite his being in a clearly weakened physical condition) presided at the ceremonies.

Seven months later, after serving thirty-one years as Grand Exalted Ruler, Wilson died on February 18, 1952, of complications from his long struggle with diabetes.

Robert H. Johnson, the Grand Esteemed Leading Knight, filled Wilson's unexpired term and then was elected Grand Exalted Ruler for three more terms through 1960. Hobson Reynolds served in the capacity from 1960–1982, and Donald P. Wilson from 1982 to present.

The next big IBPOEW event at the John Brown Farm occurred in mid-summer of 1953. Redacted from the Grand Lodge Minutes—On July 4, 1953, a large and enthusiastic crowd assembled at "the National Shrine, the John Brown Farm, Harpers Ferry, West Virginia" in part to celebrate the success of a night school for literacy in Memphis, Tennessee. Among the festivities of the two-day event was a performance by "Marge Majors and Her Band" said to be "Direct from Club 421 N.Y. City."

An article in the *Morning Herald* on July 6, adds a number of colorful details. The event was described as a "Freedom Day Program." Hagerstown's "Mayor Winslow F. Burhans welcomed the throng in a brief talk… Among the hundreds of visitors were eight busloads from distant New York and uncounted dozens of cars including a big delegation from Harrisburg. The group… talked over more elaborate projects like the construction of a freedom tower." This report shows that the Freedom Tower, whose foundation would seem to have been dug in the 1949 ground-breaking ceremony, was still in the planning phase four years later.

The Black Elks' 1953 Grand Lodge was held later that summer in Atlanta, Georgia. There had been some trepidation that holding the convention in its hitherto most southern city would lead to "undesirable reactions of various types... which would affect the status of the Negro."

The official IBPOEW financial report listed assets that included, "Cost, John Brown Farm... $30,000; John Brown Farm Improvement... $30,000; John Brown Farm Equipment... $5,500."

The Grand Auditors expressed a concern over "slow development" at JBF, urging state associations and lodges to shoulder their parts of the program for the erection of bungalows and of conducting excursions and attending celebrations on special days.

Fortuitously, the Fourth of July celebration at John Brown's Farm in 1954 was a tremendous success, with a crowd of over three thousand in attendance. The first state association cottage, that of Pennsylvania, was dedicated. A cottage funded through a national campaign by the Daughters of the Elks also had been erected during the year for the use of the Grand Daughter Ruler.

The August, 1954, Grand Lodge was held at the Corpus Christi Center in Chicago, Illinois. Several reports mentioned John Brown's Farm, including its initial purchase price of thirty thousand dollars and subsequent expenditures of one-hundred thousand dollars. That latter figure may have included a cottage on the opposite side of Chestnut Grove road—specifically for the use of the Grand Exalted Ruler and other leading officials. (The Pennsylvania State Association and Daughters of the Elks cottages were situated up the hill behind the auditorium. A fourth cottage, probably the aforementioned sample cottage, lay to the north of the auditorium.)

In his report, Grand Secretary Hueston referred to John Brown while pronouncing the goal for the Farm property was: "to enlarge, beautify and extend the usefulness of this National Shrine for ourselves and our children, preserving

Elijah P. Lovejoy Medal

Beginning in 1949, the IBPOEW annually awards its prestigious Elijah Parish Lovejoy Medal "to that American who shall have worked most successfully to advance the cause of human rights, and for the freedom of Negro people."

Lovejoy was a Presbyterian minister and publisher of the anti-slavery newspaper, *The Saint Louis Observer.* He was killed in 1837 by a pro-slavery mob while defending the warehouse and press from which he printed abolitionist materials. The notification of Lovejoy's death prompted John Brown to consecrate his life to the destruction of slavery.

The Lovejoy Medal is a coveted award—one which exemplifies the prestige, social connectedness, and political power the IBPOEW enjoyed during its ownership of John Brown's Farm and which continues to this day.

Lovejoy Award Winners during the years the IBPOEW owned the John Brown Farm: [66]

1950 Alfred E. Driscoll, Governor of New Jersey
1951 Ralph Bunche, Diplomat
1952 Branch Rickey, Baseball executive who recruited Jackie Robinson for the Brooklyn Dodgers
1953 Mary McLeod Bethune, President of Bethune-Cookman College
1954 Thurgood Marshall, Lead Counsel in Brown v. Board of Education
1955 Marian Anderson, Metropolitan opera soprano
1956 Martin Luther King, Jr., President of Montgomery Improvement Association
1957 A. Philip Randolph, President of Brotherhood of Sleeping Car Porters
1958 Lester Granger, Executive Director of National Urban League
1959 John H. Johnson, Publisher of *Ebony* and *Jet*
1960 William P. Rogers, Attorney General of the United States
1961 Roy Wilkins, Executive Director of the N.A.A.C.P.
1962 Adam Clayton Powell, Congressman from New York
1963 Gerald A. Lamb, Treasurer of CT; Leroy R. Johnson, GA State Senator; Edward R. Brooke, Attorney General of MA
1964 Harry Golden, Editor, publisher, and civil rights activist
1965 Whitney M. Young, Executive Director of National Urban League

Dr. Martin Luther King, Jr.

Dr. Martin Luther King, Jr. Accepts the Lovejoy Award

Twenty-seven-year-old Dr. Martin Luther King, Jr. was the winner of the 1956 Lovejoy Award. King had a longstanding relationship with the IBPOEW. As a fifteen-year-old in 1944, King had participated in an Elks oratorical contest by delivering a speech entitled "The Negro and the Constitution."

Below is the text of a letter of acknowledgment Dr. King wrote to Judge Hobson R. Reynolds, then Director of the Elks Department of Civil Liberties.

Dear Judge Reynolds:

This is just a note to acknowledge receipt of your letter of May 18, and to state how happy I was to hear from you. It was a real pleasure having you in our city and in our home. You were a real inspiration to the whole community in our struggle. I am looking forward with great anticipation to receiving the "Lovejoy Award." Let me again express my appreciation to you and the members of the committee for choosing me for this great honor. I will accept it with great humility and profound gratitude. Please feel free to contact me concerning further details.

Very sincerely yours,

M. L. King, Jr.

President Jimmy Carter Accepts the Lovejoy Award

August 15, 1977, was another busy day for President Jimmy Carter at the White House. That morning, President Carter met in his private office—called "The President's Study"—with Arthur Burns, Chairman of the Federal Reserve System, and then with National Security Adviser Zbigniew Brzezinski. Later in the morning, Carter would meet with his Press Secretary Jody Powell, and speak on the phone with former President Gerald R. Ford.

In between those two sets of appointments, President Carter walked over to the Oval Office to receive the 1977 Elijah Lovejoy Award. Several members of the press and a number of officials from the IBPOEW were present, including Grand Exalted Ruler Hobson R. Reynolds, Donald P. Wilson, and Carl O. Dickerson.

in our memories a man who stands as a sainted leader of men, who fought for the freedom of american Negroes, in their struggles for a decent, just, equal place in the sun."

In late August, 1955, the 56th Annual Grand Lodge, held in Atlantic City, New Jersey, once again honored John Brown. Convention attendees were issued delegate badges that featured a purple and white ribbon from which hung a brass medallion sporting the stern visage of the old abolitionist. The pendant was approximately the size of a fifty cent piece and appears to have been modeled on the 1859 "Black and Batchelder" photograph of the long-bearded Brown.

The following summer, delegates to the Grand Lodge of 1956 were reminded that the purpose of buying the farm had been to turn it into "a museum to tell the story of the heroes who died in John Brown's raid, to all the world, for generations to come." The minutes noted that each member should be assessed "ten dimes" during the upcoming year to sustain the farm.

In 1957, the Grand Lodge minutes describe a groundbreaking for a chapel on the JBF property. They also suggest an interest in establishing "a museum for Elks' relics, papers, and other memorabilia" onsite.

The next large Fourth of July "Freedom Celebration" was held at the farm in 1958. An eleven-inch by five-inch program booklet from the event was found among a trove of John Brown's Farm-related materials secured by Bo Morgan upon his purchase of the property from the IPBOEW in 1966. The program shows that the Elks termed John Brown's Farm its "National Shrine." Its schedule of events included speakers, hymn singing, and a 3 p.m. concert by the Morning Star Lodge Band, conducted by Chester Wood.

The cheery mood of that mid-summer event belied some rumbles in the distance. The August 18, 1958, edition of *The Carolina Times* (a black-owned newspaper in Durham, North Carolina) featured an article anticipating the 60th anniversary of the IBPOEW Grand Lodge. Details concerning the upcoming convention scheduled for August 23–30 in Washington, D.C., included this information on the event's opening:

> *"The convention opens with a pilgrimage Saturday, August 23, to the famed John Brown Farm located 60 miles west in the... Maryland mountains."*

The article went on to read,

> *"The IBPOEW owns the 255-acre farm which has since become a bone of contention among certain disgruntled factions of the Order."*

The September 6 edition of *The Carolina Times* included no record of disgruntlement, however. Instead, it featured remarks by Jackie Robinson, a 39-year-old, recently retired baseball star. Robinson, the Co-Chairman of the NAACP Life Membership Committee, addressed the three thousand Convention attendees at Metropolitan Baptist Church on R Street.

Robinson's exhortation, as reported by the *Times*, included that it was "quite a shock to hear President Eisenhower say we must educate the people into compliance of the mandates of the United States Supreme Court's decision on segregation. How in the world can we do that, if we are going to continue to educate them separately in a Jim Crow school system? We [Negroes] must take the bull by the horns and unite to fight our own battles to get our civil rights."

For the next several years, the development of the farm's facilities was less than spectacular. The development of the music scene at the site, however, was spectacular indeed!

The Neighborhood and Neighbors of John Brown's Farm

One of the many remarkable features about the music scene at John Brown's Farm is its location—hardly on a major thoroughfare, geographical or cultural. Southern Washington County was in 1950 a world unto itself. The nearest

---

Dargan's two-room red brick schoolhouse made national news in 1970. Ten parents were arrested, tried, and found guilty attendant to their protesting the Washington County School Superintendent's decision to close the beloved grade school that had served that rural community since 1914. Photo by Judi Maliskas.

hamlet to John Brown's Farm was (and still is) Dargan. The village's principal architectural features are its two-room red brick schoolhouse and Lily's Tavern.

Nearby Samples Manor is listed on most maps, but nearly all of its inhabitants are "six feet under." The gravestones of Samples Manor Cemetery are dominated by a dozen names prominent in the area: Giffin, Grimm, Hanes, Holmes, Houser, Ingram, Jamison, Knight, Moore, Myers, Reynolds, and Waters. These families have been related by marriage for generations—tightly knit, unvaryingly white, and generally distrustful of strangers, including law enforcement.

The two Washington County sheriffs during the JBF era were Edward L. Rowland from 1950–1958 and the widely-beloved Charles Price from 1958–1974. Neither man very often made his presence felt in the southern part of the county, however. The current Washington County sheriff, Douglas W. Mullendore, described this area as having been virtually self-policing: "Back in the day, even up to the 1990s, if a problem came up down there, they usually addressed it themselves."

One-time sheriff's deputy Greg (Bruce) Johnson remembered Francis "Skunk" Knight being referred to as the "King of Dargan," and that Knight would "take care of things" or, when absolutely necessary, turn in someone to the Sheriff's Department.

Lloyd "Pete" Waters, the premier chronicler of Dargan life, once wrote, "Skunk reminded me of Popeye the Sailor Man. With his raspy voice and small frame, he was always full of energy."

Long-time Hagerstown attorney George W. "Bill" Knight, Jr. was Skunk's first cousin. When asked about Skunk's purportedly running the southern part of the county, the lawyer allowed that he thought that was "giving him a little more credit than he deserves." Bill Knight continued, "After returning from serving in the Navy during WWII, Skunk ran the dump behind the Dargan Fire Company, so he knew everything going on."

As to the Darganites' resolution of disputes, Bill said, "People didn't often call the police; folks just used moral 'suasion. They mostly talked it out... All the Knights are pretty mouthy, including me."

Apparently that was not the only trait the family had in common. While interviewing Mr. Knight in his downtown Hagerstown law office, I asked if he could shed any light on a person mentioned to me by the moniker "Wild Ass" Knight. He could not, but obligingly phoned one of his brothers and asked, "Do you know of a 'Wild Ass' in the family?" After a moment's reflection, the brother glibly replied, "I don't know. It could have been any one of us."

Among Francis Knight's several nicknames ("Skunk," "Monk") was the colorful "Pot-head." He got that handle not for his proficiency in smoking marijuana, but rather for a hairstyle he once sported. His wife, Whylmenia, would bluntly trim his hair along the bottom of a big cooking pan she pressed onto his noggin as she administered a haircut akin to that of Moe of the Three Stooges.

One story (perhaps apocryphal) long-circulated in the Dargan area is that a black family attempted to settle there c. 1940. Supposedly, on the night that the family planned to (or perhaps did) move in, a note was pinned to the front door with a knife and reading something like, "Leave tonight. If you don't, you won't have another chance."

Having heard persistent rumors of Klan activity in the Dargan area, I asked Bill Knight for his insights. His opinion was that it was "just a rumor that the whites propagated coupled with some unorganized pranks to try and scare the blacks. The so-called KKK was mostly mouth."

When I asked one older Dargan native about the attitude of the local whites at the time to the Black Elks coming to the area, he said that a common reaction (not his own) was that "the niggers are moving in."

Undeterred by the potential adverse sentiment of the Darganites, the Elks moved in with remarkable efficiency. By late September, 1951, the JBF's farmhouse had been updated, the barn renovated, one cottage with plumbing had been erected, and a new, large auditorium (50' x 124') was completed.

Yarrowsburg

In a contrasting vignette of life in southern Washington County, Lee Best, a white man, lived on the east side of Elk Ridge near Yarrowsburg, a smattering of thirty or forty houses about a mile from JBF. Lee had to sit out fourth grade during the Depression of the 1930s because of a lack of shoes. He basically spent that winter inside the electricity-less house.

The Bests lived on a hillside next door to a black family (rare in the immediate area) with whom they shared Sunday meals on a regular basis. Years later, when Best left southern Washington County and got a job working for the railroad in Washington, D.C., he was shocked to encounter the separate bathroom situation for blacks and whites.

A feat such as this required a lot of workmen using a lot of materials in a relatively short span of time—one of the largest construction projects in the history of the area. I was curious about how this was accomplished and what impression this onrush of activity made on the surrounding white community.

I was able to interview a handful of people from the immediate neighborhood who were old enough at the time to have been conscious of the construction over sixty years ago. Sadly, none of them had been aware of it. Over the course of some five years of interviewing well over a hundred persons, I had been unable to get a definitive answer as to how the construction proceeded.

Dargan natives George "Bill" Knight, Gene Hardy, and Robert Grimm, however, were all "pretty sure" that the Elks did not use local contractors to build the auditorium and the other buildings, but brought in the materials and the labor from Washington, D.C., and other places. Gilbert Everline, then a meter reader and pole climber for Potomac Edison, recalled much of the construction work being done on Saturdays. He suspected that that practice was indicative of volunteer labor rather the work of a professional contractor.

The discovery of an article in the September 24, 1951, edition of the *Morning Herald* revealed the answer to the question I had fruitlessly asked interviewees hundreds of times: "Members of the lodge are doing all the construction work."

Once the buildings were up and available for the activities of the IBPOEW, what would the future hold for their relations with their white neighbors? Animosity? Vandalism? Reprisals?

What ensued, rather, was a remarkably amiable long-term relationship between black Elkdom and white Frog Hollow. I have yet to meet a person, black or white, who had personal or even second-hand knowledge of interracial animosity during the decade and a half that the Black Elks held the property. The relationship appears to have been congenial from the onset.

A critical cog in the long-term viability of the IBPOEW's ownership of the property would be their relationship with the locals. The selection of a suitable point person, the on-site caretaker, would prove all-important. The Elks found their ideal man in Maynard Henderson.

Maynard Henderson

Maynard Henderson was a member of one of the oldest black families in the area. He was born c. 1911, one of the younger children of Daniel and Mary Henderson's many. Maynard's oldest brother, Roy, has birth dates listed variously from 1905 to 1907; his youngest sister, Virginia Simms, was born in 1921.

The Henderson family's homestead of origin hugs the eastern ridge of South Mountain, the northern extension of the Blue Ridge Mountain range—technically five miles from JBF, but easily twice that distance via the winding mountain roads.

The Henderson properties are located quite near the Appalachian Trail and roughly halfway between the village of Burkittsville, Maryland, and Gathland State Park.

Long-time JBF property caretaker Maynard Henderson (second fron left) is flanked by IBPOEW officials.

Outerbridge Pry

Many a time this author felt that he had run out of wild gooses to chase concerning this wonderful story. On one such occasion I was trying to locate Virginia Simms, the ninety-something-year-old sister of Maynard Henderson. I had heard that she lived somewhere near Burkittsville, Maryland, and, running out of leads, decided just to drive down there one rainy day and see what I might be able to turn up.

Several kind people in the area gave me well-intentioned but incorrect information concerning the whereabouts of Ms. Simms. I was just about to head back to Hagerstown in the drizzle but had a random notion to knock on the door of a prosperous-looking farmhouse south of Coatsville—just to give it one last, probably useless, shot.

I knocked and waited. Knocked and waited. Giving up, I headed out through the rain to my car. Just then, I saw a man and woman, perhaps a generation or so older than I, coming off the main road and up the puddle-filled lane on a tractor. I got back under the house's overhang and waited to see what might-could happen.

The lady of the house jumped off the tractor to field my questions while her husband put the rig in the barn. As she comprehended my strange tale, she declared, "Young man, you have come to the right place. My husband is the local amateur historian. If anybody can tell you what you want to know, he can!"

She started out to the barn, but I persuaded her to join me under my dinky little umbrella, and we walked toward the barn together. I remember thinking, "If that farmer turns the corner right now, what with me snuggling up to his wife under this umbrella, he's going to shoot me for sure!"

Well, he didn't shoot me, and he was very helpful, putting me in touch with several older African-Americans in the area. On a subsequent occasion, during the time I was preaching for a year or so at a Christian and Missionary Alliance church in nearby Rosemont, Maryland, my wife agreed to stop in with me after church to meet this lovely farm couple, Richard and Patty Pry. "But," my wife Judi insisted to me, probably with a finger waggle, "we are *not* staying for lunch."

We knocked on the door and greeted the Prys. Almost immediately, Mrs. Pry asked, "Have you had lunch?" Judi jumped in to say, "We just wanted to stop in for a few minutes." Mrs. Pry scolded here with a surprising vehemence toward someone she had just met, "I didn't ask how long you wanted to stay; I asked, 'Have you had lunch?'"

We stayed., and we had a wonderful time and a wonderful lunch: hamburgers that tasted the way they did a half-century ago, the meat from one of the Prys' own freshly butchered, grass-fed cows. The home-made apple dumpling was just as good. But that wasn't the Richard Pry story I most wanted to tell.

The story I do want to tell is how Richard Pry's father's name came to be Outerbridge Pry. Well sir, once upon a time, Richard's grandfather, Luther Calvin Pry, was renting a piece of farm property from a neighbor, the wealthy octogenarian Outerbridge Horsey IV.

On January 19, 1900, Luther Pry walked over to the nearby Horsey distillery to announce the birth of his son. Horsey asked Pry, "What did you name him?"

Pry answered, "We haven't named him yet." Outerbridge plunked down on the counter a twenty dollar gold piece—a good week's salary in those days—and declared, "Here, name that boy after me!"

Luther Pry pocketed the twenty dollars and hiked home cogitating how to explain to his wife that she would henceforth be changing the diapers of one "Outerbridge Pry."

Among the Hendersons who still live on what some locals refer to as "Spook Hill" are Maynard's younger sister Virginia, her son Larry Henderson, and Roy Henderson, the son of Maynard's older brother, Roy "Red Buck" Henderson.

One interviewee related a local legend concerning the origin of the name "Spook Hill." Heading east on Gapland Road as you cross South Mountain toward Burkittsville, there is a little stretch of road where your eyes can play tricks on you. This optical illusion makes you think that you are heading downhill when in fact you are heading uphill. Put your car in neutral, and you'll be surprised to find it "rolling back up the hill," so to speak. Folklore contends that this counter-intuitive process occurs because, "The spooks are pushing your car."

The Henderson family first acquired their land near Crampton's Gap some time prior to the Civil War. They received the land from Thomas Sim Lee the younger as part of the voluntary manumission of his slaves. Lee had been given the name of his grandfather, who was the first Governor of Maryland. Lee the elder was elected in 1779 by the Maryland Legislature under the Articles of Confederation prior to its ratification. Governor Lee's plantation comprised

Rye Whiskey

The first cousin of Thomas Sim Lee was an interesting fellow with an interesting name—Outerbridge Horsey IV. Horsey's mother was Lee's aunt; his father was a two-term Senator from Delaware. Horsey was a lawyer and also a distiller at Needwood who advertised his product as "The First Eastern Pure Rye Distillery of the U.S." Horsey became a successful businessman and was well-connected politically in Washington, D.C. He reportedly remained an avid connoisseur of "Old Horsey" up to his death in 1902, at 83 years of age.

some two thousand acres near Burkittsville and was home to the mansion he named "Needwood."

AN ELUSIVE DETAIL

Precisely how Maynard Henderson landed the position as caretaker of John Brown's Farm was difficult to ferret out. Arnetta Doleman, a fountain of knowledge about black history in the Hagerstown area, said that Henderson was working for the railroad when he was approached by the Black Elks to consider the job. Henderson's sister Virginia Simms, on the other hand, was adamant that her brother had never even worked for the railroad.

Clarice Henderson, when asked if she knew how Maynard got the job, replied, "I wouldn't know. Nobody talked about those things when I was a child. We were in one room while the adults talked about business in another room." Her answer is illustrative of a general value in mid-century America of not letting other people "know your business." So there the story sat for a time.

Later, I was referred to Melvin Henderson who helped take care of Maynard in his declining years. Melvin is of the opinion that "Maynard probably got the caretaker job because he belonged to the Elks Lodge #278 here in Hagerstown."

At the Hagerstown Historic City Farmers Market (a Saturday breakfast spot for my wife Judi and me), I met Arnetta Doleman's son Anthony. I asked him how Henderson may have gotten the caretaker position and was delighted to hear him relate that in the late 1960s he had worked with Maynard at erecting scaffolding for bricklayers. Mr. Doleman's understanding was that Henderson belonged to the Hagerstown Elks and that when it was time to recruit a caretaker, his connection to the area was valued.

I met Anthony Doleman again (perhaps two years later) attending his mother Arnetta's funeral. While chatting, I queried him again about Henderson's getting that caretaker position. This time he recalled, "Seems to me that Maynard had a good job that he quit to take [the caretaker job], but I can't remember what it was." I tendered, "Was it with the railroad?" Immediately he and a friend named Washington both exclaimed, "That's it!"

So, apparently the combination of Henderson's Elks membership, his familiarity with social realities in the area around the farm, and his established work ethic placed him in a unique position to fill the position of caretaker. His character enabled him to prosper in it.

A MAN'S MAN

By all accounts, it seems Maynard Henderson was a complex man. Following are several (often paradoxical) character appraisals, as given by friends and neighbors:

> *"He was happy-go-lucky, but don't cross him." said Henderson's sister Virginia Simms. She added, "He could take care of himself. People out here have to take care of themselves."*

> *"He was a heck of a nice guy. He got along with everybody," Melvin Henderson said. "You wouldn't want to get him mad, though; he had a bad temper."*

> *"When I was a little boy, he seemed like a man that everybody was afraid of. He was a good man. He was a very protective man when it came down to the kids," recalls Reginald "Mop" Johnson.*

> *"He was a second dad to me," said nephew Joseph "Junior" Henderson softly, followed immediately by an animated, "He was evil; he would cut you off if you said the wrong thing or something to the wrong person."*

> *Henderson's nephew Gerald Barnett put it pithily concerning Maynard Henderson: "He was a man's man."*

One of the earliest written records concerning Henderson involved his getting into trouble during his late teens. The *Morning Herald* on July 18, 1929, contained an article titled, "Tried to 'Break Up' Game; Gets 30 Days."

> *"Maynard Henderson, colored, was fined $10 and [court] costs and sentenced to three months in jail at Frederick yesterday as the result of an attempt to 'break up' a crap game near Burkittsville. Fourteen other participants of the game were assessed $1 each and costs. Henderson's jail sentence was suspended. It all happened on June 30, when Henderson wanted to get in the game without any funds. He asked for a stake, was refused and then secured a gun and slightly wounded one of the party. The shooting was believed accidental."*

Antietam Red Tops

Attorney George W. "Bill" Knight, Jr. related that back in the 1940s, the hamlet of Antietam, Maryland, had a semi-pro baseball team called the Antietam Red Tops. Among the teams they played was the Shepherdstown Red Sox, an all-black team from just across the Potomac River in West Virginia.

Because some white teams were reluctant to play at a black team's home field, the Red Sox crafted an ingenious business model. Knight related, "If they came to your town to play, you had to pay them nine dollars for travel. If you would play a return game at their park in Shepherdstown, they would pay you back the nine dollars."

Into his early adulthood, Henderson was athletic. Bobby Morris grew up near the Hendersons in Burkittsville, and said that he and Maynard played baseball together for "Kaplans out of Williamsport." Morris played second base while Henderson pitched. That tidbit came as a surprise to Junior Henderson who remarked, "I don't remember Uncle Maynard ever doing anything athletic, even pitching horseshoes."

In the absence of definitive evidence, it would appear that Henderson assumed the caretaker position at John Brown's Farm perhaps as early as the summer of 1950. One of the several clues concerning the dating is the testimony of Gerald Barnett, who was born in September, 1947.

In his infancy, Barnett had been placed into the care of his "Aunt Mame" Barnett and her common law husband, Maynard Henderson, whom Gerald called "Daddy." The couple had year-round custody of Barnett until he was six. He related, "[Maynard] was a man that came from small beginnings. He was a self-made man. He wasn't an educated man, but there wasn't anything that he couldn't do. He could read a blueprint the way he read a book," Gerald recalled of him. "I'm blessed that he raised me."

Mame, a woman of medium stature, was described by shirttail relative Margaret Barnett: "Mame was a very nice, a very fine woman. She loved children. She was a housewife and helped Maynard run the farm by picking potatoes and picking eggs from under the chickens."

Gerald remembers living as a pre-schooler "in the log house" without electricity or plumbing; rather they used lanterns and an outhouse. In September, 1953, he was trundled up to Hagerstown and transferred to the care of Mame Barnett's cousin Madeline Adams in order to attend first grade. He returned to live at the farm during the summers until he was about sixteen years old.

Indicative of the couple's familial generosity, for a time in the 1940s when they lived near Asbury Park, New Jersey, the couple helped raise another relative, Mame's nephew Henry (Buck) Barnett. Roy Henderson, Jr. said that he also "lived in the farmhouse for a year or so with uncle Maynard" when he was a child.

Henderson delighted in, and was effective at, his all-encompassing management of the property. Irma Branch recalled how much her uncle "loved running the farm." Gerald described Henderson as "the catalyst for everything that happened on the property," and added, "He ran a tight ship."

Henderson's duties included cutting the grass, making general repairs, cleaning the exterior block bathrooms behind the auditorium, purchasing supplies, keeping the ledgers, managing the lockbox he stored in a safe, and depositing monies in the bank. He also delegated tasks to others.

As Gerald Barnett grew older, he was given several summertime chores attendant to the dances. Those included spreading sawdust on the dance floor, cleaning the guest cabins, helping unload Pabst Blue Ribbon beer trucks, traveling around with Henderson to put up the posters announcing the dances, forming hamburger patties, and polishing the floors with a buffing machine the Elks owned.

As young adults, Wallace Brooks and John Henry Henderson helped "Uncle Maynard" by doing various tasks, including painting the barn and farmhouse.

At one point, Henderson engaged a couple of the local white kids to tidy up the grounds after dances. As Larry Morrison recalled, the deal was that he and his brother Glenn could keep anything they found, except they had to turn in keys and eyeglasses. The most money Larry remembers ever finding was "eight to ten dollars"—not bad for the early 1960s when minimum wage was a dollar an hour.

EVER THE ENTREPRENEUR

In addition to Maynard Henderson's regular responsibilities and remuneration, he engaged a number of his other talents to make a buck. Donald Morris, a Dargan native, remembers Maynard as "always working. He had hogs that he would feed from mashing up left-over bread in fifty-five-gallon drums." Neighbors George and Alma Morrison remembered that Henderson supplied them with firewood for their stoves by cutting dead trees on the John Brown's Farm property.

It seemed to his nephew Junior and others that Maynard partnered in running the auditorium kitchen for profit during the dances at the farm. Beverly Dykes King, who as a girl frequently worked the kitchen with her mother Lucille Dykes, said, "Mr. Henderson purchased the chicken in bulk, by the crate. It was his task to cut up the chicken." Joe Dixon, who sometimes worked at the dances, remembered Maynard buying chicken in bulk from "Bags" Lyons, owner of Lyons Grocery Store in nearby Keedysville.

Henderson was known to dabble in chemistry, too. Several people remembered peach trees on the property, and his niece Irma recalled that he "liked to make some homemade wine." Hagerstown native Rudy Russ noted that Henderson also made "jump steady" (distilled spirits) at three to four dollars a fifth. Seeking to corroborate that assertion, I asked Greg (Bruce) Johnson if perhaps Maynard may have made moonshine. He replied impartially, "Down there everybody did."

Henderson was also willing to support the industry of others in the production of that local commodity. Darganite Gene Eichelberger related, "[Maynard] used to buy moonshine from my dad, Don Eichelberger."

Henderson also had a life-long interest in animals of various kinds. Roy Henderson, Jr. recalled that one of his uncle's many pets was "an old brown Chihuahua." Another little dog of his with black and white markings was called "Skippy." Henderson had "Skip" for perhaps fifteen years before the poor thing, by then blind, met its demise by being backed over by a beer truck.

Henderson also raised pigs and chickens. A hog pen and chicken coop sat well behind the caretaker's house. There was also a butcher shack. Greg Johnson related, "My daddy once took me to the farm for a pig-butchering with Maynard. A little smoke house sat between the dance hall and barn, closer to the barn." Rick Barnett, son of Mame Barnett's nephew Henry, cites the same location. Their recollections are corroborated by an old photograph that shows a small building fitting the description just to the north of the farmhouse.

Sprigg Lynn relayed to me a story told by a woman he once met. As a girl, she lived in New York City but in the summers came to visit relatives in the Charles Town area. They would sometimes bring over her to John Brown's Farm. One of the sights she witnessed was particularly amazing—or horrifying, given her urban upbringing. As noted above, Maynard kept chickens on the farm, and often would let them roam the place—the original "free range chickens." If someone were interested in purchasing one of the chickens, either to take home or barbecue there, Maynard would whistle for his dog "Skippy." The dog would

Moonshine

Bonnard J. (Bo) Morgan, who bought the JBF property from the Elks in 1966, still lives just up the road. Morgan described the southern end of Washington County back in the day as the "moonshine capital of the United States." Upon surveying his newly-purchased farm, he remembers finding on its acreage perhaps ten stills, multiple barrel hoops, and numerous whiskey bottles with "Frog Hollow" labels.

The story goes that during Prohibition days, "Frog Hollow" whiskey shipped out on a train from Brunswick, Maryland, to Pittsburgh, Baltimore, and Washington, D. C. One or more train conductors were said to have been in on the action.

On one of my excursions down to the Dargan area, I was beckoned to "come on up and get out of the sun" and onto the porch of a house where two women sat on rocking chairs. It turned out fortuitously to be the house of the notorious Francis "Skunk" Knight's widow, Whylmenia, who sat rocking with her daughter, Doris (Knight) Shoemaker.

Skunk had held an extensive notoriety as a moonshiner, but because I was a guest on his former porch, I put my question about his erstwhile activities to his daughter delicately: "Doris, would you happen to know anything about moonshine?" She surprised me as she leaned in, held out two fingers horizontally, and chuckled conspiratorially, "I have about that much left in my bottle."

then chase down one of the chickens and bring it back to Maynard who would, in turn, wring its neck and butcher it on the spot. Welcome to the country, city girl!

The site also housed a little pear orchard beyond the barn to the southwest. A springhouse lay about halfway between the road and the historic farmhouse. A three-unit guest cottage with its distinctive cupola was situated on the opposite side of Chestnut Grove Road.

During Sunday afternoon picnics and other family-oriented gatherings, Henderson would volunteer to lead the children around on his pair of horses. Hagerstown native Thelma Waters was one of the many who took him up on the offer to enjoy a horse ride. Roy Henderson, Jr. remembers attending one Fourth of July picnic, eating ice cream provided by a dairy farm near Middletown, and riding the ponies. Roy's father Red Buck owned some of those ponies and would truck them over to JBF for special events.

Joe Dixon recalled a man named Henry Hunter from Georgia, in the area to work on the construction of Interstate 81, as having gotten thrown off a mule on one such occasion.

Maynard and his brother Red Buck both periodically bought and sold horses in West Virginia. Rick Barnett remembers that on one occasion, "A man named Bobby Armstrong told Maynard about a mare that was for sale. Maynard bought the mare, a Morgan horse. Turns out she was in foal with a colt sired by a Palomino. Aunt Mame, with the help of a man named Charlie Ware in a wheelchair, delivered the foal, Champ."

Maynard trained the colt. He would put a carrot in his pocket to teach Champ to follow him. According to Rick Barnett, Champ in turn, "trained cattle." (The author feels a wee bit gullible for not having asked a follow-up question to that last assertion.)

Ike Wilson, whom I met at the Hagerstown City Farmers Market, said of Champ, "No one could ride that horse but Maynard." According to Junior Henderson, Maynard would generally warn folks, "If you want to think about riding that horse, [you'd] better come see me first." Some people, however, did not submit to that wisdom.

Junior recalls that, "People would get their legs broke and everything else trying to ride that horse. One guy tried to ride him. Champ flipped him off. Kicked him on the way down before he even hit the ground. Broke his leg." Rudy Russ remembers that at one of the family-oriented events a man named James Baltimore tried to ride the gray stallion, fell off, and broke his arm.

Maynard, on the other hand, could just call for Champ, and he would oblige straightaway. Junior Henderson delighted, "The horse would come running. Maynard would grab him by the mane and flip [himself] up onto his back."

A local white man, Harold "Buck" Gay, grew up around Antietam Village and remembers that as youngsters he and his buddies "didn't have much sense." They would "drink a few beers and get into a bit of mischief, like just about everybody did in those days." As an adult, he moved into a house "two fields over from Maynard's place, down in the hollow." Gay would saddle up his Palomino, "Duchess," and ride over to John Brown's Farm. Henderson would mount "Champ" and off the two horsemen would go. On one occasion they rode the twenty mile round-trip to Williamsport. Gay recalls, "I was sore for a week. I don't know how those old cowboys did it."

Their typical excursion, however, was to ride up and down Mt. Lock Hill Road, just north of the farm. On one particular trip, Gay was riding behind Henderson when Duchess took delivery of a solid kick in the muzzle from Champ. Henderson mumbled an apology and suggested that they switch positions for the rest of the ride. It wasn't long before Gay heard a "whoomp," turned, and was surprised to find Maynard standing on the ground next to Champ. Henderson unperturbedly explained concerning the apparent equine retaliation,

The post-fire remnants of caretaker Maynard Henderson's private residence are seen in the right foreground. Photo by Winston Pitman.

"Your horse kicked Champ out from underneath me."

Given his love for animals of all kinds, life on John Brown's Farm suited Henderson. At some point (perhaps in 1954), he got the go-ahead from the Elks to construct a house for himself at his own expense on the property. This authorization apparently came with assurances that, all things being equal, he and Mame could think in terms of homesteading there for many years to come and probably on into retirement.

The resultant block house was situated just 10–12 feet north of the auditorium, and was luxurious in comparison to the old farm house. It had a metal roof and a full basement with a fireplace, in addition to the modern conveniences of electricity and indoor plumbing. Maynard kept a garden behind the house and according to a c. 1970 aerial photograph, an otherwise unmentioned corral off to the right of the garden.

I was curious as to the means by which the house had been constructed. Several sources said simply "Maynard built it." Others said that it was built by his kinfolk. Others mentioned "friends" helping. Junior Henderson alluded to some forty people pitching in on building the house and that it went up quickly. Gene Hardy, who grew up in the Dargan area, recollects whites from the area helping as well. Probably all of this is true. The collaborative enterprise points to both Maynard Henderson's character and to the most important responsibility of his job description.

Henderson, as did the Elks generally, had a commitment to and a knack for getting along with his Dargan area neighbors. Local Donald Morris mentioned that Henderson often came into Dargan, sometimes on his riding lawn mower. Morris reminisced, "I drank a few beers with Maynard. He was a right nice fellow; never said a harsh word."

Doris Shoemaker, Skunk Knight's daughter, said that when she was a girl of maybe ten or twelve, Henderson would often swing past her father's house in his old station wagon or pickup truck to stop and shoot the breeze with her dad. Doris described her father as generally a "hard to please kind of guy, but he loved chewing the fat with Maynard."

Shoemaker remembers Henderson as "well-mannered" and "kind." For instance, he had a little white and brown dog named Susie and gave Doris one of her pups. He would frequently invite the Knights and others to come to the farm and enjoy the festivities.

Doris remembers there sometimes being multiple buses and several hundred people at those festivities. She always felt welcome at the events, although she and her family were often the only whites among hundreds of blacks. Maynard assured them that he would be keeping a watch out for their safety—and not to worry.

In a similar testimony, long-time area resident Gene Eichelberger recalled that Henderson invited his father, Don, to an event at JBF by saying, "You'll be the only white guy there, but I've got a gun. I'll take care of you."

Eichelberger added, "Busload after busload of black people would come down through Antietam [Village] on a Saturday afternoon."

Dargan resident Henry Ingram is the grandson of Snow and Lily Ingram, who ran Lily's Tavern. When he was in his late teens, Henry and a buddy nicknamed "Packle" trucked over to the farm one afternoon to play five-card draw for money with Henderson. After the experienced caretaker had relieved the rubes of their stake, he invited them back to attend the dance that evening "on the house" saying, "Come on over and enjoy the night. Nobody will bother you."

The two young men got to see Fats Domino perform. Ingram remembered of the occasion, "[We] stayed until about midnight. … It was the experience of a lifetime—to be around so many people of a different color. Maynard was our protection. He treated us like one of them. You couldn't ask for a better host."

Rumbles in the Distance

THE ELKS STRUGGLE TO SAVE JBF

Year after year, Maynard Henderson capably carried out his administrative and civic duties in a manner that the Black Elks deemed invaluable. It seemed to everyone that Henderson would keep the position that he so loved throughout the rest of his working days and on into retirement. However, as the years went by, a combination of circumstances conspired to make the property more difficult for the IBPOEW to sustain.

A ROAD PAVED WITH GOOD INTENTIONS

For one thing, its members grew increasingly frustrated with the ongoing lack of improvements by the State of Maryland and Washington County to the roads leading to the farm. The back road from Harpers Ferry along the river is

The John Brown Farm site as it looked soon after its sale by the IBPOEW to Bo Morgan in 1966.

Harpers Ferry Road today as it turns northward from the Potomac River in the background toward John Brown's Farm. Photo by Winston Pitman.

yet today very narrow and winding in places—surely no better than a one-lane gravel road in the early 1950s. A photograph of Chestnut Grove Road taken in 1966 shows barely one full lane of tar and chip.

The primitive road conditions in the immediate area of John Brown's Farm had long frustrated one of the goals the IBPOEW had set early on concerning the property: to develop "an organized public relations campaign to attract a continued flow of visitors to the historical site." [67]

A November 14, 1961, article in the *Morning Mail* reported that a contingent of Black Elks headed by an esteemed Baltimore physician, Dr. Bernard Harris, and including Hagerstonians Leonard Curlin and Russell Snively, met with the Washington County Board of Commissioners. "The purpose of the group in appearing before the Board," Dr. Harris said at the time was, "to determine if the county is planning any improvements to roads in [the Southern Washington County] area."

It had always been difficult for the Elks membership to get out there from places like Steelton, Pennsylvania; Baltimore; and Washington, D.C. Dr. Harris, who served as president of the Tri-State Association throughout nearly the entire JBF era, went on to illustrate the problem: "Many of the visits of lodge groups are by bus, and bus drivers and bus companies have complained of the difficulty and the hazards involved in buses using the roads that lead to the farm because of their inability to pass [oncoming] vehicles at some points on the roads."

Hoping for a positive and prompt county action, Harris dangled the Elks' enterprising goals for the property, which included the establishment of a convalescent home and the construction of a youth center as well as additional cottages. A commentary written by Harry Warner for an undated Hagerstown newspaper mentioned additional potential uses for the property by the Elks, including its becoming a headquarters for their activities.

The estimated total cost for these proposed projects approached five hundred thousand dollars—equal to nearly four million in today's dollars—which would have been an enormous boon to that part of the county. The commissioners understandably and immediately "expressed approval of the idea."

But Harris cautioned, "The development is contingent upon the assurance that the present winding, narrow, and hazardous county roads leading to the site be improved to permit the passage of large buses."

According to the November 15, 1961, *Morning Herald,* County Board president Lem Kirk bade the Elks to meet with "representatives of the County Roads Department and agree upon a plan as to which of the several roads should be developed and improved." Commissioners Harry Snook and Charles Downey acknowledged budget limitations but suggested that "the county should start [repairing] the worst section first and then work to the general improvement."

The Elks representatives had some reason for being hopeful. A decade earlier the County had made improvements to Chestnut Grove Road about a quarter mile northeast of the entrance to the farm where stood a one-lane stone bridge. There, about five hundred feet north of Mount Lock Hill Road, a little lane named Rocky Road juts off to the east. According to Bill Knight, "at that spot there were a couple of little bitty streams, gullies really, that dumped into a low spot right there. The road there had a very tight S-curve where accidents often happened. Apparently the county straightened the road up a little right there in the 1950s." However, according to one-time JBF owner Bo Morgan, it was still several more years before the county finally dug up the old asphalt road running through that swampy spot, mixed the old base with cement, and laid down a more modern five-inch blacktop road.

Despite the positive reception and good intentions expressed by the County Commissioners in that 1961 meeting, little additional work was completed. The

Elks hoped that something could be done at the state level. The Elks certainly had an advocate there.

MAC MATHIAS

Maryland's then-future U.S. Senator, Republican Charles McCurdy "Mac" Mathias, Jr., was born and raised in Frederick, about twenty-five miles from JBF. From 1961–1969, Mathias represented Maryland's sixth congressional district in the United States House of Representatives. During those eight years he sponsored legislation to make the C&O Canal along the Potomac River a national park, and in 1963 he supported a congressional name change to make Harpers Ferry a National Historic Park.

Mathias also was supportive of a potential "Civil War corridor" cited in a June 17, 1965, article by Harry Warner in Hagerstown's *Daily Mail* which noted,

> *"Historical groups here and in nearby states have repeatedly proposed a road designed specifically for making it easy for tourists to see the history-rich area bounded on one end by Harpers Ferry and by Gettysburg on the other, running through John Brown's Farm and Antietam [Battlefield] areas."*

Unfortunately, the intervention of Mathias and the best intentions of others went for naught—at least as far as the immediate interests of the IBPOEW were concerned.

ARRANGEMENTS TO SELL JBF

As the IBPOEW waited on positive news about road improvements, they continued to cast about for ways to make the farm self-sustaining. According to its minutes, the 1962 Grand Lodge mulled over several possibilities. The chief candidates were the following suggestions, none of which, to my knowledge, ever came to fruition:

> *"(1) to promote the use of the farm to individuals and groups outside the Elks; (2) to develop a campsite for youth; (3) to rehab the house, put a museum in the old house, to have a recreation area with tennis and badminton courts, and a playground for children."*

Upon assuming the position of Grand Exalted Ruler in 1960, Hobson

Mac Mathias

As a legislator, Senator Charles "Mac" Mathias had a stellar record, not only in the promotion of historical sites, but also in the promotion of civil rights.

Working as the City Attorney of Frederick, Maryland, from 1954 to 1959, he helped desegregate the local Opera House movie theater where blacks were relegated to sitting in the back rows. Serving in the Maryland House of Delegates in 1959-1960, he voted with the majority in favor of Maryland's finally ratifying the Fourteenth Amendment to the U.S. Constitution (adopted nationally in 1868!), which included citizenship for blacks.

While in the U.S. House of Representatives (1961–1969), Mathias was a staunch advocate of fair housing and the improvement of welfare. At the very beginning of his long tenure in the U.S. Senate (1969–1987), he threatened a "rebellion" within the Republican Party unless the Nixon Administration worked harder on civil rights for blacks. Toward the end of his Senate career he pushed to establish Martin Luther King, Jr.'s birthday as a federal holiday.

How did Senator Mathias, a product of a racially-segregated community, come to be such an avid supporter of civil rights for African-Americans? An article in the February 16, 2010, *Frederick News-Post* may provide a clue.

In 1928, a nineteen-year-old black woman, Edith Jackson, began her twenty-five year stint as a live-in nanny for the white family of Richard Potts in Frederick. Miss Jackson soon was considered part of the family. "I lived with them, slept with them, ate with them." She added with a laugh, "The only reason you wouldn't think I wasn't a member of the family was by the color of my skin. They gave me a home and treated me great."

Part of Jackson's responsibilities at the Potts household was to help raise their six-year-old son Arthur and, by extension, his ever-present chum Charles Mathias. She said of the two, "Those boys were like my own children. They went everywhere together, like they were two brothers. I took them out to play ball, cooked dinner for them, washed their clothes. Mac was my little angel."

For the next eighty years, Jackson and Mathias maintained a relationship. In the summer of 2009, when Ms. Jackson, then 100, was in the hospital, she received a hand-written letter from Mathias, who was not well himself (he died six months later). She reminisced of her little angel, "He never changed when he went to Washington. He was always the same. Just a wonderful person." Obviously, given Mathias's stellar civil rights record, so was Edith Jackson.

Reynolds had made it a priority to secure a national headquarters in order to facilitate the mounting administrative load of such a large and active organization. He also wanted it to be a place where all the national committee heads could conveniently and comfortably congregate. Reynolds orchestrated several leadership meetings in Philadelphia as a possible site, but the cost of real estate and the associated outlay for a headquarters there portended to be prohibitive.

As evidenced by the article by Harry Warner about the Black Elks delegation meeting with the Washington County Board, there was some sentiment toward turning JBF into the IBPOEW headquarters. Generally, however, the organization considered the farm to be solely a "retreat" and unsuitable as a candidate for a national office location. Reynolds increasingly turned his eyes toward his hometown of Winton, North Carolina. To purchase and develop land even in that lower-cost area would stretch thin the IBPOEW financial resources.

The sixty-fifth National Elks Grand Lodge convened in Miami in 1964. The August 22 issue of *The Miami Times,* a black newspaper, welcomed the IBPOEW to Miami. An advertisement in that edition read, "The Sir John Hotel welcomes the Elks with performances by Solomon Burke [and] Joe Tex." Another article in that edition reported the news that on "Sunday night [August 16, 1964], a six-foot high cross—a KKK symbol—burned for fifteen minutes on a Miami Springs golf course."

There was also a photograph in *The Miami Times* with a caption that read:

> *"Grand Exalted Ruler, H. R. Reynolds and top Elks officials as they met with FHA officers and builders to sign the papers for the $3 million Elks low income housing project, Elks Valley View Apartments, Chattanooga, Tenn. Ground-breaking date was set at August 5, and completion during 1965."*

Although the Chattanooga housing venture had substantial government funding, the proceeds from a potential sale of the increasingly unwieldy John Brown's Farm property could certainly come in handy, whether partially financing the housing project or a national headquarters.

During the convention, Reynolds reinforced to the membership the persistent negative balance sheet at John Brown's Farm. In the course of consequent deliberations, the convention narrowed the funding options concerning its future to two: (1) assess an annual levy on all members, or (2) abandon the project without further losses.

Despite a pervasive emotional reluctance, the membership voted to sell. An article in the December 1, 1964, edition of the Washington, D.C., *Afro-American* newspaper relayed:

> *"Motion passed at Grand Lodge in Miami, Florida. Grand Exalted Ruler and trustees authorized to sell farm and establish a separate fund with the proceeds to be used in the future for a suitable shrine in a suitable location."*

The decision to sell was far from unanimous. James Griffin, president of West Virginia State Association, related that the opinion of most lodges near JBF was that it should have become the national headquarters. He added, "There was sentiment among the Elks membership in West Virginia that the property had been snatched from underneath us."

Wallace Brooks of Hagerstown added similarly, "It killed the blacks in Hagerstown when John Brown's Farm closed, 'cause that's the only place we had to go."

The gears to divest the property began to turn. Although the Elks had invested approximately $130,000 into the property over the previous fifteen years, its appraisal came in substantially lower at $91,000.

The availability of the property presently came to the attention of influential parties. In another undated newspaper article (probably late 1964), Harry Warner reported that in a recent letter to Interior Secretary Stewart L. Udall, Congressman Mathias noted that JBF was "up for immediate sale." Mathias went on to urge Secretary Udall to investigate "the possibility of acquiring the John Brown Farm and incorporating it into the Harpers Ferry National Park."

To speculate, perhaps Mathias's proposal was shoved to the far back burner because of other governmental and societal considerations. The Civil Rights Act of 1964 was passed on July 2 by the House of Representatives, with 80 percent of Republicans and 63 percent of Democrats voting in its favor. The following month, Congress passed the Gulf of Tonkin Resolution that kick-started an exponential military build-up in Vietnam. Furthermore, President Lyndon Johnson's so-called Great Society initiatives spawned a number of expansive and expensive government programs.

Whatever the reasons for the property's sale languishing, various events continued at JBF throughout the summer of 1965. The season was capped by the performance of James Brown over the Labor Day weekend—the last dance.

A New Era for John Brown's Farm

The IBPOEW lowered their asking price to sixty thousand dollars. Still no takers.

The interested public had been aware of the Elks' avowed reasons for wanting to sell and move on. In an article in the June 17, 1965, edition of *The Morning Herald*, Harry Warner wrote, "The Elks described [the farm] as too inaccessible for their purposes." Dargan-area land developer Bo Morgan concurred that, "The Elks officials told me that the property had become 'too hard to manage.'"

Additionally, as the popularity of R&B began to soar in the mid-1960s,

---

The John Brown farmhouse as it appeared during the years of Elks ownership, 1950–1966.

so did the appearance fees of the artists. For instance, in the late 1950s James Brown would play for a guarantee of a just a few hundred dollars and a fifty-fifty split of the gate. As the years went by, Brown pushed toward an eighty-twenty split, and finally to large guarantees of ten thousand dollars and upward.

The success of these talented performers who honed their skills at little juke joints and medium-sized venues (like JBF) for the time-honored and far-flung black entertainment network known as the Chitlin' Circuit led to their being recognized and celebrated by mass culture. As rhythm and blues music crossed over into white markets, it increased record sales exponentially. It also propelled its musicians onto much larger stages.

Instead of the artists primarily providing music for young black dancers, they now performed concerts for integrated audiences in large theaters, auditoriums, and even stadiums. The top acts also began to appear on television and in the movies. In so doing, they rather abruptly priced themselves out of the smaller Chitlin' Circuit venues. As a result, the Elks faced a substantial loss of rental income from the dances that had been held for fifteen years at John Brown's Farm.

The potential sale of the farm by the IBPOEW had been hypothetical for several years. It became a distinct possibility for more than a year and a half, but there had been no bidders even at the asking price of sixty thousand dollars—thirty thousand less than appraised value.

BO MORGAN ACQUIRES JOHN BROWN'S FARM

On one occasion, Bo Morgan was sitting in the waiting room of a real estate office in preparation for the closing on a purchase of rural property. Realtor Albert Zahn thrust a question at Morgan: "Would you want to buy the John Brown Farm property?"

A bit stunned, Morgan asked the selling price.

"Sixty thousand dollars," replied Zahn.

"Offer forty thousand," countered Morgan.

Zahn took the offer to the IBPOEW and they immediately accepted it without any further dickering. In Morgan's recollection, "They were happy to unload it."

Bo Morgan and his wife, Peggy, purchased John Brown's Farm from the IBPOEW in April, 1966. At the closing, Morgan remembers meeting several dignified men who then spoke of their reasons for selling, including the poor roads leading to the property, mounting operating costs, and a "concentration

In his late teens, Bo Morgan (left) won a $25 gift certificate for catching the largest trout in Washington County, Maryland. Photo courtesy Bonnard Morgan.

Bo Morgan

Bonnard (accent on the first syllable) Morgan grew up in Benevola, Maryland, about five miles south of Hagerstown on the Old National Pike, also known by as the Old National Road, Old Cumberland Road, and Old Route 40. As you probably guessed, it is an old road. In fact, in 1811 it became the first federally funded highway in the United States.

Morgan's father, Leon K. Morgan, studied art at the Philadelphia Academy of Arts. Leon began as a young man in the 1920s collecting and dealing antiques, with somewhat of a specialty in pottery and art from the 1700s.

Bo was more of an outdoor kid—and a hard worker. During summers he worked on a fruit farm picking berries and tomatoes. He fished in nearby Beaver Creek, caught "suckers," and marketed them to Mr. Stine at his Benevola store in trade for candy bars.

During the winters, young Morgan would run trap lines for muskrats in Beaver Creek and Antietam Creek and sell them at four dollars per pelt. (For reference, area resident Evelyn Best remembers buying a muskrat coat in Baltimore in 1950 for three hundred dollars.) One year, Morgan bagged two hundred twenty of them.

Young Bo came to appreciate that the muskrats in Antietam Creek were sleeker in body and coat than the ones living near farm streams, and they made for better pelts. One year he won a national muskrat-skinning contest sponsored by Sears and Roebuck and was presented the first prize award of two hundred fifty dollars at the Alexander Hotel in downtown Hagerstown. Some sixty-five years later he noted with pride, "I bought my first car with muskrat money."

Morgan graduated from Boonsboro High School in 1952. He served in the Navy Air Corps through 1956. He then attended college for two years as a forestry major, preparing for a career that would begin at fifty-five hundred dollars per year.

A lifelong characteristic of Morgan's is "trading up." He saw an opportunity to work for the Post Office for six thousand dollars a year and took it. He served as a mail carrier out of Union Station in Washington, D.C., delivering correspondence to embassies before transferring to the Bethesda, Maryland, branch for about three more years.

Morgan was prospering, making one dollar an hour delivering mail and five times that much in his side business of trimming trees and doing yard work. He was homesick for country living, however, and began looking for ways to return to southern Washington County.

At one point in the early 1960s, Morgan had an extra fifty dollars in his pocket and went back home to see what that might instigate. At a Boonsboro real estate office he overheard two men talking about a thirty-two-acre plot of land that was for sale for fifteen hundred dollars. He boldly asked if they might take the fifty dollars in his pocket as a down payment and give him sixty days to come up with the balance.

That being agreed upon, Morgan took out an announcement in a little weekly "advertiser" in Bethesda that touted "woodlands for sale." He offered the acreage (including a spring and a little stream) for $4,500, asking for $1,500 down. A prospect agreed to the price and terms. When Morgan got the $1,500, he paid off the balance on the property and pocketed the difference, $3,000—or roughly half a year's pay for half a week's work.

He then continued this pattern, buying up parcels ranging from five to thirteen acres each from the former site of the Antietam Iron Works at the going rate of thirty-five dollars per acre. Morgan then would survey the land and put in a gravel road back 250 feet or so to a picnic table. As he put it, "That was enough to entice the buyers into purchasing a little piece of wooded paradise."

He typically had a quick turnaround, often tripling his investment. Morgan went on to make perhaps one hundred ten such transactions as well of dozens of other deals. He concluded somewhat sheepishly, "I probably overdid it."

When I asked of his motivation for getting involved in all these dealings, Morgan's voice softened. "I wanted to be free," he replied nostalgically, "…I guess like John Brown wanted for the slaves."

Bo Morgan has become an important forest conservationist in southern Washington County and still lives just up the road from JBF. Photo courtesy Jonathan Kays.

on low-income housing." John Brown's Farm and its 235 acres changed hands on April 26, 1966.

The rapidity of the sale, closing, and transfer of possession of the farm seems to have caught caretaker Maynard Henderson off guard. Perhaps he had been in denial about its likelihood. Once it occurred, however, his nephew Junior described his Uncle Maynard's reaction as stunned and angry: "He was flipped."

After all the necessary documents had been signed, Bo Morgan began to move his equipment onto the property while Henderson was still moving his things out. Morgan remembers Henderson as being ticked off, in part because, "He had to sell his animals in such a hurry." Additionally, the Elks had given to Morgan an inventory of the various items and implements on the property that were part of the sale. When Maynard Henderson caught sight of the list, he bristled with the notion that he was being spied upon. Morgan graciously pocketed the paper and, moreover, told Henderson that "he could stay on [the property], if he wanted."

Henderson declined, turned in his keys, and moved back to Hagerstown. He seems never again to have been as happy and productive as he had been at the farm. Nephew Gerald Barnett noted, "Uncle Maynard never went back down there. He rarely mentioned it. I guess he thought that part of his life was just over."

Junior Henderson reflected, "That sale broke Uncle Maynard's heart because he thought he'd be there for life."

A few months after Henderson's departure, Morgan hosted a little ceremony on the property signaling the passing of the property out of the hands of the Elks, but retaining a commitment to keep alive the dream of honoring John Brown. On that occasion Leonard Curlin, the Hagerstown man who had orchestrated the property's original purchase by the Elks leadership in 1948, verbalized a sentiment common within the IBPOEW: "It is still our property."

As Morgan initially sized up his new acquisition, he was primarily concerned that it would be a profitable piece of land, but he also was aware of its historical value, as earlier in life Bo had helped his father to restore several old buildings in the area, including a stone house on Marble Quarry Road that dated from the 1700s.

Morgan recollects that early in his ownership he offered the property's historic farmhouse to John Frye, the longtime curator of the Western Maryland Collection at the Washington County Free Library. Frye was not in a financial position to accept but urged Morgan to try to keep the entire property together. However, he could find no such able buyer.

Morgan subsequently divided the property into two parts, the first being the old farmhouse from which John Brown led the raid on Harpers Ferry, and the second being a larger holding upon which sat the other buildings erected by the IBPOEW, including the auditorium that had featured so many icons of rhythm and blues.

Morgan cordoned off the farmhouse and the immediate acreage around it, giving it a separate lane and planting a protective row of pine trees between the farmhouse and nearby buildings. He also added gutters and downspouts to the rear of the farmhouse, where water had been running directly down the side of the house and causing substantial rotting, especially of the lower logs in the wall. Morgan then began the process of subdividing the remainder of his holding into smaller plots in order to facilitate more manageable sales.

From 1966 to 1972, when Morgan held the property's entire 235 acres, he allowed the AMVETS Post #10 and the local fire department to use the auditorium for social events. Morgan supplied the construction materials, and the organizations provided the manpower to make several improvements to the property.

Those upgrades included the installation of a septic system and the running of pipes from the southwest end of the block building, underneath the barn, then out to the drain field. Morgan also dug a sizable pond (about five feet at its deepest point) and constructed a sand beach for swimmers' use.

The AMVETS hoped to make the auditorium and ten acres of the property their lodge site. They also wanted to restore the adjacent historic farmhouse and furnish it with era-appropriate décor. Toward that end, a dedicatory ceremony was held on July 4, 1970. Among the guests making remarks was Leonard

Curlin, who once again embodied the desire of Elkdom to stay attached in heart to the property.

The good intentions of the AMVETS were undermined by the property's general inaccessibility and paucity of AMVET members in the southern part of Washington County, so Morgan retained ownership for a few more years before selling the sub-divided tracts.

Morgan made diligent efforts to make the public aware of the historical value of the farm. For instance, an original letter by Bo Morgan dated September 24, 1968, was addressed to a group of people on a bus tour from Hagerstown. The section "Development and Restoration Plans" included,

"Captain" South T. Lynn

South Trimble Lynn was born in Washington, D.C., in 1927. He is the grandson of Kentucky Congressman South Trimble and the son of David Lynn IV, who was the seventh Architect of the Capitol, serving under five presidents from Coolidge through Eisenhower. During David Lynn's administration, the four major buildings constructed were the Longworth House Office Building, the Supreme Court Building, the Annex of the Library of Congress, and the United States Botanic Garden Conservatory.

South Lynn joined the Navy on his seventeenth birthday and served in World War II. Reflecting on his young adulthood Lynn says, "I was a good fast-pitch softball player, football player, boxer, sailor for Uncle Sam, tennis player, and on top of it all, wild as a March hare."

South T. Lynn stands in front of the authentically restored farmhouse that John Brown rented for several months prior to his historic raid on Harpers Ferry. Photo courtesy South T. Lynn.

Following the war, he graduated from the University of Maryland with a B.S. in Business and Public Administration and started a flooring business, Universal Floors, with his brother. In 1956, South Lynn married Joann Minter, and they now have three children, Elizabeth, South, Jr., and Sprigg.

Lynn has had a lifelong interest in history. For instance, he earned the moniker "Captain" for his participation in a 1976 Civil War reenactment during which he led the 18th Virginia Regiment of Infantry, the Nottoway Greys.

"The John Brown House will be completely restored, furnished with antiques and opened to the public as soon as the local roads are made safe enough to handle the heavy tourist traffic. Also the grounds will be landscaped to shield the historic house from the recreational area and the modern buildings.

"Presently Harpers Ferry just 6 miles to the south is visited by 1 million tourists per year. About 7 miles to the northwest Antietam Battlefield is visited by only about 200,000 people. I believe Washington County is losing about 800,000 tourists per year by not having a good road from Harpers Ferry to Antietam.

"When you get back to Hagerstown please pass along my suggestion that a decent road for this area would benefit local citizens and Washington County in general by increased tourist trade."

On March 16, 1973, Morgan and his wife sold the old farmhouse and a 1.77 acre parcel of land with it to South T. Lynn, Harold W. Keshishian, and two other partners "by deed dated June 30, 1972."

In Morgan's recollection, he sold the JBF farmhouse property with assurance of Lynn's intention to restore it. Morgan remains appreciative of Lynn's intent and ability and says of him, "He was the man. He was the one that got it done. Right time, right place, right person."

SOUTH T. LYNN BUYS JOHN BROWN'S FARMHOUSE

Lynn explained to me how he became involved in the property:

"I had a friend who was a Congressman from Montgomery County, Gilbert Gude. We had gone to the same high school in D.C. There was a picture of him and the old house in an edition of the Evening Star.

"After Bo bought the house, [Gude] was trying to drum up interest in the National Historic Landmark idea. I was approached by a real estate agent who knew that I was a history nut since he had sold me the property that I built my present home on. He knew about the Kennedy Farm and talked me into going for a look-see.

"I was sold on the fact that it was historic and for sale. An opportunity to buy

a real piece of American history was of great interest to me. A lot of people firmly believe the American Civil War started right here in this dining room. I told Bo if he would lease the place to me for one year with an option to buy, I would sign up for it.

"I used the year to explore the house at the Enoch Pratt Library in Baltimore and the Library of Congress in D.C. to confirm that the house was really what Bo and others said it was. After convincing myself, I talked three friends into joining me, and I bought the house with minimum land for forty thousand dollars."

Lynn then set out to secure additional interest, expertise, and funding in order to restore the old farmhouse to its appearance in 1859—the year of John Brown's raid on Harpers Ferry. For instance, he says he "convinced the [Maryland] State Board of Public Works" to contribute $109,128.

While the restoration plans were coming together, the Lynn family used the property as a weekend retreat. Younger son Sprigg lived in the farmhouse for two school years while he attended Shepherd College (now Shepherd University) in nearby Shepherdstown, West Virginia. South, Jr. also had lived in the farmhouse for a brief time as a college student.

South T. Lynn has been honored repeatedly and rightly for his long-term diligence to see this important historical landmark preserved and restored. In his affection for the property, he echoed the sentiments of the IBPOEW, particularly those members who yearned to have been able to retain it. According to Lynn, "The Elks worshiped John Brown, and the house represented that [reverence] to them. It was Brown who started the war on slavery. If they had to take horses, they would have come out there."

Once the farmhouse's restoration was completed, Reverend Leonard Curlin, the man who decades earlier had recommended the property to the IBPOEW, was "invited to deliver the invocation at the dedication of the restored farmhouse," Lynn says.

Under its corporate name, The Kennedy Farm was designated a National Historic Landmark on November 7, 1973. It is located at 2406 Chestnut Grove Road near Sharpsburg, Maryland, and is thus far open for tours by appointment only.

In January, 1973, Morgan sold the portion containing the auditorium to two men, Stephen Belschner and James E. Sickafus, who operated a notorious nightclub there for a time. At one point the two bought a large supply of straw—ostensibly for chickens they hoped to buy—and then stored it in the barn. The barn burned down within weeks. Several area residents intimated that an "insurance fire" was the probable cause.

The pair was unable to keep up payments, however, and the mortgage was assumed by area resident Freda Williams in the autumn of 1979.

THE FREDA WILLIAMS ERA

Freda Conner Williams was born in 1930 in tiny Albright, West Virginia. As an adult she worked for several restaurants and hotels in and around Washington, D.C. Perhaps that is where she met future husband James Williams, more widely known as "Nature Boy Williams."

"Nature Boy" was one of the most beloved figures of the Indianapolis Clowns baseball team. The Clowns' most famous alumnus is Hank Aaron, who made his professional debut with the team in 1952. (Aaron signed later that spring with the Boston Braves organization.)

Originally part of the Negro Baseball Leagues, the Indianapolis Clowns later became baseball's equivalent of the Harlem Globetrotters. Williams was described by one person as "The best comic ever for the Indianapolis Clowns." (Another of the Clowns' entertainer-athletes was "Goose" Tatum, who also played for the Harlem Globetrotters.)

Williams was a good athlete. The May 26, 1955, issue of *Jet* magazine contained an article entitled, "Barefoot Boy Makes Six Hits in Game."

He also became a solid businessman. The December 17, 1959, issue of *Jet* reported,

> *"Nature Boy Williams, the cavorting first baseman of Syd Pollock's touring Indianapolis Clowns baseball team, sold his Los Angeles Beauty Show and became a member of the City Employment Center, Washington, D.C., as an employment counselor and personnel administrator."*

Years later, the May 1, 1980, issue of *Jet* conveyed,

> *"James (Nature Boy) Williams, 50, retired first baseman for the Indianapolis Clowns baseball club, died of a heart attack at Southern Maryland Hospital Center. He is survived by his widow, Freda, and step-son, Francis Bucklew."*

Freda Williams lived her later years at John Brown's Farm. She rented out the former IBPOEW cottages to various tenants. Toward the end of her life she apparently became a bit senile. According to one long-time Dargan denizen, Williams "would often get lost while driving her little red truck."

Her brother, Earl Emery Conner, for many years lived in a trailer behind the now deteriorating auditorium and served as a security guard of sorts. According to one Dargan resident, Conner—a former Korean war vet, coal miner, and carpenter—had come to the attention of local officials because of his "stealing things out of area mailboxes."

Conner died at 81 in the trailer on February 8, 2009. A local rumor has it that Conner's corpse was eaten by his dogs. A representative of the Bast-Stauffer Funeral Home in nearby Boonsboro was kind enough to phone and (thank God!) to refute the rumor.

In January, 2011, less than two years after her brother's death, Ms. Williams also passed away on the property. At that point the ownership of the auditorium (the erstwhile dance hall) and some twenty acres around it passed into the hands of her son, Francis G. "Buck" Bucklew, Jr. Bucklew subsequently listed the property with one and then another real estate agent.

Meanwhile, several interested parties, including members of Save Historic Antietam Foundation, investigated means by which the property might be obtained for historic purposes. They feared that its loss to real estate developers would thwart efforts to extend the acreage associated with the nearby Antietam Battlefield. Additionally, South Lynn was concerned that the isolated beauty of the restored farmhouse would suffer from commercial encroachment.

On June 8, 2013, I was delighted to receive the following email from Captain Lynn:

> *"My son, South, and I have purchased the land around Kennedy Farm, all 20-some acres. I appreciate your help to date, and will need some in the near future as we will have to clean up and restore the Chitlin' Circuit entertainment parlor as part of the Kennedy Farm history."*

According to South Lynn, Jr., "Bucklew ran into some financial problems, and the property was scheduled for a tax auction. We made a quick deal in early June, I believe, while the vultures were circling." On June 5, 2013, the estate of Freda Williams conveyed the dance hall and its surrounding property to the Kennedy Farm LLC.

Laborers take advantage of unseasonably warm weather in late winter, 2016, to make extensive repairs to the dance-hall roof. Photo courtesy South Lynn.

OUT OF THE ASHES

Since that time, the Lynn family and many friends have made remarkable progress on clearing the former dance hall of multiple truckloads of junk. They also have scoured from the grounds a dilapidated trailer, overgrown vegetation, and other debris. Furthermore, improvements have been made, including repairs to the fireplace and the installation of a new roof.

On August 11, 2013, South T. Lynn emailed an update.

> *"I am clearing the land of an accumulation of burn-outs and junk left by previous owners. I am thinking very seriously of restoring the Entertainment Parlor built by the Black Elks in the 50s. I'd like to put [mannequins of] Ray Charles back at the piano and James Brown doing the "splits" on the dance floor."*

Co-owner South Lynn, Jr. filled me in a few weeks later,

> *"We are trying to make the building functional so as to save it. We have cleaned the interior in order to allow access to damaged roof rafters. We are working on raising funds to get a new roof."*

Highest honor should be given to the IBPOEW, Bo Morgan, and the Lynn family for their roles in preserving John Brown's Farm. Without their respective attentions, the old farmhouse could easily have been lost to history. Truth be told, however, there were misunderstandings along the way that led to some hard feelings.

At this point much of it is water under the bridge, but a significant number of IBPOEW members from lodges nearest the farm harbor emotions ranging from disappointment to anger that the place was ever sold. Some have said without specifics that "it was stolen from us." Others feel that the leadership of the IBPOEW in the mid-1960s was less than forthright about the need to sell and about the conditions of the sale.

I shared with Lynn, Sr. my discovery of the 1965 newspaper article in which Harry Warner wrote, "The Elks described [the farm] as too inaccessible for their purpose."

Lynn testily countered, "What they are telling you are merely excuses for giving up on saving their unpolished historic pearl. They really did nothing in saving the landmark, nor did Bo."

Lynn continued, "Bo was in the real estate business and dug the lakes to make the farm more attractive to buyers. I believe he would have torn down the farmhouse if he felt it was in his interest in selling the property."

I mentioned Lynn, Sr.'s long-simmering grievance to Morgan, who was more distressed than angry at the misunderstanding in earnestly responding, "I was certain it had to be preserved. I realized the importance of it. I wanted to see it preserved, but I didn't have the resources or the pull." As evidence of his intention to have kept the historic farmhouse protected and disconnected from the rest of the acreage, Morgan offered, "I put a private drive into it separate from the one to the pond and the dance hall."

When I relayed Morgan's explanation to Lynn, the latter received it in peace.

{PART II}

The Participants

The Man Behind the Music at John Brown's Farm

John Brown's 1859 strategic use of the Farm property is alone wholly sufficient for it to be regarded as a premier American landmark of liberty. The property's subsequent service as a virtual headquarters for an influential black fraternal organization during the height of the Civil Rights Movement adds to its glory. The property's third distinct employment, and the one that prompted this book, is every bit as significant in the struggle toward racial equality in the United States.

John Brown's Farm became a vital and beloved stop on the Chitlin' Circuit. Every summer from 1950 to 1965 young people flocked to the Farm to revel in live performances by nationally renowned recording stars.

John Bishop, the entrepreneur responsible for bringing the giants of R&B to John Brown's Farm, is pictured from the early 1950s. Photos courtesy LaVerne Bishop.

The music that they experienced had long-standing roots, but only then was clearly becoming the favorite of America's youth — first black, and then white. Just a few years earlier, in 1948, *Billboard* magazine's Jerry Wexler had coined a new name for it: "rhythm and blues."

At a typical event at John Brown's Farm, hundreds of (primarily) young adults congregated to experience a unique communal event. They set out from more than a hundred different black communities. They ventured over the dark and serpentine roads of southern Washington County in cars, trucks, buses, motorcycles, and taxis. Upon arriving, they renewed acquaintances, danced until they dropped, and built precious memories that endure to this day.

This upcoming section explores the dizzying array of components that converged during an event at the Farm. Who were the young people who attended? Where were they from? How did they get there? Who were the musicians? How did they know about the venue? What did the property look like? How was the auditorium laid out? How about the dances themselves—what went into their planning and execution? Was there ever any trouble there? Who was in charge? Whew! Let's take a breath and answer that last question first.

JOHN BISHOP

The prime mover of the music scene at John Brown's Farm was a gifted black entrepreneur named John Vernard Bishop.

Professionally, Bishop was known for his calm demeanor and sophisticated style. Family friend Reginald "Mop" Johnson described him as "sort of a quiet, shy person, but a good businessman." Charles Town resident Jim Taylor typed him as "a very, very classy individual." Bishop's periodic professional collaborator Leonard Harris portrayed him variously as "laid back" and "business-fied."

Politically, Bishop eschewed partisanship. According to an article in the August 11, 1966, *Daily Mail,* "Bishop strictly prohibits members of his [enterprises] from taking part in civil rights demonstrations." Bishop clarified, "I try to promote integration in my own humble way each day by being a good citizen and above all a gentleman."

Temperamentally, Bishop was mild-mannered. His niece, Betsy Miller, brimmed over with superlatives in describing her "Uncle Vernard" as a "humble, intelligent, peaceful man with a kind and giving spirit."

Physically, Bishop was nearly six feet tall and slender. Leonard Harris recalled him being "a very well-dressed man—curly hair, nice-looking man."

John Bishop in his U.S. Army uniform just prior to being deployed abroad during WWII. Photo courtesy of LaVerne Bishop.

Musician Kenny Hamber described Bishop as "fair-skinned," while another acquaintance typed him as "the Billy Dee Williams of his day—which is to say that women were attracted to him."

Bishop (1919–2006) was originally from Suffolk, Virginia. He and his brother Morris Bishop joined the Armed Services during World War II. Morris served with the segregated 92nd Infantry Division, the Buffalo Soldiers, seeing combat in Italy, while John (called by his middle name "Vernard" by some within the family) served in the Quartermaster Corps for supply and services in the Pacific, where he sustained an injury.

During an interview with Morris before his passing in 2014, he recalled how "John was injured when the side of a truck he was riding in collapsed. He and others fell out onto a rough coral road. He was badly scraped up and was eventually sent back to the States to the Newton D. Baker General Hospital in Martinsburg, West Virginia, to recuperate."

Upon regaining his health, John made his way the fifteen miles from Martinsburg to Charles Town, West Virginia. There he soon met his match—professionally and romantically.

SYLVIA RIDEOUTT BISHOP

By the time Bishop met Sylvia Rideoutt (1920–2005), she was already a graduate of Storer College, an accomplished horse trainer, and heir to the well-known Payne's Hotel and Rooming House—the only hotel in town for blacks in Charles Town, West Virginia.

Sylvia had been raised in large measure by her godparents and oft-time guardians, William and Lavinia Payne. According to LaVerne Bishop, her grandmother (Sylvia's mother, Bertha) "had gotten sick and had to parcel out her kids to friends."

The Paynes bought Sylvia a pony when she was five years old, which

John and Sylvia (Rideoutt) Bishop on their wedding day. Photo courtesy LaVerne Bishop.

initiated her lifelong love of all things equestrian. Soon after the Charles Town Race Track opened in 1933, young Sylvia began riding her bike there to work with the horses. At age seventeen she bought her first horse.

According to a February 22, 2002, article written by Sarah Mullin for *The Herald-Mail,* Sylvia became "the first licensed African-American woman thoroughbred trainer in the United States." Bishop said she "earned the license when she was eighteen or nineteen years old." Over the course of her sixty-five-year career, Ms. Bishop trained her own and others' horses—as many as twenty-five at a time.

A 2002 West Virginia House Resolution recognized Ms. Bishop for her various achievements and for enduring "the intolerance and bigotry she encountered daily at the horse track and elsewhere with grace and dignity." The fifty-thousand-dollar Sylvia Bishop Memorial Stakes, a seven-furlong race for state-bred fillies, is still conducted annually at Charles Town.

The handsome newcomer and the established local were married on August 28, 1945. It would be quite some time before Mr. and Mrs. Bishop became parents of their only child, LaVerne. The two would spend the intervening years rapidly expanding their respective careers.

BUDDING ENTREPRENEUR

Bishop's first known venture in the Charles Town area came by way of Sylvia's acquaintances at the race track. He soon determined, however, that his opportunities at the track were too limited.

Consequently, he and Sylvia promptly developed and co-owned a tavern in the basement of Payne's Hotel and christened it the "Tap Room." In addition to the local entertainers who worked the room during regular hours, many of the hotel's famous guests such as Billie Holiday and Dinah Washington would return at the conclusion of their gigs elsewhere to participate in memorable

Sylvia Bishop, America's first black female licensed horse trainer, with husband John to her left.

John Bishop later in life with his daughter LaVerne (center) and other family members. Photos courtesy LaVerne Bishop.

after-hours jam sessions.

LaVerne Bishop recalled of one of those famous guests, "When Ray Charles stayed at the hotel, my mother would fix his dinner, and he would eat two whole fried chickens at one sitting!"

Morris Bishop and his wife Rose attended Howard University in Washington, D.C., from 1946 to1948. During that time they often would travel by train to visit John and his bride. John would send over a car from Charles Town to meet them at the train station in Harpers Ferry. Morris remembers one automobile being a DeSoto, but stressed that characteristically, "John liked Buicks."

During those visits, Morris and Rose would help John with his promotional activities attendant to his newest enterprise. In addition to the Tap Room, he was now booking bands into the Orchard Inn—a nightclub he operated on Route 340 between Charles Town and Berryville, Virginia. Interestingly, this same club later became known as the Rainbow Inn and was used as one of the settings for the movie *Sweet Dreams* about area resident and legendary country singer, Patsy Cline.

Among the many famous acts that played the Orchard Inn were Joe Liggins and His Honeydrippers. Their big band blues hit "The Honeydripper" spent a whopping eighteen weeks at the top of the R&B Chart from September, 1945, to January, 1946.

John Bishop had an exceptional capacity for long and hard work, often juggling several of his enterprises simultaneously. The August 11, 1966, edition of Hagerstown's *Daily Mail* noted of Bishop's longstanding industriousness,

> *"[He] has no relaxing spare time activities simply because he has no spare time. Even when he does get a few days off, he spends them traveling around and scouting new acts."*

PROMOTER EXTRAORDINAIRE

By the early 1950s, Bishop was clearly employing his chief entrepreneurial trait —that of a promoter. Daughter LaVerne and his one-time employee Tyrone Henszley independently described his penchant for promotion, moreover, as a "calling." He loved discovering talent and putting it to use.

Bishop's long-time friend, Richard "Dickie" Moore, has been for many years the Director of Racing at the venue now known as Hollywood Casino at Charles Town Races. He recalls, "John was quite a visionary. He knew how to entertain—not just black people, but white people as well." Reginald Johnson expounded along those lines, "He knew what people wanted." And he was thorough about their getting it.

A specimen of Bishop's networking and promotional diligence surfaced when several bags of memorabilia were rescued at virtually the last minute prior to the demolition of Payne's Hotel. Among the loot was one sheet from among many in Bishop's extensive hand-written contact list for "East North Street" in Charles Town. It was displayed at a September 24, 2011, event graciously sponsored by the Jefferson County NAACP at Fisherman's Hall in Charles Town. There, about a dozen people reminisced about their personal experiences as attendees of the dances at John Brown's Farm.

Mr. Bishop's entrepreneurial instincts and his successes at the Orchard Inn furnished him with the confidence to ratchet his operation up a notch. He was ready for a bigger venue.

BISHOP BRINGS HIS TALENTS TO JOHN BROWN'S FARM

One of the unfortunate remaining obscurities of this story is precisely how Bishop initially hooked up with the IBPOEW in renting the JBF property.

There had been an Elks Lodge (now defunct) in Charles Town, so maybe the connection originated there. Perhaps Bishop was aware that the Elks themselves had sponsored several musical events at the property—possibly even bands that he had booked for them—and speculated that they might be willing to rent the auditorium to him for his own endeavors.

Another possible scenario concerns Leonard Curlin, the Hagerstown Elk who had negotiated the IBPOEW's purchase of the Farm. Curlin loved attending the horse races at Charles Town where Sylvia Bishop was a fixture. Could it have been that the racetrack provided the perfect venue for the two inveterate networkers to have struck up an acquaintance?

Perhaps the most likely explanation for the partnership between Bishop and the Elks is that it originated somehow by way of Bishop's membership in IBPOEW Lodge #458 in Winchester, Virginia. Alas, at least to this point, all is conjecture.

...ANADA EXHIBITION ASSOCIATION
MIDWAY

Receipt   No 556

SHOW No. 45   SHOW Coppertone

CARRIER BOY SLIPS			CASH RECEIPTS	$	
@ 10¢			50 x 1.	50	00
@ 15¢			70 x 2.	140	00
@ 20¢			67 x 5.	335	00
@ 25¢			190 x 10.	190	00
@ 30¢					

Behind the Scenes

Once the IBPOEW auditorium was secured, a logistical quagmire lurked that only a gifted and determined executive would be able to navigate. Consider how many different hats have to be worn to pull off a safe and successful event capable of routinely accommodating four hundred-plus patrons.

The buildings and grounds must be readied, supervised, and cleaned up. Hospitality staff has to be recruited, trained, managed, and paid. Then food and drink need to be procured, prepared, and served; security personnel contracted, deployed, and supervised; music acts secured ahead of time and accommodated during the engagement; promotional materials created; money managed; and negotiations made with the landlord. That's a lot of plates for one man to keep spinning without himself coming unglued, but Bishop accomplished it in a steady and steadying manner.

An example from the Coppertone Review of John Bishop's meticulous attention to detail.

One indispensable element of John Bishop's management toolkit was his ability to be "present" at events. As Morris Bishop put it, "John was always behind the scenes." I understood this statement to mean that his brother was hands-on, but without taking the spotlight. In case I had misconstrued Morris's meaning, however, I asked Sylvia Stanton to clarify if John was literally present at JBF on concert nights. "Always!" she exclaimed. "He was always there!"

Bishop was always there psychologically, as well. He had the will and capacity to be in the moment. His skill at remaining unruffled was apropos because every "buck" at those dances stopped with him. At every event, any number of sleeve-pullers would have questions, large and small, that only he could answer, no matter how well he had delegated responsibilities in advance.

Bishop's typical evening at the Farm was spent in constant supervision. Prior to the dance itself, there was staff to get situated: sheriff's deputies, ticket takers, kitchen helpers, and bartenders. As the performers arrived, he dealt with their road manager and reviewed how payment splits for the night would be made. He also directed the band members toward the stage for setting up their equipment and to the dressing room for their costuming and relaxation.

He had to make sure that the cash boxes at the door, the kitchen, and the bar were stocked—and that no one was dipping into the till. If a fight among attendees should erupt, he would quickly assess the situation to determine if his dignified charisma would be enough to settle things down or if the deputized bouncers would need to apply further "persuasion."

If during the course of an event, the band was taking too long a break, Bishop would tap his watch and gesture toward the stage. Then, he might venture out to the parking lot to make sure things were running smoothly out there. His "whatever it takes" attitude was an indispensable trait in the fast pace attendant to the fluid conditions at the crowded dances.

He also delegated well. Tyrone Henszley observed, "He had an eye for talent." Musical skill was not the sole talent in view. Bishop had the knack of assessing people quickly and inviting them to assist him in appropriate aspects of his operations. For instance, Henszley mentioned Bishop's noticing Marion Green as having a good head for math; he soon employed her as his bookkeeper.

Bishop's brother-in-law, Harry S. Rideoutt, Jr. was his most consistent right hand man. Rideoutt was described by a later-in-life girlfriend as "tall, brown-skinned, likeable, outgoing, [and] educated." He did a bit of everything attendant to the dances from putting up the promotional posters, to "making sure everyone was okay on music nights," to taking tickets.

In 1967, Rideoutt and Bishop became co-owners of the Kleeco Supper Club in Bunker Hill, West Virginia, located near Inwood about halfway between Martinsburg, West Virginia, and Winchester, Virginia.

Rideoutt was an entrepreneur in his own right. At various times, he was a partner (with Russell Roper) in a Charles Town taxi company, a dry cleaning business, and a restaurant. Rideoutt was also involved in the running of "The Shamrock Inn" in Sandy Point, Maryland. The Shamrock operated during and, for a time, after the R&B era at JBF.

Leonard Harris was an occasional collaborator with John Bishop in booking bands at JBF. Photo by Winston Pitman.

One of Bishop's notable intermittent collaborators was Leonard Harris of Martinsburg, West Virginia. Harris was one of the founders and is currently the volunteer director of the Sumner-Ramer African American School Museum in Martinsburg. He and his wife Helen own Harris Community Care—a home care business.

During the John Brown's Farm era, Harris owned and operated the 701 Club in Martinsburg and is one of the premier authorities concerning who did and did not play at John Brown's Farm. The 701 Club had a dance floor and could accommodate perhaps a hundred people at a time. If it was convenient for him and for Bishop—and if the price was right—Harris would occasionally book into his club on a weekend night an artist that would play at JBF on an adjoining date.

John Bishop and Leonard Harris had another recurring collaborative venture. Sometimes Bishop would be offered a high-priced musical act for the Farm on short notice. On the rare occasion when Bishop was unable to raise the cash quickly, Harris would put up 50 percent of the required deposit and the two would split the profits from the event.

Harris shared an anecdote from that collaboration. During the course of a major event with a big guarantee to the band, he said, "We'd go back in the back room. [Bishop] had a habit; he'd put his head down; he'd say, 'Leonard, you think we gonna make it, man? You think we gonna make it? We got a lot of money out here.' I said, 'Don't worry; we'll make it. We'll make it.' And then Bishop he'd start walking [pacing]."

Although occasionally by the skin of their teeth, they always did make it.

CARR'S BEACH

John Bishop's most important business collaboration, however, was with Rufus Mitchell. Mitchell (1911–2003) was for over two decades the general manager of a large segregated resort in Anne Arundel County, Maryland, called Carr's Beach.

In the early 1900s, Fred Carr, a black grocer and farmer, had purchased a 180-acre swath of land on the Annapolis Neck peninsula of the Chesapeake Bay. Upon his death in 1927, his four daughters inherited the acreage. Two of them developed the waterfront portion of property just north of the then brand-new Annapolis Golf Club. (The site is now an upscale development known as Chesapeake Harbour.)

Elizabeth Carr Smith opened Carr's Beach in 1929. Mary "Florence" Carr Sparrow launched the adjacent Sparrow's Beach in 1930. As the sisters added such amenities as motels, picnic tables, rides, and concessions, the two resorts constituted an incredibly popular destination for black families up and down the East Coast. Carr's Beach gradually became the preeminent of the two and developed into a major stop on the Chitlin' Circuit.

Ms. Sparrow continued to oversee her property into the 1950s, but following Ms. Smith's death in 1948, the ownership of Carr's Beach came into the hands of a consortium of owners known as the Carr's Beach Amusement Company. They were primarily financed and directed by "Little Willie" Adams.

William Lloyd Adams (1914–2007) began his business career as a numbers runner. As his activities expanded, he came to dominate the West Baltimore liquor trade as well as the related businesses of juke boxes, vending machines, and pinball machines. In 1946, "Little Willie" opened The Sphinx (pronounced with a hard "p"), a swank members-only nightclub for the black middle-class on "the stroll" of Pennsylvania Avenue, which included the legendary Royal Theatre.

Under Adams's leadership, $150,000 of upgrades and additions were made to the twenty-acre Carr's Beach property. They included the installation of

Rufus Mitchell was the general manager for Carr's Beach, a premier black entertainment venue on the East Coast. Mitchell referred many of the top R&B artists to John Bishop and John Brown's Farm. Photo courtesy Kevin Coombe.

one-armed bandits (legal in Anne Arundel County), upgrades in sanitation facilities, enlarged picnic grounds, and the construction of a large pavilion and dance floor.

On weekdays, various churches would utilize nearby Sparrow's Beach for day camps, church picnics, and baptisms. On the weekends, "The Beach" complex became a magnet for blacks seeking to flee not only the oppressive summer heat, but also the oppressive racism that most of them endured in the marketplace Monday through Friday.

In 1949 Adams (later described as West Baltimore's "one-man Small Business Administration") hired Rufus E. Mitchell as his general manager for Carr's Beach. Mitchell, a Jacksonville, Florida, native, had moved northward to Baltimore as part of the Second Great Migration. He served for two years in the United States Army at nearby Fort Meade during World War II. Upon his discharge, he opened a dry cleaning business to which he added a tuxedo rental enterprise.

Mitchell's responsibilities at Carr's Beach included the oversight of up to thirty summertime employees. The staff served as lifeguards; operated the Ferris wheel, merry-go-round, and other rides in the small amusement park; and manned the concession stands and clean-up operations.

Mitchell also booked the music acts for the festivities that ran from Memorial Day through Labor Day. Events and operations under his purview included bathing beauty contests, the jazz-oriented Bengazi Room, and the 1951 boxing exhibitions by Joe Louis.

It is Rufus Mitchell's role as booking agent that most interests us. His part in making Carr's Beach "The Entertainment Capital of the East Coast" can hardly be overestimated. During his tenure, Carr's Beach became a regional hot spot where Saturday evening R&B performances were attended by hundreds and hundreds of adults. The Sunday afternoon events, however, were of an almost unimaginable magnitude.

On Sundays, especially after church let out, the various roads into Annapolis would clog to a literal standstill. Thousands of black families from Philadelphia to Newport News, Virginia, streamed out to Carr's Beach by bus, car, and truck. The early afternoons were spent in picnics and swimming. As three o'clock approached, however, the picnickers tidied up, the swimmers toweled off, the sunbathers brushed off the sand, and everyone flocked to the pavilion.

On any given Sunday, the crowd would be treated to R&B royalty. In the early 1950s, entertainers included Ella Fitzgerald, Louis Jordan, Billy Eckstine, and Louis Armstrong. In the mid-50s, people danced to Count Basie, Big Jay McNeely, and Ray Charles. The late 1950s brought Sam Cooke, Little Richard, James Brown, Etta James, the Coasters, and the Drifters to the pavilion. The Shirelles, Patti LaBelle & the Bluebelles, and numerous performers from Detroit's newly-formed Motortown Revues highlighted the early 1960s.

An enormously popular feature of those splendorous Sunday afternoon gatherings were live broadcasts of the music via the 1,000-watt daytime radio station WANN (1190 AM). "Bandstand on the Beach" was emceed by WANN's beloved disc jockey, Charles W. "Hoppy" Adams.

Those broadcasts had a far-reaching cross-cultural effect. Veteran Baltimore-area music historian Larry Benicewicz explains, "Although, for the most part whites were excluded from the audience, there wasn't a Caucasian teenager in these parts who claimed to be hip if he didn't listen to the Sunday afternoon broadcasts."

For the black community, Carr's Beach displayed a cachet of wholesome good times and a sense of togetherness that is sadly missed yet today. In a 2009 article about Carr's Beach by E.B. Furguson, one can feel the yearning of interviewee Larry Griffin as he reminisced, "We need to find that sense of community again. If I could only [regain] the feelings I have about the beach… it was something else."

Rufus Mitchell's commitment to bringing in artists on the cusp of their popularity burnished his résumé within the music industry. Although he did not launch his own Ace Booking Agency until the early 1960s, he had been functioning for more than ten years in that capacity as a liaison for several large talent agencies headquartered in New York City.

Soul singer Kenny Hamber recalls Mitchell's connections with ABC

(Associated Booking Corporation): "He was tight with everybody." Winfield Parker, a regular performer at the JBF dances, cited Mitchell as also working with the Shaw Agency and Queens Booking Agency.

As the experienced chief promoter for Carr's Beach, Mitchell was not overmatched when dealing with those large and reputedly mob-connected agencies. As Hamber put it, "Rufus was a big, strong player."

THE MITCHELL-BISHOP CONNECTION

The specifics of how Rufus Mitchell and John Bishop initially connected business-wise are probably lost to history. However, based upon the quality of the talent Bishop booked earlier into the Orchard Inn, their connection may have been made as early as 1950.

It is evident from the success and duration of their collaboration that the two clicked both personally and professionally. As Kenny Hamber described it, "John and Rufus were like two peas in a pod." Essentially, if an act that Mitchell planned to book at Carr's Beach had an open date on either side of the calendar, Bishop had first dibs on adding a second performance at John Brown's Farm.

It seemed to Winfield Parker that Bishop must have also contacted the big agencies directly in order to ascertain situations wherein JBF was conveniently situated time-wise and travel-wise for bands who were between two higher-paying gigs at venues other than Carr's Beach. As that occurred, then he could reduce his expenses by piggy-backing on existing travel and fee arrangements. Bishop's daughter, LaVerne, attests to her father making several trips to New York City to visit one or more agencies for just such purposes.

Joe Dixon also mentioned Joe Dasher as a promoter out of Washington, D. C., who referred bands to Bishop.

A document unearthed from the materials rescued from Payne's Hotel prior to its demolition revealed that Bishop also had dealings with Universal Attractions Agency of New York City. That same stash also disclosed that Bishop called his own operation "Bishop Attraction."

The most common Rufus Mitchell/John Bishop collaboration concerned the artists playing the Sunday afternoon extravaganzas at Carr's Beach. Following their appearance at the Beach, the groups would tear down their equipment, drive the ninety miles from Annapolis out to John Brown's Farm, set up again, and get ready for another show on Sunday night.

Friday and Saturday night performances at JBF were also frequent, with the artists often playing the Farm first and then Carr's Beach on Sunday afternoon. There also were recurring "Midnight Dances" at JBF that ran from midnight until three a.m., primarily on holiday weekends. Joe Dixon remembers, "We'd leave [Hagerstown] at eleven thirty for the midnight dances and get back to town at daybreak."

Mitchell and Bishop were flexible and solicitous toward one another. Each had the other's economic interests rather constantly in mind. Based upon their joint trust, the mutually beneficial arrangement prospered for the better part of twenty years.

As far as their financial arrangement went, they seem to have followed the standard agreement at clubs along the Chitlin' Circuit. The terms of contract incorporated "the guarantee," an appearance fee negotiated ahead of time, from which came the agent's cut. Sometimes the entire guarantee was due up front; most often only an agreed-upon percentage was required.

Several contracts discovered at Payne's Hotel between Bishop and "Stanley Jackson featuring Sammy Fitzhugh" followed that pattern. For instance, one contract stipulated a $150 appearance fee from the nightclub with $25 due at the signing of the contract.

Another provision of the typical contract was "the privilege," an agreed upon percentage split of the gate beyond the guarantee. Incorporating several of the above-listed elements, a standard Mitchell-Bishop deal would go down as per the following example.

Mitchell might say to Bishop, "I have Little Richard available on July 8. Do you want him at a one thousand dollar guarantee and a 60/40 privilege?" If Bishop did, then he would sign a contract for that amount and pay Mitchell $150 (15 percent) up front—refundable only if the act failed to show. Mitchell would then forward a portion of the up-front money to the pertinent NYC agency.

On the evening of the concert, then, at intermission, Bishop and Little Richard's road manager would tally "the gate." If the money in the till at that point was already, say, $2,400, then Bishop would disburse to the road manager the $850 balance of the guarantee to fulfill the contracted one thousand dollars. Then, Bishop would keep the second thousand dollars for himself.

Out of that one thousand dollars, Bishop would cover his own expenses: the rent to the Elks, the cost of promotional materials, plus the wages of his security guards, ticket takers, and other helpers—not including those working

Discovered and managed by John Bishop, renowned comedian Dap Sugar Willie emceed for numerous dances at John Brown's Farm. Photo from the author's private collection.

the kitchen and bar; they were part of a different arrangement. Then Bishop would split that next four hundred dollars at the pre-arranged 60/40 ratio, leaving $240 for Little Richard (minus 15 percent for the talent agency) and the remaining $160 for Bishop.

At the end of the night, Bishop and the artist would count any additional gate money that had come in since intermission. If it was a national act, the split was generally 50/50 (although it eventually would become 80/20 in James Brown's favor). If it was a local act, Bishop probably kept everything beyond the guarantee, sometimes more. Bishop would occasionally and somewhat imperiously "fine" local bands for sloppy appearance, playing half-heartedly, being inebriated, or otherwise acting in an unprofessional manner.

There is the notion floating around that the Mitchell-Bishop professional relationship became increasingly informal as the years went by, meaning less paperwork and more "I'll scratch your back if you scratch mine."

At least a few of the dances at JBF were relatively short-notice affairs wherein the booking agencies and the musicians' union apparently were willing to turn a blind eye to some of the contractual fees and conditions. Thus, the artists could work for a little less and still pick up good "gas money" toward the next gig.

Leonard Harris elaborated, "Different people would call you. When [the artists] would be coming through, their agency would call, and if you could hold them and if you had the cash, then they would come through because that's just a drop-off, so they could pick up extra money. This might not be their regular gig, but they were coming through the area."

The Coppertone Review

Beginning in 1960, The Coppertone Review, owned and managed by John Bishop, became a constituent part of Amusements of America, owned by the five Vivona brothers who billed their enterprise as "America's Largest Traveling Amusement Park." Each year, the entire colossal troupe set up and tore down more than a dozen times at smaller venues like the Hagerstown Fairgrounds and made longer stays at various larger festivals and state fairs.

The annual caravan started in the South in the spring; made its way north to Trois Riviéres (Quebec) and Ottawa, Canada, in mid-summer; slipped southward to Binghamton, New York; and trekked down the East Coast to Macon, Georgia, as autumn approached.

Such traveling carnivals often were comprised of independent sub-units. Vendors would run the shooting gallery, house of mirrors, bingo parlor, ring toss, or kiddie rides. The Vivonas owned and operated larger rides in the vein of the Octopus, the Whip, and the Tilt-A-Whirl.

Additional attractions might include a motorcycle daredevil like "Speedy McNish and his Wall of Death." A "Cavalcade of Wonders" would include the kind of sideshows that creeped me out as a kid: a bearded lady, a lizard man, "Carl the Frog Boy," or a tattooed sword-swallower.

Promoter John Bishop's brother Morris explained his brother's operation. "The Coppertone Review was so named because it was black. It used to be called 'The Jig Show,' which was a kind of a minstrel show with snake charmers, dancers, and the like."

Although just a sub-set of the Vivona's corporate enterprise, Bishop's Review was still a sizable operation. To acquire the roustabout help that he needed, Bishop often recruited locals. For instance, when the Review came to the Great Hagerstown Fair, Bobby Roland worked as a bouncer. Roland, a Charles Town native, knew John's wife Sylvia Bishop because he worked with horses. Freddy Lee Gardin, more of a regular, "ran the spotlights" as often did Joe Dixon.

Bishop ran a tight ship. He screened potential employees and, once hired, he imposed upon them twenty-five dollar fines for such offenses as swearing, excessive drinking, fights, and "acting in an ungentlemanly or unladylike manner." He also docked workers for more trivial offenses such as lateness and chewing gum on stage.

"Supe" Henzsley, a Hagerstown native, got his initial assignment as a "gopher" because he knew Bishop through their acquaintance at John Brown's Farm. Henzsley tells an amusing story about one of his first experiences with the Coppertone Review. A frequent front man for Bishop's musicians was the flamboyant vocalist, Sammy Fitzhugh—a man whose appearance was memorable: tall, rain thin, light-skinned, and sporting bright clothing and dyed blond hair.

Young and naïve, Henzsley had heard that one attraction of the Amusements of America troupe was the "freak show." Upon seeing glitzy Sammy Fitzhugh for the first time, the startled Henzsley reasoned to himself, "Damn, that must have been a freak!" When he later related that first impression to Fitzhugh, Henzsley said, "A cussin' match ensued, but later we became good friends."

In contrast to the ad hoc enlistment of relatively unskilled roustabouts, Bishop typically hired his musicians and dancers for the entirety of the warm-weather fair season. Those musicians were impressive to a young T. J. Tindall.

Today, Tindall is a veteran session guitarist in the Philadelphia area. His credits include work with the O'Jays, Billy Paul, Harold Melvin & the Blue Notes, Robert Palmer, and producers Gamble and Huff.

"Girls in their panties" dancing in Bishop's "Coppertone Review." Photo courtesy LaVerne Bishop.

Tindall related that he and a childhood buddy would, "always go to the Trenton State Fair and see the Coppertone Review, which was a black dancing-girl type of review. We were too young to get into the show, but the guys in the band and some of the girls would do a sort of preview out on the midway before the show and [we] would get right up front to watch the band play. These guys were funky. Shark skin suits, processed hair, old dented saxes. I remember one guy's guitar had the neck held on with tape wrapped around it. Amazing; but boy, could they play!"

Winfield Parker played sax in the Coppertone Review along with Sammy Fitzhugh and the Moroccos. Rudy Hall of Frederick, Maryland, had a sister, Sandy, who was one of the singers. Rudy remembers his sister warning him concerning the Review, "Don't go home and tell mama what you seen." Which was what? "Girls in their panties" – including dancers Gloria, Sandy, and Linda.

The Coppertone Review routinely retained the services of the Hortense Allen Dancers. An iconic dancer from Philadelphia, Hortense Allen (Jordan) served as choreographer, seamstress, and creative consultant to Bishop. Joe Dixon, a trusted employee of Bishop, related, "If there was any trouble [with the dancers], she would replace them." Dixon also related that some of Ms. Allen's dancers would alternate between working for Bishop and for James Brown.

Several of the dancers in the Review became well-rounded professionals. In addition to studying at the Alvin Ailey American Dance Center and being on the Faculty of the Philadelphia College of the Performing Arts, Faye B. Snow cited in her distinguished resume that she "danced with the Coppertone Review"!

Bishop employed as his emcee for the Review (and not infrequently at JBF) the comedian Dap "Sugar" Willie. Bishop had traveled to Philadelphia specifically to scout the young comedian who was performing at a local club, and he immediately signed him up. Willie (born "Willy Anderson") was also an actor and played the recurring role of Lenny on "Good Times" starring Esther Rolle, John Amos, and Jimmie "Dy-no-mite" Walker. Willie also played himself on four episodes of "Sanford and Son" (1975–1977) with fellow comedian, Redd Foxx.

In the August 11, 1966 edition of Hagerstown's Daily Mail, Willie described his early days with the Review: "I used to clown around and run around the [circus] ring like a nut."

Freddy Lee Gardin remembered another Coppertone comedian simply as "Jules," who doubled as a performer that "danced under the limbo pole with broken glass and 'flames of fire' on the floor."

Teaser acts out on the Midway drew paying customers inside to see more of The Coppertone Review. Photo courtesy LaVerne Bishop.

The U.S. Economy During the JBF Era

It is interesting to note that during almost the entire JBF era, the United States enjoyed a rather vigorous economy. (Potential foreign competitors by and large were still digging themselves out of the rubble of World War II.) Unemployment rates in the U.S. were so low at times that employers found it hard to recruit qualified workers.

National Unemployment Rates

1950	5.3%
1952	3.0%
1954	5.5%
1956	4.1%
1958	6.8%
1960	5.5%
1962	5.5%
1964	5.2%
1966	3.8%

The average wage for black males rose 20% between 1959 and 1965, which is the latter portion of the John Brown's Farm era. The highest inflation rate during that same time frame was a mere 1.6%. For black females, the average wage over the same time period increased 40%.

To be sure, unemployment in that period was higher for blacks (nearly double) and their wages lower (about 60% of the average white worker). However, economic conditions were such that a goodly number of young black people had money enough for discretionary spending on stylish clothing, records, and other entertainment. Some had their own cars, and many had friends who did.

(Statistical sources: United States Department of Labor and Richard B. Freeman's "Changes in the Labor Market for Black Americans, 1948–1972.")

Getting There Was Half the Fun!

One of my earliest curiosities about this story was how the patrons of John Brown's Farm traveled to and from the property. I had trouble enough finding the place in broad daylight with a map (in the pre-Flood days before GPS). Thus I was eager to learn how hundreds of people, some of whom came from well over fifty miles away, could locate the place at night without even the benefit of modern street signs.

HOW THE MUSIC LOVERS GOT TO THE FARM

Indeed, the musicians themselves were often confused about where exactly John Brown's Farm was. Multi-instrumentalist Chico Vega described it as being in Virginia, and guitarist Mike Jackson recalled it being in West Virginia, rather than in its true Western Maryland location.

The "500 private cars and 20 buses" mentioned in the IBPOEW Grand Lodge's 1951 Minutes that found their way to JBF had accomplished no mean feat. The winding roads, monotonous woods, and lack of lighting and landmarks

Young dancers from a 75-mile radius loved to "car up" to get to John Brown's Farm.

made for a perplexing journey. Indeed, one clever nickname for the Farm, coined by an attendee and her friends from nearby Washington, D.C., was "You can't find it!" But find it they did, year after year.

Based on my own difficulties in locating the Farm, one of my early questions of interviewees was simply, "How did you get to John Brown's Farm?" The initial answer was often something jovial like Rose Williams's "Best way we can!" or Edwina Mason's "Whatever was moving!" or Tyrone Henzsley's "Anything that was smokin', I was on it."

Reginald Johnson described John Bishop's annual marketing strategy, "He would try to bring in a very big name act around Easter as a lead-in to the rest of the season. In the summer everybody, from Pennsylvania, from the Tri-State area, came to see those entertainers."

Al Baylor related that there regularly was a "convoy of cars from Charles Town to John Brown's Farm." Sylvia Stanton added, "Kids would meet at Fisherman's Hall and 'car up' to go to the Farm. They'd fill one car, take off, fill another, and take off."

Charles Town native Diane Puller-Williams confessed, "I started sneaking in at the very early age of seventeen. People would drop by my house and pick me up, and probably about six of us would get in the car and go together. We would always go. Carloads."

Diane Puller-Williams.
Photo by Winston Pitman.

Ruth McDaniel of Charles Town recalled a not uncommon occurrence: "You'd come down here to town as everybody else was leaving town and you'd say, 'Where is everybody?' [And somebody would answer,] 'Well, they're all gone over to John Brown's Farm.' And you'd say, 'Well, let me see if I can find a ride to go.' That was the way it was."

Jean Lee Roberts, also from Charles Town, often got stuck functioning as the designated driver. "If I couldn't find [another] way, then I would drive. I didn't really want to drive. A lot of times I would leave

Sandy Hook, Maryland, pictured here, lay roughly halfway between Harpers Ferry and John Brown's Farm and was the site of the Shamrock Club, another of John Bishop's music venues. Photo by Winston Pitman.

The Route to JBF

Folks trekking from the East from as far as Baltimore and D.C. would go through Frederick, Maryland. From there they would travel the recently widened and resurfaced U.S. Route 340 to the approach of the new bridge over the Potomac River built in 1948 at Sandy Hook, Maryland. From there, they veered over to the old Sandy Hook Road virtually stitched to the river bank.

Even today, Sandy Hook Road is so narrow in places that you wonder if you have strayed onto someone's private lane. After a mile or so, that road turns north and becomes Harpers Ferry Road, which in a couple of miles intersects with Chestnut Grove Road. From there, JBF is about a kilometer ahead on the left.

People traveling from the South, from places like Winchester or Leesburg, Virginia, would make their way across the Sandy Hook Bridge and then over to Harpers Ferry Road as per above.

People traveling from the West, from Martinsburg and Shepherdstown, West Virginia, crossed the Potomac River near the ford used by the Confederate Army in their retreat from the Battle of Antietam. The James Rumsey Bridge, built there in 1939, ushered JBF-goers east into Sharpsburg.

From Sharpsburg they could drive southeast on Burnside Bridge Road and then south on Chestnut Grove, especially when the Potomac River and Little Antietam Creek were overflowing their banks. Most often, though, people took Harpers Ferry Road south out of Sharpsburg to the left at Samples Manor onto Chestnut Grove Road.

Attendees from locales to the North, such as Hagerstown and Chambersburg, Pennsylvania, could travel south to Boonsboro, Maryland, and then onto what is now Maryland Route 67. Alternately, they could travel southward on Maryland Route 65 through Sharpsburg and join those coming from the west onto Harpers Ferry Road.

[town] early so I wouldn't have to drive, but then I'd end up having to drive somebody's car back because they done partied too much. I didn't want to drive, because I wanted to party [too]."

Russell Roper.
Photo by Winston Pitman.

Russell Roper said of his Charles Town taxi service, "We had two cabs and we made a lot of trips back and forth, back and forth, to JBF on the nights that they had dances."

Janet Jeffries lived in a rural area on Berryville Pike near the Virginia/West Virginia state line. "Being the country girl that I am, what I would do on a Saturday evening was go down on the highway and thumb a ride to Charles Town. Believe it or not, anybody that I caught a ride with my father knew. So I'd catch a ride to Charles Town and meet up with several of my friends to go to John Brown's Farm."

Ethelene Clinton said of her crew from Kearneysville, West Virginia, "We would start about three o'clock in the evening. We would meet at the Friendly Inn and we ate steamers (similar to a Sloppy Joe)... We would have a good time there, and we'd make sure about nine o'clock we head over to Ferry Hill (opposite Shepherdstown, West Virginia). [There] we'd get our little 'refreshments' (alcoholic beverages) and we would head to John Brown's Farm."

The contingents from the west—Kearneysville, Martinsburg, and Shepherdstown—sometimes would be met by carloads of folks coming up from the south. James Taylor of Charles Town explained about the route along Sandy Hook Road, "Sometimes after a heavy rain, the road that we usually traveled to the Farm would get washed out, and we had to go through Shepherdstown on into Sharpsburg and to a right onto Harpers Ferry Road. And we had to take that route into the Farm. That was the long way around [but] we wanted to get there!"

As an adult, Laurence Bailey served as the first black assistant director of the United States Conference of Mayors. He also functioned at the White House in

James "Jim" Taylor.
Photo by Winston Pitman.

a prestigious and influential position as Deputy Assistant for President Jimmy Carter. As a teenager, however, Bailey worked summers at the Goose Creek Golf Club in Leesburg, Virginia. At the end of his Saturday shifts he would dash out to the parking lot and hop in his 1951 Plymouth. He detailed, "I would change into my dancing clothes in the car and make a beeline to John Brown's Farm."

Freddy Lee Gardin of Charles Town drove his chrome and tail-finned 1957 Chevy Bel Air to JBF. One of the ladies in his neighborhood would let no one other than Freddy drive her daughters there and back. He recalled that when he pulled up in front of the house and honked for the girls to come out, their mom would say, "Who's driving that car? Step out and let me see you." Freddy would oblige and the girls were free to go.

Leonard Cooper related, "Sometimes we'd thumb a ride, but generally people would say 'You know you got a ride, Leonard; you can go with us.' Sometimes I'd ask, 'Can I bring somebody with me?' And they'd say, 'Sure, you can bring them along.'" Cooper continued, "Most of the people that drove didn't drink. Some of the little uppity boys, their parents let them drive, but didn't let them drink. In fact, my mother would warn them not to drink."

The Hagerstown convoy was somewhat smaller than Charles Town's, but they too found various and ingenious ways to get to the dances. Reginald Johnson said, "We didn't have as many cars going down, but every one of those cars had five to eight people in it. If you wanted to ride, you paid fifty cents for gas."

Johnson continued, "People in Hagerstown would start planning on Monday to go down to John Brown's Farm on the weekend. People would say to somebody driving down, 'Hold my seat, man, 'cause I'm going!' You had those several days to hustle up your three dollars for the two-dollar ticket, the fifty cents for gas, and for a little something to eat or drink while you were there."

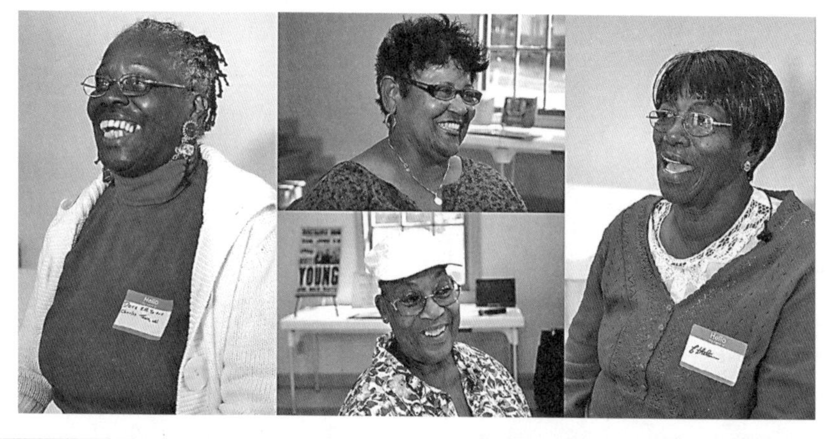

Former patrons of John Brown's Farm who shared their experiences at an NCAA-sponsored event at Fisherman's Hall in Charles Town, West Virginia, included (clockwise from top) Gloria Puller-Johnson, Ethelene Clinton, Janet Jeffries, and Dora Roy Yates. Photos by Winston Pitman.

Beverly (Johnson) Owens-Gaither of Hagerstown said, "We always found a way to get the three dollars to go to the dances. I would babysit; I collected soda bottles, put them in a wagon, and took them to the store to get the three cent deposit on them."

Dora Roy Yates clearly appreciated the value of a dollar in saying, "As far as Mr. John Bishop, he had all of the good people that come in there, and what you expected of them is exactly what you got. It was worth our money. Our money back then was hard to get, and you had to save. As your mama said, 'You wanna go, you better get your money.' So we got our money. And then when it went up to maybe four or five dollars, it was only because they had bigger bands. But we got our money. And we got our money's worth."

Rudy Russ of Hagerstown rustled up his entertainment dollars by caddying at the Fountain Head Country Club for about two dollars, then cadged coins downtown for perhaps another dollar or two, went home, got dressed, and headed for JBF. "Cars would leave left and right to go down there. It was a party."

Anthony Doleman recalled, smiling, "People would tap on your house window on a Saturday night and say, 'Hey, do you want to go to John Brown's Farm tonight?'—and you just got up and went."

The Berryville bunch recounted numerous trips to JBF from Virginia. Doris

Green's brother, George, once carried several people up in the cab of his sod truck. Rose Williams and her friend Edwina Mason remembered once siphoning gas out of a lawn mower in order to partially fill somebody's tank for the trip. On yet another trip, they ran out of gas entirely and waited in the car by the side of the road while the driver walked with a gas can to the next service station and filled it so they could continue on.

Thelma Waters of Hagerstown and her late husband drove their own car and loaded it up with others heading down. When I asked her if that was before they had children, she negated my faulty premise in replying, "I never had children; I kept my panties up."

Gloria Puller-Johnson, yet another Charles Town native, described a time when she and her then-husband got to the property—and the adventure was just beginning. "We were having car problems. We got as far as the gate and we paid, but his transmission went out so we couldn't get up the hill. We were holding up traffic, so we had to push the car out of the way," she said, to let some other patrons get past. She chuckled, "We had to turn around and back up the hill. It was just so embarrassing! But we went in, and we had a good time anyway."

Leonard Cooper was known for his dancing ability and for a snazzy wardrobe, which can be seen in this picture of him as a young man (left), and still today. Photos courtesy Leonard Cooper.

Squeezed between the Potomac River and South Mountain, Sandy Hook Road juts north here and becomes Harpers Ferry Road. Photo by Winston Pitman.

A WWII and Korean War Army veteran (who politely declined to give me his name when I buttonholed him in a Hagerstown grocery store) said that on several occasions he rode up from Baltimore with his riding club, the Roadrunners. They would travel in a group of a dozen or more and then meet up with other motorcycle clubs at the Farm. His crew tried to get there early to stake out a good area to park their bikes and to roll out their sleeping bags and other camping equipment.

Another Army veteran related that he and other soldiers stationed at Fort Detrick, Maryland, piled into cars on numerous occasions to make their way to the dances at JBF.

Louise Morris of Burkittsville said of her husband and herself, "We drove ourselves—not going over Elk Ridge, but on down to the Potomac River and back up."

Just about everybody recalled that the trips to and fro were fun in themselves. The Berryville bunch loved to spend their travel time singing. One time however, they pushed their chauffeur's patience too far. The over-decibeled driver made the warblers get out and walk for a while.

Al Baylor recently drove out to JBF from Charles Town and noted, "The ride seemed much longer than it did when I was just a kid. It was a long trip, but [back then] we were laughin' and jokin'."

Most nights at JBF, you could find someone who had driven the forty-five miles from Chambersburg, Pennsylvania; fifty miles from Front Royal, Virginia; sixty miles from Warrenton, Virginia; seventy miles from Baltimore and D.C.; and even one hundred miles from Steelton, Pennsylvania, where there was a large and active IBPOEW lodge. Curious visitors from as far away as Philadelphia (175 miles), New Jersey, and New York City (260 miles) also came.

The record distance would have to be the four hundred miles covered by several Marines stationed at Camp Lejeune, North Carolina. Rose Williams and Edwina Mason gossiped that the leathernecks came home on leave and stopped by JBF even before going home to visit their families in Millwood, Virginia.

Most of the attendees came from the towns listed below. The population figures cited are from the 1960 U.S. Census.

Municipality	Population	Blacks	Black %	Miles to JBF
Shepherdstown, WV	1328	218	16.4	10
Brunswick, MD	3555	146	4.1	12
Charles Town, WV	3329	989	29.7	15
Ranson, WV	1974	196	9.9	15
Martinsburg, WV	15,179	818	5.4	20
Hagerstown, MD	36,660	1716	4.7	20+
Frederick, MD	21,744	2349	10.8	25
Leesburg, VA	2869	495	17.2	30
Winchester, VA	15,110	1190	7.9	35+

Additionally, there were a number of smaller African-American enclaves within driving distance of the Farm. Below is a sample from just the northeastern part of Clarke County, Virginia:

Blackburn Town (wide spot in the road)

Gaylord (unincorporated)

Josephine City (now part of Berryville)

Lewisville (unincorporated near Franklintown, West Virginia)

Pigeon Hill (unincorporated, south of Berryville)

Rattlesnake Springs (wide spot in the road)
Stringtown (unincorporated, near Lewisville)
Webbtown (unincorporated, east of Berryville)

According to the book "African Americans of Jefferson County" by the Jefferson County Black History Preservation Society, there were twenty-four African American communities in Jefferson County, West Virginia, alone.

Extrapolating from the Clarke and Jefferson County concentrations and from anecdotal evidence given by the various interviewees of people traveling from Baltimore, Washington, and their suburbs, it would appear that people from well over a hundred discrete communities large and small came to John Brown's Farm on a recurring basis.

"WE WATCHED FOR THOSE POSTERS EVERY WEEK!"

How did so many people from so many places even hear about the dances at the JBF? The answer is simple: posters. Although a good deal of promotion was done by word of mouth, it was primarily achieved through those colorful, widely-distributed posters designed and printed by the Globe Poster Printing Corporation of Baltimore.

Bishop almost certainly made his connection with Globe Poster through Rufus Mitchell from Carr's Beach. Bishop followed the typical Globe Poster customer process of telephoning in the minimum basic information required: place, date, time, and artists. (Charles Town native Norvel Willis remembered also seeing ticket prices on the posters.)

Globe Poster eventually came to be run by the Cicero brothers—Joe, Jr., Bob, and Frank. Globe Posters had a distinctive look with bold type and eventually Day-Glo colors. They were designed to be loud and legible. One of the Ciceros' design mantras was "clarity and color." Their posters were meant to be seen primarily by passing motorists, so they needed to attract attention and convey essential information quickly.

The promoters entrusted Globe with the design of the poster itself. Frank Cicero remembered the standard poster size as being 14" X 22" and a larger size of 22" X 28". Upon completion of the printing, Globe would package the posters in appropriately sized cardboard boxes and ship them off to the various promoters employing their services. The next step was for the promoter to circulate the posters to places advantageous to their purposes.

Globe Posters

Globe Poster Printing Corporation of Baltimore has become world-famous for its iconic posters featuring bold print, Day-Glo colors, and publicity photos of the stars of rock and roll and R&B.

The man heading the operation for nearly five decades after its founding in 1929 was owner Norman Shapiro. (He changed the pronunciation of his last name to "Sha-PIE-ro," believing that it sounded more Italian.)

Shapiro sold the company to his long-time right-hand man, Joseph J. Cicero, in 1975. At various times, Cicero's sons Joe, Jr., Frank, and Bob Cicero also came to work at the company and eventually to inherit it from their father. During the brothers' tenure, it was a going concern—literally. According to Bob Cicero, "We moved several times. We actually started at 113 S. Hanover Street, then to 123 Market Place, then 1801 Byrd Street, and finally to 3705 Bank Street."

While they were working their long and often hectic schedules, the Cicero brothers tended to view their work as just a hurry-up, blue-collar printing business. Today, however, their craftsmanship is prized as artwork and is sought after by individual collectors and museums.

In 2011, the bulk of Globe Poster's machinery and artwork was acquired by the Maryland Institute College of Art. The college's staff is in the process of sorting out the vast collection, but MICA students already are making use of the old letterpress under the weekly tutelage of Bob Cicero.

Globe Poster devotee and champion, John Lewis, is working toward the completion of his documentary "Say It Loud!" that chronicles the history of the company and its legacy.

Bob Cicero, former co-owner of Globe Poster, was kind to create a replica poster celebrating the classic elements of John Brown's Farm. Posters are available for purchase at www.johnbrownsfarm.com

From Front Royal in the west to Chambersburg in the north, and from Baltimore in the east to D.C. in the south, John Bishop maintained an astonishing four thousand square-mile network of poster pounders. His "John Brown's Farm" posters adorned the telephone poles and business windows of dozens and dozens of black communities on a weekly basis throughout the summer months.

Bishop and his brother-in-law Harry Rideoutt seem to have done most of the poster-putting themselves in the early days, but they soon enlisted a cadre of helpers over a huge area. In the little community of Millwood, Virginia, people remember at various times John Bishop and Delores Harris (Leonard Harris's wife) fastening posters to several telephone poles in town. One of those Millwood poles still sports the staples. The nearest telephone pole to Fisherman's Hall in Charles Town is riddled with them.

Leonard Harris supplied additional insight into the process. "If (Bishop) had something at the Farm, he would say, 'Hey Leonard, we got to get these bills [posters],' twenty-four inches by twenty-six inches, 'we got to get them out.' We would get them from Baltimore. At times we might have to drive down ourselves to get them—to make sure they would be on time. Globe Poster. It was Globe Posters. They used to have the word "Globe" at the top. You could get different colors—orange, white. To get them in the real fancy colors, it cost more."

Gerald Barnett remembers helping his uncle, Maynard Henderson, circulate the posters. "He kept some in the car and would put them up as needed."

Reginald Johnson, Jr. dated Harry Rideoutt's daughter for a time. He rode around with Rideoutt at first but later became the main guy to put up the posters in Hagerstown. Johnson tacked them on telephone poles and abandoned houses in addition to placing loose copies in a pool hall and other businesses. For doing that chore, he got into the dances for free. "The first time I put my [admission] money in the window, Mr. Rideoutt told me not to do that again. Doing the posters was my pay."

Johnson remembers, "We hated the Farm to close each Sunday night because then you had to wait a whole week. People immediately started asking, 'Who's it gonna be?! Who's coming next week?!' People thought I had inside knowledge because I put up the posters." (Actually Johnson often did have some advance information, but kept it a secret that Rideoutt sometimes slipped him the posters a week ahead of the next event.)

Authentic Globe Posters for contemporaneous events at other venues now carry a hefty price tag. Although I have searched far and wide and deep for one of the old posters from John Brown's Farm, the quest may be futile. As Reginald Johnson glumly noted concerning their apparent extinction, "At the time we just took them for granted."

UPON ARRIVAL

Posters alerted the public to the performers and dates of the various events. The serpentine byways steered them toward the property. Let us now explore what the young attendees would experience upon setting foot on John Brown's Farm.

Once the would-be revelers arrived at the pillared entrance to the Elks' property, they would head up a long gravel lane. On their right they could see the old farmhouse—if they happened to look. In my experience, fewer than half of the people who attended the dances had any idea why the place even was called John Brown's Farm. James Taylor admitted, "Honestly, I never noticed the farmhouse at all."

Al Baylor said that he "assumed that the farmhouse was just a barn on the property." Virtually none of the dance attendees understood at the time that the farmhouse was the very building John Brown had rented for over three months in 1859. They had little to no idea that this was the place from which he had led the Raid on Harpers Ferry that precipitated the Civil War and the liberation of many of their grandparents from slavery.

As the cars made it about halfway up the gravel road, it was time for the attendees to dig into their pockets and purses to pay the admission fee. Norvel Willis remembers a little gate astride the road. Daniel Jackson, Jr. elaborated, "You had to go through the front gate and they would check the car, make sure nobody was in the trunk of the car, you know, try to get in free or laying down on the floorboard, and then you would go on through."

Sylvia Stanton worked that post. "Cars would come in. We would count heads and charge whatever the rate was for the night. Some people would duck down in the seats or hide in the trunk, but most people honestly paid up."

One man that I interviewed in Frederick, Maryland, along with Dorothy Johnson and "Half Pint" Thomas, was one of those occasional exceptions. John Henry Morris admitted, "We used to sneak in sometimes by hiding in the trunk so we wouldn't have to pay at the gate."

Coppertone Review's Joe Dixon recalled, "Some cars would have a couple people in the trunk. When we suspected that, we'd say something like, 'You have to open up your trunk, man.' For the really big stars they would take tickets at the door to make sure every head got counted." Dixon cited the typical cover charge as "two dollars; more if it was somebody famous."

For cost comparison purposes, I found an advertisement in the October 6, 1962, edition of *The Miami Times*. For two dollars on the weekend, you could see artists like Gene McDaniels or Clyde McPhatter at the "King O' Hearts Club." McPhatter was only one dollar for the teen matinee on Sunday afternoon.

John Bishop would set up the ticket-takers with a table, a cigar box, and a little cash to make change. Then he and Harry Rideoutt would head off to scrutinize activities inside, including the kitchen operation. Bishop would come back out periodically to collect the money. Sylvia Stanton expressed that she "never experienced any danger or even threat of trouble at the gate. People back then were honest, respectful, raised differently than they are today."

I asked Sylvia and a friend what the age-mix would be in a typical night's crowd. They thought that it was fairly evenly distributed between those of late high school age (not many under 17), the 19–22 age group, and 23 and older. It was not uncommon, however, to see people in their forties and even fifties, depending on who the artist was. Al Baylor concurred in describing the typical crowd as being late teens to mid-twenties with other attendees into their thirties.

Having paid the admission fee, patrons were waved on back toward the auditorium. Once the various parties got to JBF—whether by bus, car, motorcycle, or sod truck—finding a parking spot could take a little while. No big deal. There amongst the parked cars a party already was happening. As Rudy Hall of Frederick put it, "You could have a bigger party on the outside than you had on the inside!"

Edgar Young from Mt. Airy had this interesting anecdote to share: "Down at John Brown's Farm we would set up a [makeshift] baseball diamond and play fast pitch softball before the dances started. My team was the Mt. Airy Nightcrawlers. One time after we beat a bunch of guys from Frederick, they pretended like they weren't going to let us go into the dance. They said, 'We're not going to let you beat us in softball and then take our girlfriends, too!'"

On nights when the entry fee was collected at the front door, helpers like Beverly Dykes King stood at a little wooden table, received the cover charge, and gave the customer his or her ticket from a stock roll of generic tickets. Norvel Willis recalled, "Nobody carded at the door for proof of [being] twenty-one." As needed, the helpers also would stamp patrons' hands for re-entry using a little ultraviolet lamp to help them see the stamps.

The young revelers, having devoted their weeks to scrounging up money for tickets and refreshments, boning up on their dance moves, and orchestrating their rides, were now lined up to bound through the front door into the auditorium throbbing with potential. What lay immediately ahead was the idyllic and halcyon experience of the fullness of John Brown's Farm.

Experiencing John Brown's Farm

In 2009, this author first sought to explore the auditorium of John Brown's Farm. I had to wrench aside a rotten piece of plywood in order to squint through a broken window into a dark and dank room. As my eyes adjusted, at last I beheld the fabled old dance hall—literally filled with junk.

Finding a rickety door ajar, I entered the room and traipsed gingerly across the slippery floor, crunching glass underfoot, and hoping desperately not to startle some raccoon or skunk into action. In the dim light, I picked my way past clusters of bottles, damp furniture, and rotting old clothing—the rain-soaked remnants of what looked like a long-forgotten neighborhood yard sale gone bad.

Contrast that dismal condition of the venue in 2009 with the vibrant

The auditorium at John Brown's Farm as it looked to the author on his first visit in 2009. Photo by Winston Pitman.

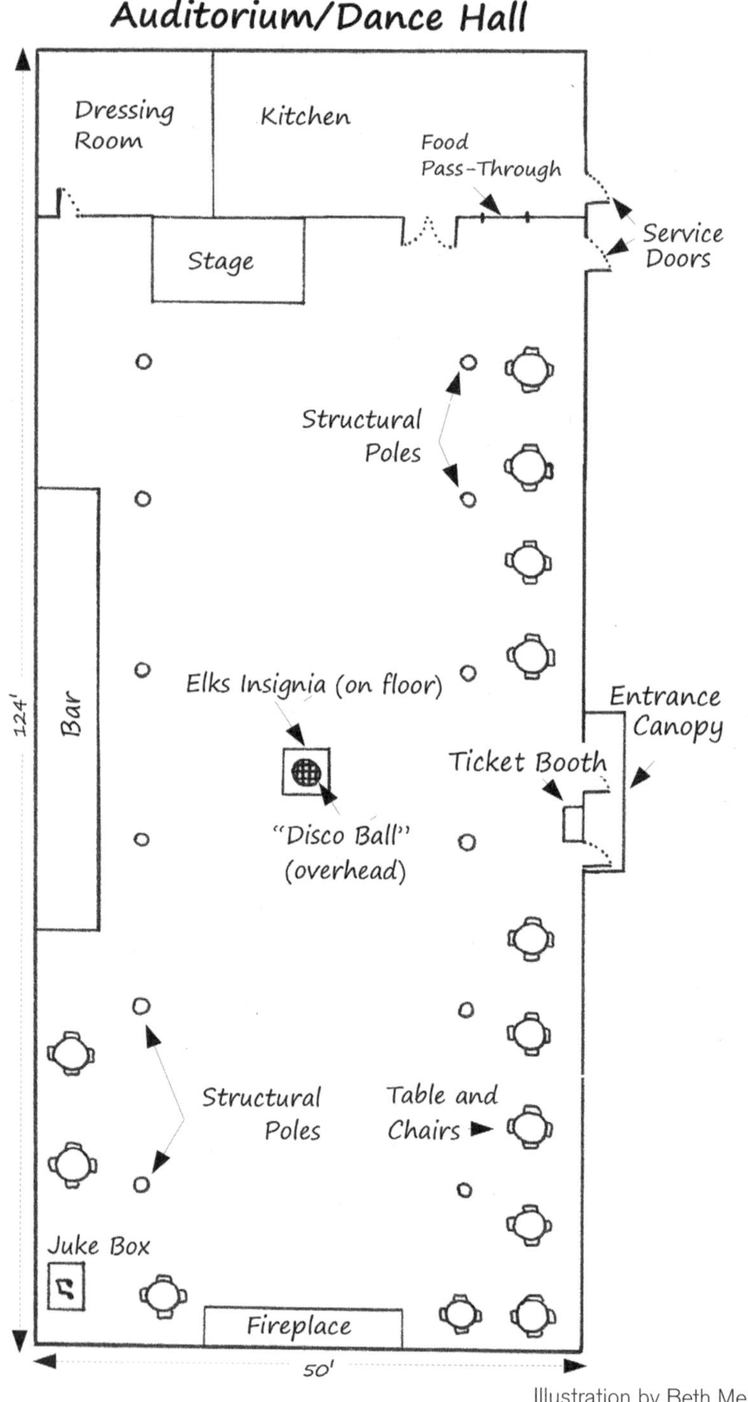

Illustration by Beth Meier

If hell had a yard sale, it might look something like the interior of the dance hall did in 2009. The tattered remnant of what later became known as a "disco ball" hung directly over the Elks insignia on the dance floor below. Photo by Winston Pitman.

expectancy of a typical summer weekend fifty years prior. Here is what the young attendees back then would have seen.

The squat auditorium, where so many famous musicians played late into the night, was a 124-foot-wide by 50-foot-deep edifice built of concrete block and topped by a flat roof. Although architecturally charmless, its manifest homeliness was mitigated by a fresh coat of white paint and green awnings over the windows and doors. Emblazoned across the top of the facade were painted the initials I.B.P.O.E.W., marking it as the proud national shrine of the Black Elks.

The expectant dancers poured into the building's main entrance, respectfully skirting the Elks insignia gracing the center of the floor. The open, 108-foot by 50-foot main room hummed with energy, dominating the interior floor plan. The tiled dance floor, where so many of the night's moments were spent, occupied the lion's share of the room. Spotlights directed toward a "disco ball" produced shiny little dots throughout the room.

As young attendees entered through one of the dance hall's two main doors, they could opt for the comfort of tables and chairs situated to the right and to the left. On the left-hand wall stood a large, hand-crafted fireplace. Beyond the fireplace the large jukebox presided, spinning records when no band was present.

The bar, straight ahead, was stunningly elaborate, filling much of the room's long, 108-foot wall. A steady crowd would keep its three bartenders busy throughout the evening, buying beer, wine, sodas, and "set-ups" for their own carried-in liquor. Perhaps purposefully reminiscent of Grand Exalted Ruler J. Finley Wilson's cowboy days out West, the design was, as described by Reginald Johnson, Jr., "really a beautiful bar. Like an old-style cowboy bar with a brass railing and everything."

When the attendees shifted their eyes across the room, they would find the fabled bandstand nestled in the far right corner of the dance floor. A wooden performance stage was ensconced there—about three feet high and roomy enough to accommodate six or seven musicians. Larger groups and/or active performers like James Brown and Tina Turner necessitated some of the musicians moving down to floor level.

Many groups brought their own sound systems, but the stage also furnished the Elks' house P.A. system and a well-used upright acoustic piano. It was described as "generally in pretty decent tune," by Gerald Barnett, who also supposed it was his Uncle Maynard's job to have it tuned periodically.

Musicians readied themselves for the night's performance in the sixteen-foot-square dressing room located behind the stage. From there they could check out the crowd's increasing anticipation through the single door with its eye-level porthole.

Saloon-style double doors connected the dance hall to the kitchen, which hustled and bustled all night long. Food ordered through an efficient pass-through window in the far right-hand corner of the main room kept the kitchen busy and dancers' bellies satisfied.

Having gotten one's bearings, what might a young reveler expect to experience?

SOUL FOOD

The kitchen at John Brown's Farm had been constructed and equipped to handle events as large as the Elks' gatherings on the Fourth of July and Labor Day when upwards of three thousand people attended. Thus, the servicing of a typical dance night's crowd of four to five hundred people was considered challenging but manageable.

Beverly Dykes King was the principal source of information about the food operation in the kitchen at JBF. As a teen, she worked the dances with her mother, Lucille Dykes. According to King, the kitchen itself had "big, deep sinks" and "an old-time stove" where they pan-fried chicken in a "big old iron skillet." Gerald Barnett remembered several big skillets and "a nice-size range" that was situated under a large exhaust hood.

For dances, caretaker Maynard Henderson purchased chicken in bulk, by the crate. It was his weekly task to carve up the chicken. For an average event, they would utilize Sylvia Bishop's batter from Payne's Hotel but cook the chickens

The Great Debate

Far and away, the biggest controversy among interviewees who had attended the dances concerns this all-important topic: "What were the restrooms like?"

What is there now is clear enough—behind the crumbling auditorium are two intact and sturdy little block buildings: a men's and a women's lavatory with toilets and sinks. Folks agreeing on what was on the property in, say, 1959 is another matter altogether!

At one end of the spectrum, Norvel Willis says he remembers no indoor bathrooms ever and not even outhouses initially. He offered perhaps too much information in adding, "The guys would provide lookout for their girlfriends as they relieved themselves behind a car or a tree."

Gerald Barnett lived on the farm year-round as a pre-schooler, and during the summers until he was sixteen. He cited as one of his chores, "cleaning the outside brick (cinder block) bathrooms." (He recalled no sinks, but didn't rule them out.)

After hearing such varied lavatory reports, I asked Winfield Parker about whether or not he thought there were bathrooms inside the auditorium back in the day. He hooted at me incredulously, "Of course there were! Ray Charles was there! Do you think Ray Charles was gonna go outside?!"

Hmm. I hadn't thought about that one. In fact, I wish I could stop thinking about it now.

To put an end to the controversy, however, Bo Morgan, who bought the property in 1966, confirmed that there had been no inside bathrooms until the Amvets helped him install them, probably in the spring of 1967. They built the bathrooms as an addition to the south side of the auditorium and ran a sewer line out to a septic field on the far side of the barn (which has since been razed).

To corroborate his story, Bo Morgan, while sorting through some of his records, found a copy of the Souvenir Journal for the 1951 Grand Lodge National Convention held in Buffalo, New York, in late August. On page twenty three, an aerial photograph (probably taken earlier in the summer) clearly shows that the exterior block bathrooms had been built prior to the auditorium.

The term "built like a brick outhouse" applies in this circumstance. These two still-standing outhouse structures were among the first erected by the IBPOEW upon assuming the property in 1950. Photo by Winston Pitman.

in the kitchen at JBF. Several people mentioned that for expected high-traffic events, John and Sylvia Bishop would cook additional chicken at their hotel and transport it out to the Farm.

LaVerne Bishop remembers Saturdays being busy at the hotel as her mother made potato salad and her batter. The chicken was used for sandwiches, which were one-quarter chickens cooked and then placed atop a piece of bread. King remembers the price to have been $1.75.

Avid dancers Rose Williams and Edwina Mason of Millwood, Virginia, made it a practice to order those sandwiches at the end of the dance to eat on their way home. A welcome treat after dancing all night!

The kitchen also offered hot dogs and hamburgers. Thelma Waters of Hagerstown remembers fish and potato salad being sold there—what she called "good country cookin'." One person recalled the serving of "pigs' feet," but several people pooh-poohed that notion as perhaps wishful thinking.

According to King, concern was shown to be discreet about where the kitchen cash was kept. "When taking the money for the food, we would go back out of sight to the cash drawer, out of the customer's sight, then bring back the change and hand out the food."

Another memorable aspect of the John Brown's Farm experience was the liquid refreshments. As for soft drinks, Ms. King remembers the kitchen selling "Coke, Barq's root beer, and also other flavors of Barq's."

Recent excavations on the property unearthed pop bottles from Rock Creek Ginger Ale Co. out of Washington, D.C. Also discovered were milk bottles dating from the mid-1950s from the Hagerstown Dairy Company.

The refreshments staff, whether in the kitchen or over at the bar, poured drinks from bottles into paper cups and then handed the cup to the patron. The staff retained the bottles as perhaps too tempting for use as an emergency weapon if tempers began to erupt.

King remembered the Elks having a liquor license but selling only beer. Gerald Barnett expressed certainty that the license was for beer-only.

Some attendees brought their own adult beverages onto the property. George Bumbaugh of Hagerstown remembers "riding down in a Studebaker that had a built-in beer cooler in the back seat."

Other folks bought hard liquor elsewhere and brought it onto the Farm. Rose Williams and Edwina Mason recounted that they often chipped in to buy a bottle of liquor from the owner of "the bar at the top of the hill" (Lily's Tavern in Dargan). They recalled that, "The lady [Lillie Mae, the wife of Snow Ingram] was quick to remember what each customer liked and could get it to them in a hurry." The two then would slip flasks inside their pocketbooks and take a swig from time to time throughout the evening.

A more common way to get hard liquor at the dances, however, was to sidle up to one of the "bootleggers" scattered here and there about the grounds. One of the on-site purveyors of potent potables was, according to Williams and Mason, "a moonshiner named Pete Carter who had a stash of half-pints in each coat pocket."

Recently deceased Charles Harris from Winchester, Virginia, primarily attended the daytime family functions as a youth, but recognized that "you could bring your own alcohol and pay for a 'set up'—glass, soda, and ice."

KEEPING THINGS IN LINE

The events were first-class affairs. People generally dressed well and came to dance and socialize, not to get in trouble. But the natural volatility level of masses of energetic young people coupled with the presence of an abundance of alcohol were certain to result in a number of fights. And yet at the same time, virtually everyone interviewed said they never felt the least bit threatened.

Thus, it seems that if you wanted to get in a fight, you could. If you wanted to stay away from them, you did. Leonard Harris recalled that characteristically, "People would get a few drinks in them and have a ball."

The demeanor and policies of John Bishop and Maynard Henderson set an orderly tone to the events. Bishop carried himself in a paternal and business-like fashion. Leonard Harris clarified, "When you went to one of [Bishop's] places, you took care of business because he set an example."

Dora Roy Yates.
Photo by Winston Pitman.

LaVerne Bishop's memory of her father's typical cautionary address to club-goers was, "You're welcome to come in, so long as you act like a lady or like a gentleman. But if you don't, you gotta go."

Maynard Henderson could be more threatening as needed. Junior Henderson noted that his uncle "carried a gun" and that his attitude toward the attendees was, "You're gonna act right or you're not gonna come back here no more."

Was there potential for inter-racial animosities at the dances? Dora Roy Yates minimized that notion in saying, "There was always some white people there, but we all came there for a purpose—to dance and have a good time and get something to eat, get in the car and come back home. It wasn't none of that other friction. Where the friction was, we kept it out. We didn't come up like that, so we didn't need that. And we don't need it now."

Yates additionally noted, "There were [few] fights because if you started a fight inside, you was walked completely off the grounds, and you was not permitted to come back on the grounds."

And if decorum, admonition, or threat of expulsion weren't sufficiently persuasive, then up would step Bishop's paid security guards: full-time Washington County sheriff's deputy Bill Mason and under him several part- and later

On the Jail

Mr. Bill Mason was the first black police officer in Washington County and worked for the Sheriff's Department for 16 years, the last five serving as Captain.

Mr. William L. "Bill" Mason

The Washington County Jail was at one time situated at the south entrance to Hagerstown's Jonathan Street. Former sheriff's deputy Greg Johnson and Frank Keyes, III (son of former sheriff deputy "Sonny" Keyes) both likened some of the jail's departmental practices to that of "The Andy Griffith Show." That is, the lock-up's magistrate routinely allowed relatively harmless boozers "Woody" and "Monk" to check themselves in and out of their cells a la Mayberry's Otis Campbell.

Today at that former county jail site stands a plaque honoring JBF's principal law enforcement officer.

On Deputies

How Sheriff's Deputy Bill Mason, who was originally from Martinsburg, West Virginia, and the others came to be deputies is interesting. Greg Johnson explained that back in the day, "The position of sheriff was a political one that gave the person holding that office the authority to lay off [if he chose] the entire department. The County Sheriff's Department had no merit system, no job security. You were a deputy of the sheriff."

full-time assistant deputies.

During the JBF era, the sheriffs of Washington County (Edward L. Rowland 1950–1958 and Charles Price 1958–1974) grasped the wisdom of having black deputies on staff, especially when it came to matters such as policing dances at the Farm.

While patrolling the property, Bill Mason (1928–2005) and the other deputies were considered "on duty" and had the authority to make arrests. They wore their uniforms, carried guns, and had a special assistant—Mason's black and tan German Shepherd.

According to Greg (Bruce) Johnson, a former sheriff's deputy who worked later with Mason and another deputy, Frank "Sonny" Keyes, "If necessary, Mason would turn the dog loose on an unruly person and he'd take a chunk out of your ass."

Current Washington County Sheriff Doug Mullendore said of Mason, "He was like a big, likeable bear, but he could get the job done." The "bear" simile had

Sonny Keyes (left) and Vernon Johnson (center) were two top assistant deputies to Sheriff's Deputy Bill Mason (right).

to do in part with his physical stature.

Johnson described Mason as 6'2" and 240 pounds (a bit lighter when younger). Linda Irvin-Craig, Executive Director of the Washington County Historical Society, described Bill Mason as "tall, handsome, well-built." Apparently his facial features would adjust quickly when he was on high alert. For instance, when asked to describe Mason, George Bumbaugh offered, "Big, tall, ugly. He'd bust some heads up real quick. He didn't go around to start trouble, but he didn't take none, either."

Or, as Tyrone Henzsley, a one-time employee of John Bishop, starkly described Mason's default protocol, "He would blow you away if you stepped out of line."

Mason's first assistant deputy was Vernon E. Johnson in the mid- to late-1950s. Johnson (1920–2000) was a tad shorter and lighter than Mason at perhaps 6'1" and 225 pounds. Ronald Johnson described his father as a "no-nonsense kind of guy, but a nice guy. Everybody in the neighborhood called him 'Dad' and called my mom 'Mom.' Sometimes after working the Farm, he would come home and amaze us kids as he emptied his pockets of knives, guns, and brass knuckles onto the table."

Another of Mason's early assistants was William "Henry" Stewart. By day, Stewart was at various times a barber, the manager of the North Street YMCA in Hagerstown, and the first black man to run for Hagerstown City Council.

White deputies Harold McCarty and William Oscar (Bill) Lum, a county constable from nearby Mt. Lena, also sometimes worked the events.

Bill Mason's primary partner, and the one most often recalled by attendees, was Frank M. "Sonny" Keyes, Jr. Keyes began working with Mason in about 1962. Former colleague Major Robert (Bob) Hafer described Keyes as perhaps 5' 9" and 185 pounds, and added, "He could handle himself." Keyes's brother, Reginald, deemed Sonny to be a bit larger—5'10" and approaching 200 pounds.

Frank Keyes, III said of his dad, "Everybody loved him. As a result, all of his children could go into stores and be invited to have some candy or something from the cookie jar." But as Reginald Keyes noted with some younger brotherly admiration, "If you did something wrong, [Sonny] could put you in your place quick."

Most of the patrons of John Brown's Farm remember the tandem of Mason and Keyes as being simply part of the landscape—a friendly and even comforting presence. For instance, Charles Town's Leonard Cooper mentioned, "If I was a little short on cash, Mason would let me slip in."

However, as Greg Johnson related, "If somebody created a big enough commotion or was belligerent, they could and would be carted off to jail."

Leonard Harris elaborated, "They didn't play. [Mason] had to show the people that he was for real. He had to bang some heads. Some of us all didn't think it was right maybe the way he did, but to get their attention he had to whip some heads."

Inside the auditorium, the management of JBF had several ways to thwart potential outbreaks of hostility among the patrons. Gerald Barnett remembers that, "There was a ledge above the bar where a chaperone or bouncer could take stock of things, to look for fights."

Leonard Harris recalled, "At times you would have these fights and all. Bishop would be in the corner and sometimes I'd be on the other side, and he would just hold his hand up at me. 'We need help.' And [the deputies] would come in there and take [the offenders] out."

Keyes and Mason routinely patrolled outside the auditorium, the latter with his leashed German Shepherd. Larry Togans of Charles Town said of the dog, "I was scared of him." Sheriff Mullendore recalled that "Sonny" Keyes was scared of him, too. But one time Keyes apparently forgot that he was—or should have been, according to Major Hafer.

Hafer chuckled repeatedly as he told a story of working one evening at the former county jail on North Jonathan Street in Hagerstown as Mason and Keyes were gearing up to head down to JBF. "Bill Mason's dog was a German Shepherd named 'Satan' and he lived up to his name. Keyes was agitating the dog in the parking area. Mason warned him, but Keyes kept it up until the dog bit him. When I told the story a couple of days later at work, Mason thought it was funny. Keyes did not."

Daniel Jackson, Jr.
Photo by Winston Pitman.

Despite all the various precautions, fights did erupt from time to time, and it appears that Mason and Keyes would sometimes allow them to occur—within limits. Someone likened the tactic to a wise hockey referee who understands that, to a large extent, the players are self-policing. Trying to keep a lid on things by calling too tight a game violates the ethos of the game and actually can cause tempers to erupt out of control. Better to let the players enforce "playground justice" by way of a short physical altercation, letting off steam so that things don't boil over entirely.

Reginald Johnson, Jr. described the reality, "There was always going to be a fight, but I didn't really feel endangered. Personally, I never saw any weapons. People knew that Mason and Sonny (Keyes) weren't jokes. They had your name, your height, your hometown."

Winfield Parker relayed a telling bit of information about why at least some fights would occur. "The bootleggers outside sold hard liquor. Guys would get a few drinks in them and get upset if somebody danced with their girlfriend."

Once while probing a woman's sense of safety at the dances, I ventured to Hagerstown's Thelma Waters, "I suppose you had your husband to stick up for you." She snorted in rebuttal, "I didn't need nobody to stick up for me; I stuck up for myself!"

Leonard Cooper acknowledged, "We had our fights. West Virginia people in those days liked to fight—the race track guys against the apple pickers. That

Four top dancers at John Brown's Farm c. 1960 were (L–R): Charles Town's Margaret Ramseur, Leonard Cooper, Juanita (Mickey) Ramseur, and Arnold McDonald. Photo courtesy Leonard Cooper.

sort of thing. But after the fight was over, they'd all become friends and start partying together."

Cooper was certainly in a position to make such an assessment. Among the young attendees of the dances, no one was a more central figure than he was. Reginald Johnson remembered of him, "He was a happy-go-lucky guy. He was comical. He had his entourage. Leonard was one of the best dancers, one of the best dressers, and had all of the women hanging around him all the time." He also might have been the toughest guy there.

Laurence Bailey, a former Division II All-American basketball point guard at West Virginia State University, smiled at the mention of Leonard Cooper's name, saying, "You didn't want to get Leonard mad." Bailey paused and waggled his head in amused reflection. "Once he got started, there was no stopping him."

When asked about Leonard Cooper's prowess in that arena, Nedra Keyes, Sonny Keyes's daughter-in-law, remarked, "The whole Cooper family could fight, from the mother on down!" Keyes seems not to have been exaggerating. As Leonard Cooper tells it, "One time my sister punched a man in the face—

knocked him out."

Reginald Johnson, Jr., however, did seem to be hyperbolizing when he said, "Leonard Cooper would beat Muhammad Ali! He would waltz all over John Brown's Farm with you!"

When told about Johnson's comment, Cooper appreciated the accolade, but clarified, "I didn't really fight too much. If you fought a couple of times, then you got a reputation. And then you didn't have to fight too much after that."

Al Baylor agreed, "The norm was that the people never had harsh words, fights, or troubles of any kind." He remembers seeing only one fight—but it was memorable.

One night, the dapper and constitutionally mild-mannered Cooper and his entourage (mostly girls and other friends) made their entrance. He wore a set of clothes he had designed and sewn for himself, which Baylor described as "kind of like a Zorro outfit, including the cape. Three guys—I can tell you their names: Alfred, David, and Lionel—kept picking at Leonard and eventually backed him into a dark corner. I can still picture it. A minute later all that could be seen was Leonard's cape flying all around and those three guys come flying out of the corner one at a time!"

Given the last word on the subject of fighting at JBF, Daniel Jackson mused, "There wasn't much fighting, because they was more lovers than they was fighters—you understand what I'm saying. So, we didn't have to worry about too much fighting."

JBF'S HIP STYLE

Although there was no official dress code, clothing worn to the dances tended to be smart and stylish. Speaking of the sartorial standard of excellence at John Brown's Farm, Leonard Cooper said, "You had to go down there and look good!"

Beverly Dykes King stated that the attire for attendees "ranged from suits and dresses to slacks and shirts or skirts and blouses. Not many blue jeans in those days."

Al Baylor remarked about men's fashion at JBF, "It was all about sharp dressers—suits and ties." Although technically Baylor was underage for construction work, his father had gotten him a summer job as a bricklayer's helper. Thus, he made good money for a 16–17 year-old and had a goal in mind for how to spend it: "I tried my best to have a new set of clothes [for the dances] every couple of weeks."

Edwina Mason nominated Victor Burrell for snazziest dresser, recalling that he wore "fancy suits, hats, and alligator shoes." She and Rose Williams credited David and Alfred Jackson of Charles Town, West Virginia, as being "clean [sharp] dressers," and marveled at Duane and Rudolph Grey, whose "white pants stayed spotless all night."

Reginald Johnson, Jr. remembers on one occasion buying for JBF a blue shirt, white duck pants, and Converse tennis shoes. Johnson tipped his cap to Leonard Cooper as one of the best dressers.

Isabelle Johnson glowed in admiration, "Leonard was as talented as he could be. He would design and sew his own clothes, even putting embroidery on the cuffs of his pants." She also recalled Cooper having a bright yellow suit with a white hat and a matching yellow band. Her daughter, Beverly Owens-Gaither, remembered that Cooper once sported a red suit with a white cape and a white hat with a red band, while Nedra Keyes described one of Cooper's outfits having "fur cuffs on his shirt and pants."

Cooper recounted how he began tailoring his own wardrobe:

"Somebody gave me an old sewing machine, and I learned how to use it to make alterations. It was one of those where you had to pump the pedal to make it work. I started with handkerchiefs to learn my way around it. I did one outfit where I took a black suit and made plaid cuffs for the pants and shirt, and a plaid cummerbund. Another time, I made a black tie and connected it to a cape, so that when I undid the tie (as he demonstrated with a twirl), the cape would come loose, too."

Cooper mentioned fashioning an ensemble in what he said people called "Ivy League Style." He cut slits in the ends of the pant legs and shirt sleeves, and re-connected them with little fabric "belts." He did something similar with the back of a jacket by cutting a slit along the center seam and connecting the two panels with a fabric belt that had a little "buckle" in it. He added, "Another one of our styles was to wear real tight pants with short legs showing white socks—like Michael Jackson did later. We did that."

To top things off, Cooper sported a variety of processed hair styles. Joe Dixon remembered of his friend, "Leonard dyed his hair blonde and other colors, and wore a strong musk scent."

The women at John Brown's Farm were not about to be outdone by the men. Nedra Keyes remembers from her childhood the adults getting ready to go to JBF. She relished the memory in relating, "They were all dressed up!—with their hair all done up in pineapple curls," which were accomplished by gelling the hair, putting on a wide-webbed hair net, and pulling the curls partway through.

Most women wore dresses or crisp blouse and skirt ensembles. Dora Yates described the process in almost breathless earnestness: "We would start on a Thursday or Friday lining up our clothes—what we were going to wear for [the dance] Saturday. Talking about the clothes we wore—oh, we were just sharp! The earrings and everything had to match."

Edwina Mason remarked concerning footwear, "The girls wore shoes with three inch heels." Her lifelong pal Rose Williams piggybacked in laughter, "Maybe five inches!" (Given the fervor with which so many hit the dance floor, one can imagine that the ladies' pumps began the evening at five inches and by the end of a night's activities were down to three.)

The fashion sense at John Brown's Farm was top notch, but not its most magnetic feature. Although fighting did occur, it was not the main attraction. Socializing, as important as it was, wasn't the biggest allure either. Truth be told, the Farm's chief appeal wasn't even the fantastic singers and musicians. The centerpiece of the scene for the regular attendees was the dancing.

Dancing the Night Away

Al Baylor put it succinctly, "Our primary concern was to dance." Friends Williams and Mason agreed, "We couldn't even wait to get there." One time on the way, they stopped the car for a while and danced in the headlights to the radio. When they got to JBF they said, "We went *in* dancing."

The earliest personal testimony of someone attending a dance at JBF was one by (surprisingly to me) a white guy, George "Bill" Knight. He was from the immediate area. In fact, in the summer of 1941, as a nine-year-old, he had worked on the Farm. He pulled weeds and mowed the grass for Mrs. Davis, a widow who rented the place from Alfred Ankeney and lived in the farmhouse.

Knight was home on leave from the Army in September, 1952, when he went to a dance held in the JBF auditorium. He said that that particular audience was mixed racially—far more whites than blacks—and that the band was all-black. Upon hearing this ultra-early date stamp, I eagerly quizzed him about if he knew who might have booked the band. He laughed, "A young guy goes

Summer after summer, young dancers like these from Page-Jackson High School in Charles Town, West Virginia, packed the dance floor at John Brown's Farm.

down there to see the girls, not to see who runs the place!"

It seemed that just about everybody there danced. Some people were experienced dancers and other people were novices, but as Williams put it, "There were no wallflowers."

Larry Henderson from nearby Burkittsville recalled of JBF, "That's where I learned to dance; a young lady taught me the two-step."

Williams and Mason said that they often brought along a white friend, Paul Thomas, and bragged, "We taught him to dance!"

The bell-shaped curve of dancing ability included the vast majority—people like William Shanton, who said of himself, "I thought I was a pretty fair dancer."

Competent hoofers like Junior Henderson of Hagerstown answered more positively: "Did I dance? Oh, definitely! Are you kiddin' me? I didn't go down there to be a wallflower. I could boogie. Boogie, boogie, boogie."

Ruth McDaniel glowed in recollection, "Everybody was so friendly. It was a place to go to have a joyous, wonderful time—to dance and just feel good. If you were a good dancer, you didn't even have to worry—you danced every dance, because somebody saw you and said, 'Well, I want to dance with her.' And so you

Leonard Cooper

John Brown's Farm's arguably most memorable character keeps adding to his legacy. Perhaps you have heard the Toby Keith lyrics, "I ain't as good as I once was, but I'm as good once as I ever was." They apply to Leonard Cooper. And then some.

In April of 2009, Leonard Cooper was sitting in his barbershop, "Just Us Hairstyles," on Jonathan Street in Hagerstown. He was reading his Bible and waiting for the next customer to arrive. Instead a young ski-masked man brandishing a knife walked through the door, demanding money.

Mr. Cooper set aside the Bible, stood up, and turned his pockets inside out hoping to convince the intruder that he was cash-less. Unpersuaded, the thief thrust his free hand into Leonard's pocket to see for himself. At that moment the then 69-year-old barber seized the younger man by both wrists and a struggle lasting several minutes ensued.

Cooper narrated, "All I'm worried about is the knife. It was so fast. We were moving fast." Becoming a tad winded and sensing that the robber was resolute on hanging on to the 8-inch blade, Cooper switched tactics. He picked the man up and threw him through the glass front door!

Later in the day Cooper, nicked up and stitched up from the flying glass, thanked the Lord for being his protector. He summarized, "It's been a... wow... It's been a day." He's had a lifetime of them.

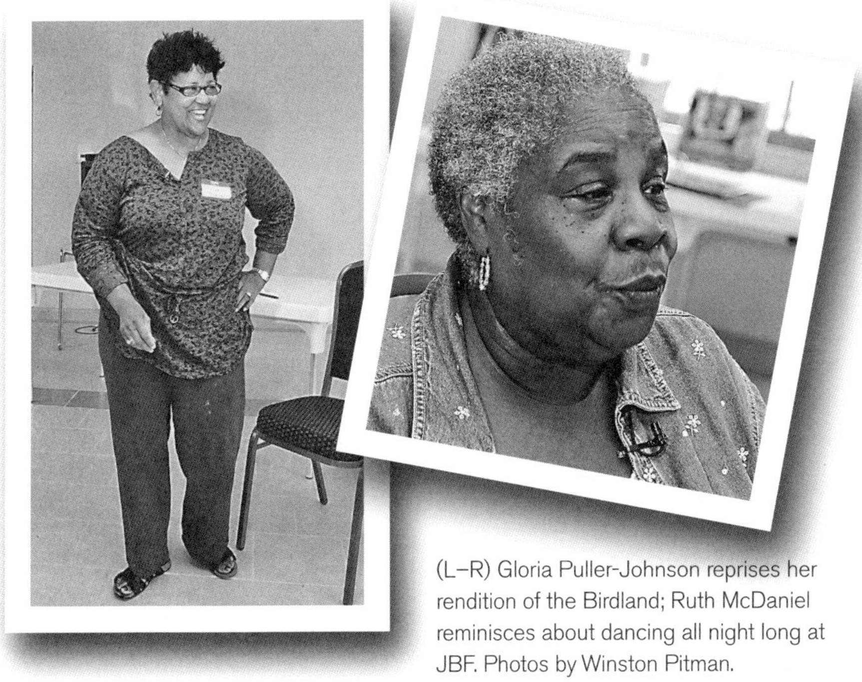

(L–R) Gloria Puller-Johnson reprises her rendition of the Birdland; Ruth McDaniel reminisces about dancing all night long at JBF. Photos by Winston Pitman.

danced with whoever asked you."

Jean Lee Roberts voiced a similar sentiment. "I just loved to dance with anybody. We met a lot of people from the Leesburg area, Winchester, Hagerstown. Every once in a while there would be somebody from D.C. or Philadelphia or something like that. As a little girl I always loved to dance."

At eighty-something, Thelma Waters recounted her fun in carrying on at JBF. She proudly demonstrated with a little shimmy-shake in her rocking chair, "I always dance wherever I go."

I smiled at her vivacious display and offered, "I bet you were the ticket back then."

She tooted in all earnestness, "I'm *still* the ticket!"

There was also an upper echelon of dancers, and the air up there could be quite spirited. Laurence Bailey said that at JBF he recognized guys from other towns from contesting with them in high school athletics. He added knowingly, "The competition would extend to the dance floor."

Certainly Leonard Cooper could compete in the dance department. During a group interview in what I have nicknamed "The Alley Fellowship" in

Hagerstown (an alley a half-block west of Jonathan Street where "jokey folks" socialize), one female participant said that her mother used to dance with Cooper. She added, rather indelicately, "Leonard Cooper could dance his ass off."

Another "star" of the scene was a guy from Charles Town named Clarence "Rock" Stanton. As Al Baylor noted emphatically, "When he arrived, you knew you were seeing a dancer coming in."

Margaret Ramseur of Charles Town nominated fellow townsman Lawrence Johnson as one of the best hoofers. Rose Williams cited Theodore Pendleton as another accomplished male dancer. When asked who were some outstanding female dancers, she mentioned "a girl named Ramona" and "Edwina Mason." (Ms. Mason, sitting immediately to her left, did not out of false modesty contradict!)

Dance styles came and went between 1951 and1965, but dancers frequently cited the Pony, the Bird, the Twist, and the Mashed Potato. Gloria Puller-Johnson added that the Birdland was popular. (To the delight of the attendees of the NAACP-sponsored event in Charles Town, she performed a spunky reprise of her Birdland moves!)

There were sundry versions of those dances. Al Baylor explained, "People from different towns had different dances. For instance, the Mashed Potato had local variations. It looked different in Winchester than it did in, say, Frederick."

There were also other distinctive permutations. According to Nedra Keyes of Hagerstown, "Leonard Cooper's family members had a different dance for every song!"

The Coopers were indeed a dancing family. Leonard reminisced, "At home Mom would do the San (probably short for the San Antonio Shuffle) and Daddy would buck dance. My sister and I learned to do all those dances at home." He continued, "I used to dance with all my cousins. We learned to line dance in the streets outside our house. We would set out a music box at night and dance in front of the [street] light."

As they got a bit older, the Cooper clan shifted its activities over to a youth-oriented venue attached to Venning Twyman's house, which was known as "Doc's." The club sported a pool table and little dance floor.

As the Coopers perfected their craft further, they moved up to more adult-oriented establishments. He recalls, "They used to pay my sister Peggy and me at Rankin Taylor's and buy us drinks to see us dance. Older people at the Tap Room liked to see younger people dance, too. They gave us free beers there."

As Cooper approached his upper teens, "[My friends and family] used to say, 'We can't wait to get old enough to go to JBF.' [Initially] we came to watch other people dance, but we always out-danced them. We planned out our dances ahead of time. We would dance and dance, then take a little break to get something to eat or drink, and then hurry back out on the dance floor. You can't let that music go by."

A popular line dance of the era was the Madison, a dance step originating in Columbus, Ohio, in 1957. In addition to its basic up-and-back and side-to-side movements, a number of regional variations cropped up. Among them were such "called steps" as the Double Cross, the Cleveland Box, the Rifleman, the Jackie Gleason ("Away we go!"), and the Basketball—a dribble sometimes accompanied by a Wilt Chamberlain dunk. The Coopers created a great deal of levity among the other attendees as they rendered their own comical addition to the Madison, "the Old Lady," in which they stooped over and pretended to walk with a cane.

So popular a dance partner was Cooper that, as he told it, "Girls would want me to come out to the Farm to dance with them, so they would get money together to pay my way in. I had money; I was already cutting hair, but I wanted to spend it on other things, so I kept it in my pocket. Sometimes I would get to the door and [John] Bishop would say to me, 'Come on in; the girls already paid your way.'"

When asked to recall young ladies with whom he liked to dance, Cooper cited "Pauline Brown, Dora Roy Yates, and Raymonda Williams—they could keep up with me." And that took some doing, because a typical dance night was a workout of several hours' length.

The jukebox provided the early music for dancing, then the bands played, and then the jukebox cranked again during bands' breaks. The dancers would keep it up all night long. Al Baylor remembers one time "looking down and seeing sweat coming through my shoes."

Seeing Stars

In the heyday of John Brown's Farm, its patrons witnessed the emerging genius of Ray Charles, the acrobatic physicality of James Brown, the combination of raw energy and rough elegance of Tina Turner, the innovative choreography of the Cadillacs, and the visual vigor and vocal virtuosity of Jackie Wilson. The evolution of American music unfolded week after week on that very stage.

It was my recurring privilege to locate and interview those patrons of JBF in order to record their memories of those captivating entertainers. Among the most vivid remembrances are the following:

FAYE ADAMS

James "Jim" Taylor made his first trip out to John Brown's Farm soon after he got out of the Navy in 1955. One of his earliest memories of the Farm was the performance of Faye Adams singing her enormous 1953 hit record, "Shake a Hand" (ten weeks atop the R&B chart). Taylor described it as "a night that everybody

John Brown's Farm patrons were already familiar with the music of their favorite artists—and doubly thrilled to see them in person.

was sort of happy, because that's all we did that night was shook hands—every time she sang [the lyric], "Shake a hand, shake a hand."

JAMES BROWN

Senator Joanne Benson delighted in her recollection of "The Hardest Working Man in Show Business": "When James Brown came, oo-wee! He just acted up!"

William and Nancy Shanton both recalled seeing James Brown, specifically in 1959. Bill described the performance as "Very moving. He kept dancing and singing and sweating, and they put the cape on him, and he left the stage." Nancy remembered it as being a black cape with red lining. Brown had changed from using a towel or a blanket to using a cape for "Please, Please, Please" in 1959, so the JBF faithful were among the first to see that new version of his iconic routine.

Leonard Harris, then-owner of the 701 Club in Martinsburg, West Virginia, collaborated several times with John Bishop in bringing James Brown (and others) to the Farm. "To us James was always polite, calling us Mr. Bishop and Mr. Harris. He was wild," (carrying a handgun, for instance), "but he was all business. He had to be. He had bus drivers, singers, musicians, and roadies to pay." Harris added in a different interview, "He had a little room [in his tour bus] that we used to go in. He also had like a body-guard. James used to carry a pistol. He had a suitcase with a pistol in it. James Brown was really all about business."

As the years progressed, the percentage of the gate going to Brown tipped more and more in his favor, with him eventually getting 80 percent and the promoters getting twenty. As Harris puts it concerning the last few splits with Brown, "He'd go out with a suitcase full of money and us with a little purse."

RAY CHARLES

Norvel Willis from Harpers Ferry remembers seeing Ray Charles perform "What'd I Say?" Willis sat just a few feet away from Charles as he played. He joked, "If he'd 'a' fell off that stage, I'd 'a' caught him."

Leonard Harris offered this observance: "I remember the one time when they had Ray Charles… We know Ray was blind. But I saw a fight break out down at John Brown's Farm. Ray was the first one to get out of there. He left his [assistant] and everything. I said, 'I don't know how a man could be blind and get out of John Brown's Farm that fast.'"

Daniel Jackson, Jr. from Harpers Ferry remembered the same event: "I'll never forget the time when Ray Charles was there. They had a gun battle and he was the first one off the stage!"

CHUBBY CHECKER

Leonard Cooper said of the time that Checker appeared at the Farm, "I'll never forget that day! Everybody was twistin'—cats, dogs, even the cockroaches were doing the Twist."

FATS DOMINO

Nancy Shanton reflected, "Both Fats Domino and James Brown, with all that hair, looked very much like they did in their promotional pictures."

ETTA JAMES

Reginald Johnson said of Etta James, "When she came in the room I saw this [overweight] yellow-skinned woman—very unattractive, I thought. But when she opened her mouth, she could sing!"

Dora Roy Yates from Charles Town said of the songstress, "Etta James, my goodness, when she opened up her mouth we just screamed worse than some of the women would scream for the men—and, oh, we were just in heaven."

PATTI LA BELLE AND HER BLUE BELLES

Daniel Jackson, Jr. was a relative of the Farm's caretaker, Maynard Henderson. "When I went there [to see] Patti, she pulled me up on the stage. And I was young and dumb and you know playing around, and so we got to be friends."

LITTLE WILLIE JOHN

On the night frequent patron Beverly Gaither saw Little Willie John, she pestered and even begged him for the gold tie that he had been wearing on stage. He repeatedly and unbendingly refused—but eventually did give her another of his ties.

CURTIS MAYFIELD

Senator Joanne Benson recalled, "When Curtis Mayfield played there, the women were taken aback by his voice."

BOBBY PARKER

Junior Henderson said concisely of Parker, "He could chirp" (sing).

LLOYD PRICE

Reginald Johnson remembered, "I had a great time when I saw Lloyd Price." Diane Puller-Williams was impressed that he put on an especially good show.

OTIS REDDING

Tyrone "Supe" Henzsley summarized the sentiment of a number of people in saying that he "could not have predicted that [Redding] would be a success by the way he dressed in his early days: white shirts smudged and crinkly, shoes 'run over,' and cuffed shirts rolled up because of no cuff links."

Once Redding had become a star, however, he was acknowledged as a snappy dresser. Dora Yates remembers trying to get a good view of him on stage as she stood behind two friends. Yates recounted in a hushed and almost reverent tone, "[My friends] were stretching their hands out so that they could just touch him." Then Yates brightened up to add, "We said [to our friends blocking our vision], 'Just get over so that we can just see him *and* hear him!'"

One night that Otis Redding played at JBF, his backing band was the Rocking Cabanas comprised of young musicians from Newport News, Virginia. During a break, Beverly Johnson Gaither, her friend Geraldine, and Beverly's father, sheriff's deputy Vernon Johnson, were talking to Redding near the stage. Otis had noticed the girls had been singing along to his music, and so he invited all of them back into the dressing room.

There, Redding suggested light-heartedly that he just might take Beverly and Geraldine on the road with him as back-up singers. Beverly's father stepped up and growled, "You might take Geraldine, but you're not taking my daughter," and then playfully added, "because she can't sing a lick!"

"It was true," verified Beverly. "I couldn't carry a tune!"

BILLY STEWART

Beverly Dykes King met Billy Stewart while she was working the kitchen. She recalled that Stewart "carried a big dog with him to the dressing room, but would leave it there while he was performing."

IKE AND TINA TURNER

Al Baylor typically didn't just stand and watch the bands; he was into dancing. When Ike and Tina Turner played, however, he did just stand and gaped at the leggy female vocalist. He said, "I was as close to Tina as I am to you" (three feet or so). Baylor remarked concerning his and his buddies' impressions of Ms. Turner, "We thought we'd died and gone to heaven."

Turner was just a year or so older than Baylor, but she looked to him like a woman fully-grown. Baylor revealed, "I remember my thoughts at the time exactly. I was thinking, 'They don't have women in Charles Town like this.'"

Laurence Bailey said simply, "I remember seeing Tina Turner." (For some strange reason, none of the guys remembered very much about Ike.)

Beverly Gaither remembered something about both Ike and Tina. During one of the band's breaks, Tina was heard hollering from the dressing room behind the stage. Sheriff's deputies Bill Mason and Vernon Johnson, Beverly's father, burst through the connecting door behind the stage to find Ike viciously beating Tina.

As Beverly peered through the open door, she saw her father throttle Ike and, as she described it, he "jacked him up in the corner." Deputy Johnson then glowered, "You wanna beat somebody, try beating me!" Ike wisely backed down. Ms. Turner gamely covered her contusions with make-up. Minutes later she went out on the stage and on with the show.

ARTISTS AND AUDIENCE SOLIDARITY

A number of people expressed a sentiment indicating a sense of commonality of purpose with the artists. Daniel Jackson, Jr. mused, "It was joyful just to have [the artists] here to collaborate with because they really brought a sense of dignity and togetherness at that particular time to be black going to a black social function. It was a nice place to go and nice to be there. If you wanted to see a star, you just go across the bridge [from Charles Town] and you'll see all the stars you want to see."

Janet Jeffries took Jackson's general sentiment and made it specific. "I really loved Tina Turner. As I always say, we got her started. A lot of the bands back then, we were instrumental in getting them started, because if they did good here, they could go elsewhere and do it, too."

The Memories Live On

LONG NIGHTS MAKE FOR SHORT MEMORIES

On a closing note, it was frustrating that so many attendees remembered so little about the artists, other than the mere fact that they saw them. Why was that? Something about my interviewing? Was it perhaps because many of the acts were on the way up, and people came to recognize their fame subsequently? Reginald Johnson, at least, discounted that idea by saying, "I already knew most of them."

The most plausible explanations for why most interviewees remembered relatively little seem to be that (1) people came primarily to dance and to socialize; (2) the last dance at the Farm was Labor Day, 1965—fifty years ago; and (3) adult beverages often were involved.

Ruth McDaniel weighed in with a piece of evidence supporting conjecture #1 above. "I loved to dance. That was my thing. I loved to dance. I don't remember any of the bands... I didn't go because certain people were playing over there; I went because I was going to a *dance*."

This earliest known photo of the interior of the auditorium illuminates how tightly 400–500 young people pressed themselves to dance to the world's best rhythm and blues.

ENDEARING TIDBITS

As I asked interviewees what they remembered about John Brown's Farm, their initial responses occasionally were quite awkward. For some folks it had to do with the slightly naughty reputation that the Farm had in some circles. Betty Newman from Shepherdstown, West Virginia, the nearest sizable black community to JBF, confessed, "I used to sneak down there with a bunch of girls."

Sometimes a guarded reaction seemed to have arisen from potential guilt by association. As one person put it, "People did their dirt there in the cars and out in the woods." For others, the discomfiture may have been about getting teased—like when a buddy ribbed frequent patron Anthony Doleman about the time he "stepped on a cow pie" after parking the car out in the field behind the auditorium.

For yet others, the embarrassment was merely that what little they did remember seemed to them trivial and inconsequential. Frequently, however, those tidbits were especially endearing.

Rudy Hall attended dances while still a child but was confined to an area near the dressing room side of the stage. "My sister, Sandy, sang in Winfield Parker's band, but she also had to baby-sit me. I had a little spot I had to sit in," he said.

Rose Williams and Edwina Mason recalled being more than just bystanders. "If the stars saw you singing along, they sometimes would invite you up on stage or hold the microphone out for you to sing," they recalled.

Reginald Johnson remembered there having been a battle of the bands with several groups from Newport News: the Rocking Cabanas, the Rocketeers, and Bobby Marshall and the Crystals.

"I DANCED TILL A QUARTER TO THREE"

Singer Gary U. S. Bonds made that boast in the lyrics of his 1961 Number One hit. Staying up that late on a Saturday night did not always work out so smoothly, however, especially for those who went to church on Sunday morning. Al Baylor said that at first his parents allowed him to go to JBF only on the condition that he be home by eleven p.m., because he "had to be up and out of the house the next morning to Sunday school and church."

Friends Rose Williams and Edwina Mason spoke rapidly, piggy-backed on what each other said, and even finished one another's sentences, so I'm not

George Bumbaugh

George Bumbaugh is a white man from Hagerstown. Although several people said that it was not uncommon for white people to be at the dances, Bumbaugh was the first—and one of very few—I was able to find who was there. His experience is illustrative of several realities, racial and otherwise, in Washington County in the late 1950s at the time he began working his first job.

George got his start as a "sanitary engineer" working from the back end of a garbage truck, known facetiously as a "honey wagon" as it certainly attracted flies! At that time, the collecting of Hagerstown's food waste was contracted out to private firms, in this case "J & J Collection" owned by the Resh brothers, John and James.

Back then, food waste was picked up three times a week in the summer and twice a week in the winter. That garbage was hauled out to a nearby hog farm to supply the porkers their feed. Two trucks serviced all of Hagerstown. The pay was one dollar per hour, the federal minimum wage at the time. The work "day" began at eleven p.m. and continued until the work was done—"hardly ever less than eight hours a day, with as much as seventeen not unheard of," said Bumbaugh.

When he began working for the Resh brothers, one truck was staffed by three white men and the other truck by three black men. As the Reshes desegregated the operation, Bumbaugh was transferred from the all-white truck to what became an integrated truck.

He said that he got along well with his two black truck mates because, "I was half-crazy like they were." (He can remember neither of their names.) When they invited him to attend a dance at JBF he reasoned, "I like to do different things." So he went.

Bumbaugh attended the dances at John Brown's Farm "eight or nine times" and added, "I might have gone more often, but the long hours on the truck made only Saturday nights possible." He rode down to JBF in the back seat of a 1952 Buick Roadmaster owned by the driver of the garbage truck. Bumbaugh related that he typically wore to the dances "blue jeans and a sweatshirt or a shirt my mother made out of feed sacks, which I also wore to South Hagerstown High School."

Describing his experience at JBF, Bumbaugh said that he "mostly stayed outside" and remembered vaguely that there was "nothing fancy about it." He remembered vividly, however, that he was working the garbage truck on November 22, 1963—the day John F. Kennedy was shot.

(L–R) James Taylor and Daniel Jackson, Jr. share their experiences of John Brown's Farm with an appreciative audience at Fisherman's Hall in Charles Town, West Virginia. Photos by Winston Pitman.

---

exactly sure who said what. However, they certainly shared a good chuckle in recalling how they used to stay awake in church on Sunday mornings by "chewing gum and eating mints."

Beverly Owens-Gaither related that, as an adult, she would come home to Hagerstown to go to JBF and would stay overnight with her parents. Her father would wake her up Sunday morning to go to church and insist, "You spent eight hours with the devil; you can spend one hour with the Lord!"

THE JOURNEY HOME

As each event's final song came to a close, the lights came on, and the worn-out dancers began to locate their ride-mates to head for home. There were still more adventures to come, however. Until I heard the next several travel stories, I had wondered exactly what James Taylor meant when once during a group discussion he interjected, "Coming back [home] was the rough part!"

Daniel Jackson, Jr. elucidated, "The onliest problem we had was coming back from John Brown's Farm. [People] would miss that curve down by Sandy Hook and they all landed in the Potomac River. They all landed right there. So if you [couldn't find somebody], you knew they was down in the river!"

Henry Ingram and another white friend once left JBF following an afternoon of card playing with Maynard Henderson. As they headed south-bound, they sideswiped an oncoming bus full of Elks on the way to the Farm. As Ingram described it, "One of us got over too far and we bumped fenders pretty good."

As the drivers of both vehicles stopped to inspect the damage, Ingram said that he was "scared to death" at the thought of being confronted by a mass of potentially angry black people.

As it turned out, everything was cordial. The black sheriff's deputy, Bill Mason, was quickly dispatched with his German Shepherd from his service at JBF to help sort things out. Upon his arrival, Mason reassured the still-jittery Ingram, "Don't worry; you'll be fine."

The road leading northward could be equally treacherous. Gilbert "Buss" Everline (Bo Morgan's boyhood Scoutmaster) was a lineman for Potomac Edison in the 1950s. Everline recalled being summoned multiple times to come straighten up or replace a power pole standing dangerously near an S-curve in the macadam road, which had been crashed into by inebriated revelers leaving John Brown's Farm.

Ethelene Clinton shared her "going home" story. "I liked to dance, so I didn't miss no records," she said. "I was up there dancing. And I'd be tired and we'd go out to the car—and my brother-in-law was the one who took us over there—and he said, 'Ya'll ready (to go home)?' And we'd say, 'Oh, just two more music selections.' And he'd [threaten], 'All right now, I'm going to leave you all.' And so finally he did leave us. And it was dark and I was scared. I was standing around looking at how dark it is, and thinking how far it is that I have to walk home. Finally [a guy] came and picked us up and took us back to Kearneysville."

Isabelle Johnson, in her 90-plus years, has never had a driver's license, but one dark night she had to serve as the designated driver for the trip home from John Brown's Farm. Johnson recollected that her "cousin Robert liked to drink Maynard Henderson's home-made wine" but would sometimes overdo it. On one such occasion following a dance she said, "Robert got in the driver's seat to drive home but slumped over the steering wheel, which began honking the horn." I asked, 'What are you doing?' and he said, 'I'm tooting at my girlfriend out in the field.'" (There was nobody in the field; he was seeing things.)

At that point, Ms. Johnson—though having only a learner's permit—barked at Robert, "Get your ass from behind that wheel!" He obeyed. She slid into the driver's seat and maneuvered the car the dozen or so miles over the dark and winding roads north to Boonsboro. From that point, Robert proved sober

Janet Jeffries.
Photo by Winston Pitman.

enough to drive the remaining ten miles to Hagerstown.

Concerning one particularly hair-raising ride back home to Charles Town, Jean Lee Roberts recalled, "The curvy roads, the river on one side, and the mountain on the other side. I had to drive somebody's car back, and its brakes had gone. And all I got thinking about was that I would have to run into the mountain if that car done give out."

Joe Dixon remembers catching a ride from John Brown's Farm to Hagerstown with a driver who was "so drunk that we got out at Boonsboro and thumbed a ride with another car going north." Dixon said that on several occasions, "I got a ride back to Hagerstown at the end of the night with Bill Mason—with his dog breathing in my ear from the back seat."

Wendell Scott was a former moonshine ridge runner who in 1953 became America's first black NASCAR driver. His skills could have come in handy for some of the dancers' trips back home from John Brown's Farm. Hagerstown's Wallace "Goose" Brooks remembers that after a dance was over, some person or another would shout, "I'll beat you back to Hagerstown!" And off they flew.

According to Brooks, people would pass each other like crazy, even on hills and curves. On one occasion, the vehicle immediately in front of Brooks's carload spun out, flipped over, and came to rest on an embankment. As Brooks and friends approached, one of the women in their car screamed and (for some reason) flung her door open, hitting the overturned car and creating even more mayhem.

Somehow, most JBF attendees made it back safe and sound, though not infrequently still a little tipsy. Beverly Owens-Gaither noted, "We would get seven or eight in a car coming back to Hagerstown and get to town about dawn. Then we would put on the radio, get out of the car, and start dancing again in the street."

Janet Jeffries ("a country girl and proud of it") had to exercise a little faith at the end of nearly every one of her evenings at JBF. She said, "In order to get back home I would always catch someone headed back past my lane on [U.S.] Route 340. I remember a lot of the people from Franklintown, Lewisville, and Berryville who would come down this-a-way.…But it was exciting, and of course my father always wanted to know who I went with and who I came back with."

Not everyone had a harrowing adventure in getting home, however. Plucky Ruth McDaniel had uniformly good fortune getting back to Charles Town after the dances. "You rode over with one person, and then when you got there, if [your ride] wanted to come back early and you weren't ready to come back, well you just hunted around until you found somebody you could get a ride back with."

Doris Green reminisced that it was always comforting following the dances to get across the bridge over the Potomac heading to her home in Millwood, Virginia, verifying that you were literally and figuratively "out of the woods." She added whimsically, "John Brown's Farm could be entertaining—even if you weren't there!" She then clarified, "Even the times I didn't go, it was still fun to hear the stories of the night from those who did."

And they still are.

{PART III}

The Performers

The Artists Who Played at John Brown's Farm

How bright were the stars that played at John Brown's Farm? Five of the ten members of the inaugural class of the Rock and Roll Hall of Fame, "Performer" category, played there: Chuck Berry, James Brown, Ray Charles, Fats Domino, and Little Richard.

Four of the eight members of the inaugural class of the Rhythm and Blues Foundation appeared at JBF: LaVern Baker, Ruth Brown, Etta James, and Mary Wells. Fifteen of *Rolling Stone* magazine's "100 Greatest Singers of All Time" performed at the Farm, including five of the top ten: James Brown, Ray Charles, Aretha Franklin, Marvin Gaye, and Otis Redding.

The celebrity and impressive performances of such major stars made it comparatively easy to document their appearances at John Brown's Farm, but what about other and sometimes lesser stars? How does one ascertain that they did, indeed, perform there?

B. B. King, Audimax Uni Hamburg, November 1971 (Heinrich Klaffs Collection 55).

Directory of Artists who played at John Brown's Farm

Faye Adams . . . 218
Marie Allen . . . 218
LaVern Baker . . . 219
Brook Benton . . . 220
Chuck Berry . . . 221
Bobby "Blue" Bland . . . 222
Buster Brown . . . 222
James Brown . . . 223
Maxine Brown . . . 224
Ruth Brown . . . 225
Jerry Butler . . . 226
The Cadillacs . . . 227
Ray Charles . . . 228
Chubby Checker . . . 229
Claudine Clark . . . 230
The Coasters . . . 231
Arthur Conley . . . 283
The Crystals . . . 232
Bo Diddley . . . 233
Fats Domino . . . 234
Lee Dorsey . . . 235
Jimmy Dotson . . . 235
The Drifters . . . 236
The Esquires . . . 237
Sammy Fitzhugh and the Moroccos . . . 237
The Five Du-Tones . . . 238
The Five Keys . . . 238
The Flamingos . . . 239
Inez and Charlie Foxx . . . 239
Aretha Franklin . . . 240
Marvin Gaye . . . 241
Kenny Hamber . . . 243
The Impressions . . . 244
The Isley Brothers . . . 245
"Bull Moose" Jackson . . . 246
Chuck Jackson . . . 247
Walter Jackson . . . 247
Etta James . . . 248
Little Willie John . . . 249
B. B. King . . . 250
Ben E. King . . . 251
Eartha Kitt . . . 252
Patti LaBelle and (Her) Blue Belles . . . 253
Little Anthony and the Imperials . . . 254
Little Eva (Boyd) . . . 254
Little Richard . . . 255
Frankie Lymon and the Teenagers . . . 257
Gene McDaniels . . . 258
Clyde McPhatter . . . 259
The Moonglows . . . 260
Johnny Moore . . . 260
Aaron Neville . . . 261
The Orioles . . . 262
Bobby Parker . . . 262
Junior Parker . . . 263
Winfield Parker . . . 264
Wilson Pickett . . . 265
The Platters . . . 266
Lloyd Price . . . 267
Lou Rawls . . . 268
Otis Redding . . . 268
The Shirelles . . . 270
Shirley and Lee . . . 271
Billy Stewart . . . 272
Barrett Strong . . . 272
The Swallows . . . 273
Joe Tex . . . 274
Ike and Tina Turner . . . 274
Jr. Walker and the All Stars . . . 276
Dionne Warwick . . . 276
Dinah Washington . . . 277
Justine Washington . . . 279
Mary Wells . . . 279
Warner Williams . . . 280
Larry Williams . . . 280
Jackie Wilson . . . 281
The Winstons . . . 282

THE CRITERIA FOR INCLUSION

Regrettably the passing of time, the frailty of memory, and the scarcity of written documentation has made it difficult to establish with 100% certainty which artists really did play at John Brown's Farm.

The certification process is exacerbated by the fact that during the John Brown's Farm era the principal booking agent, John Bishop, also scheduled many of these same artists into two other area nightclubs: the Orchard Inn outside Berryville, Virginia, and the Shamrock Inn in Sandy Hook, Maryland. Thus some of the interviewees were not sure if they had seen a given artist at JBF or at one of those other clubs.

Consequently, a tight criterion had to be established—one that resulted in the weeding out of some artists ("Peg Leg" Bates, Clarence Carter, the Clovers, Eddie Floyd, Wynonie Harris, Paul "Hucklebuck" Williams, Big Joe Turner, Amos Milburn, etc.) who may have performed there, but whose appearance was cited by only one person.

Contrarily, even though multiple people had a vivid memory of an artist at JBF, if the artist's career clearly ended before 1950 or began after 1966, then the artist was disqualified from inclusion. One example of such an exclusion would be Al Green. Several people said they remembered him playing JBF and mentioned his cutting his tie in half to give to two female attendees. No other evidence exists, however, that Green had begun his national career prior to the sale of the Farm.

Artists were included in the following lengthy and illustrious list only if they fit one or more of the following conditions: (1) promoter Leonard Harris said they were there; (2) frequent JBF performer Winfield Parker said so; (3) two or more unrelated attendees said so; or (4) one otherwise reliable-sounding attendee had a particularly vivid memory of the artists at the Farm.

The list of performers below is in alphabetical order by last name except where the artist's last name is somewhat obscure to the general public (for instance, Little Eva or Little Richard).

The references below certain artists' names to the Rock and Roll Hall of Fame and the Rhythm and Blues Foundation ("Pioneer Award") indicate the years of induction into those respective illustrious institutions. An asterisk next to the year indicates membership in the inaugural class.

And now... a virtual "Who's Who" of rhythm and blues!

Faye Adams (1923–present)

"Atomic Adams"
Rhythm and Blues Foundation—1998

Faye Adams's approach to a melody had a rich and well-honed gospel underpinning. Her father, David Tuell, was a vocalist within the musically fertile Church of God in Christ denomination. Faye began singing at five years of age with her sisters in church and on radio shows in Newark, New Jersey, her city of birth.

While performing years later in Atlanta under her married name, Faye Scruggs, she was noticed by R&B giant Ruth Brown who secured for her an audition with band leader Joe Morris. Changing her name to Faye Adams, her first release, "Shake a Hand," went straight to the top of the R&B charts and stayed there for ten weeks in the fall of 1953. She had two additional #1s, in early 1954 with "I'll Be True" (covered by Bill Haley), and in the fall of 1955 with "It Hurts Me to My Heart."

Legendary disc jockey Alan Freed plugged Adams as "the little gal with the big voice." When well-matched with a quality song, her rich texture and gospel-oriented expressiveness was given fertile soil in which to flower. Excellent examples are up-tempo jazzy tunes such as "Somebody, Somewhere" and her last charted hit, "Keeper of My Heart," in 1957.

Miss Adams is long retired from the music industry and is reported to have returned to church and family life in New Jersey.

Number One R&B
"Shake a Hand" 1953
"I'll Be True" 1953
"It Hurts Me to My Heart" 1954

Marie Allen

"Little Marie Allen"

Marie Allen (birth and possible death dates unknown) had the perfect voice for yelling something like, "You'd better get your funky butt in the house right now!" Her sassy and gritty voice still gets some play for her 1959 song "Humdinger" fronting Chuck Booker's Band.

She also recorded two duets with Sonny Warner in 1962 that were released in the Washington, D.C., area: "Hand in Hand" and "That's for Me."

LaVern Baker (1929–1997)

Rock and Roll Hall of Fame 1991
Rhythm and Blues Foundation 1989*

If ever a rhythm and blues singer had a pedigree, it was LaVern Baker. She was related to both the renowned bar room blues singer Merline Johnson ("The Yas Yas Girl") and "Memphis Minnie" (Lizzie Douglas), the pioneering blues vocalist and guitarist.

Baker began to make her own way in the music business in Chicago in the late 1940s, initially recording under her frequently used billing as "Little Miss Sharecropper." From 1955 through 1962 she unleashed a torrent of eleven Top Ten R&B hits beginning with "Tweedlee Dee" and including a #1 ("Jim Dandy") in 1956.

While on a tour to entertain American troops in Vietnam, Baker became seriously ill and spent time recuperating in the Philippines at the Subic Bay Naval Base. A friend there urged her to consider staying on as the entertainment director at the Marine's NCO club, which she did—for the next twenty-two years.

Upon her return to the United States in the late 1980s, Baker performed at Atlantic Records' fortieth reunion at Madison Square Garden, worked on several movie soundtracks, and replaced Ruth Brown in *Black and Blue* on Broadway.

In 1989 she joined Ruth Brown in the inaugural class of the Rhythm and Blues Foundation. Two years later Baker become the second female solo artist (after Aretha Franklin) to be inducted into the Rock and Roll Hall of Fame. Miss Baker died of coronary complication from diabetes in 1997.

Number One R&B
"Jim Dandy" 1956

Brook Benton (1931–1988)

Benton began his singing career using his given name, Benjamin Franklin Peay. His record label, the legendary Okeh Records, pushed him to leave the comfort of singing background in gospel and R&B groups to become a solo artist and to use the stage name "Brook Benton."

After some time spent polishing his craft and co-penning Lloyd Price's "It's a Lover's Question," Benton moved over to Mercury Records. In 1959 he charted another song he co-wrote, "It's Just a Matter of Time," which rocketed to #1 R&B and #3 Pop. His songs sat atop the R&B list for 15 weeks in 1959 and an incredible tewnty-three out of fifty-two weeks in 1960.

Benton charted a whopping total of forty-nine singles on Billboard's Hot 100. Somehow he is in neither in the Rock and Roll Hall of Fame nor has he (or duet-mate Dinah Washington) become a Pioneer Award winner of the Rhythm and Blues Foundation. He died all too early of pneumonia at the age of fifty-six in Queens, New York.

Prominent Number One R&B

"It's Just a Matter of Time" 1959
"Baby (You've Got What It Takes)" (with Dinah Washington) 1960
"Kiddio" 1960
"Rainy Night in Georgia" 1970

Chuck Berry (1926–present)

Rock and Roll Hall of Fame 1986*
Rolling Stone's 100 Greatest Singers #41

"If you tried to give rock and roll another name, you might call it 'Chuck Berry.'" (John Lennon)

Chuck Berry is a singer, song-writer, showman, and electric guitar player—a musician who straddled blues and country in such a way that he virtually created his own genre. His familiarity with both blues musicians (T-Bone Walker, Muddy Waters) and country artists (Jimmie Rodgers, Bill Munroe) put him in position to be "the guy."

Berry grew up in a middle-class household in St. Louis, Missouri, where his father was a contractor and his mother was a school principal. Traveling to Chicago in 1955, Berry met Muddy Waters, who pointed him toward Leonard Chess of Chess Records. The savvy Chess had noticed a cooling off of the blues market and was looking for a fresh sound.

Berry's initial recording at Chess paired his signature guitar licks with clever lyrics that combined romance and cars—a primal rock recipe. "Maybellene" (said to be an adaptation of Western Swing artist Bob Will's "Ida Red") shot Berry to national attention.

Red Hot Chili Peppers' lead vocalist Anthony Kiedis once aptly described Berry as "a musical scientist who discovered a cure for the blues."

Prominent Number One R&B (and other notable hits)

"Maybellene" 1955
"Roll Over Beethoven" 1956 (#2 R&B)
"Rock and Roll Music" 1957 (#6)
"Johnny B. Goode" 1958
"My Ding-a-Ling" 1972

Chuck Berry's mastery of country music, R&B, and the blues thrilled America's teenagers and influenced the Beach Boys, the Beatles, and the Rolling Stones. Illustration by Beth Meier.

Bobby "Blue" Bland (1930–2013)

"The Lion of the Blues"
Rock and Roll Hall of Fame 1992
Rhythm and Blues Foundation 1992
Rolling Stone's 100 Greatest Singers #44

Bobby Bland, as did Sam Cooke and Lou Rawls, concocted his individual style by mixing elements of gospel and the blues. Upon returning from the military in 1954, Bland incorporated himself into the Memphis blues scene alongside Johnny Ace, Little Junior Parker, and B. B. King.

Bland's soulful sound found a wonderful niche in big band blues melodies, such as his Texas shuffle "Farther Up the Road," recorded for Don Robey's Houston-based Duke Records (featuring excellent guitar work by Pat Hare). Across the course of his lengthy career, Bland charted some twenty-three Top Ten R&B hits.

Number One R&B
"Farther up the Road" 1957
"I Pity the Fool" 1961
"That's the Way Love Is" 1963

Buster Brown (1911–1976)

At sixty-one years of age, Buster Brown had his second biggest hit, "Sugar Babe" (#19 R&B; #99 Pop), which featured his vocal energy and strong harmonica playing. His biggest hit was a big one indeed; "Fannie Mae" earned #1 R&B (#38 Pop) in April of 1960.

"Fannie Mae" was later featured in George Lucas's first big film, *American Graffiti* (1973). There the song was introduced by the legendary deejay "Wolfman Jack" who became famous while working for radio station XERF, a 250,000 watt "border blaster" operating out of Mexico.

Number One R&B
"Fannie Mae" 1960

James Brown (1933-2006)

"The Godfather of Soul"

Rock and Roll Hall of Fame 1986*
Rhythm and Blues Foundation 1993
Rolling Stone's 100 Greatest Singers #10

"The hardest working man in show business" was working hard long before he got into R&B. From a poor town (Elko, South Carolina), from a poor family, abandoned by his mother at two, and handed over by his father at six to live with an aunt who ran a house of prostitution, Brown made it a lifelong priority to take care of himself.

As an unparented child, his various street hustles included shining shoes, sweeping out stores, and washing cars and dishes. He buck danced for troops from nearby Camp Gordon. He learned to play harmonica, piano, and drums from whomever could show him a little something.

Almost inevitably, Brown's hustling began to include petty crime. He "advanced" to armed robbery and spent time (1949–1952) in a juvenile detention center. His recreational activities there included baseball and singing.

Brown's juvie baseball team played a ball club from the outside that included Bobby Byrd, a future collaborator and eventual R&B star in his own right. Byrd's family was impressed with Brown's talent, and they helped to secure an early release for him. Brown then sang in the Gospel Starlighters with Byrd's sister Sarah before joining Byrd's group. Known initially as the Avons, and subsequently as the Flames, the group was inducted independently into the Rock and Roll Hall of Fame in 2012.

Brown later became friends with "Little Richard" Penniman in Augusta, Georgia. He adopted a Penniman phrase, "Please, Please, Please" as the basis of the song that became the first hit for the Flames (#5 R&B). When Little Richard abruptly left secular music to become a preacher, the Flames stepped in to fill out the remainder of Little Richard's tour dates.

James Brown, "Soul Brother Number One," was a frequent performer at John Brown's Farm and headlined at the last dance at JBF, Labor Day of 1965. Illustration by Beth Meier.

Several members of Little Richard's backup band, the Upsetters, joined Brown's group, which provided increased professionalism to the act.

"Try Me" in 1959 became his first #1 R&B hit. His self-financed 1963 live show and attendant album, "Live at the Apollo," surprised perhaps everyone but Brown himself as it peaked at #2 U.S. and stayed on the Pop charts for over a year. His 1964 musical groundbreaker "Out of Sight" foreshadowed both the sound and the success of subsequent offerings such as "Papa's Got a Brand New Bag" and "I Got You (I Feel Good)."

Brown's fifty-year career included seventeen #1 hits among his sixty-one Top Twenty R&B chart toppers. He also scored eighteen U.S. Top Twenty hits. During his career of five decades, Brown's influence on funk, hip hop, dance music generally, and on Michael Jackson specifically is incalculable.

Prominent Number One R&B
"Try Me" (as James Brown and the Famous Flames) 1958
"Papa's Got a Brand New Bag" (as James Brown and the Famous Flames) 1965
"I Got You (I Feel Good)" (as James Brown and the Famous Flames) 1965
"It's a Man's Man's Man's World" (as James Brown and the Famous Flames) 1966
"Cold Sweat" (as James Brown and the Famous Flames) 1967
"Say It Loud–I'm Black and I'm Proud" 1968

Maxine Brown (1939-present)

Rhythm and Blues Foundation 1990/1991

Another of the many R&B artists who got started singing in church, Maxine Brown performed with several gospel groups in her teens. In 1960 she recorded her own composition, a smooth soul ballad in 6/8 time entitled "All in My Mind." That song zoomed to #2 on the R&B chart and to #19 U.S. in 1961. That same year a comparable, though better-produced, "Funny" made a similar ascent before peaking at #3 R&B and #25 U.S.

Upon moving to Wand Records in 1963, Ms. Brown recorded a string of Hot 100 hits, typically backed by Cissy Houston and the Sweet Inspirations, as well as the talented husband and wife team, Nickolas Ashford and Valerie Simpson.

Several Gerry Goffin/Carole King compositions did well for Brown on the Pop charts (during that brief period during which Billboard did not publish an R&B chart). "Oh No, Not My Baby" was a perfect showcase for her voice, and it reached #24 in 1964. She joined Chuck Jackson for several charting duets including the 1964 "Something You Got" (#10 R&B) and a 1967 cover of Sam and Dave's "Hold On, I'm Comin'" (#20 R&B).

She sang at her friend Ruth Brown's funeral in Portsmouth, Virginia, in 2006.

Ruth Brown (1928-2006)

"The Queen Mother of the Blues"
Rock and Roll Hall of Fame 1993
Rhythm and Blues Foundation 1989*

In the early 1950s Ruth Brown had so many #1 hits on the fledgling Atlantic Records label that it became known as (with a nod to baseball's "Babe" and the old Yankee Stadium) "The House That Ruth Built." She placed hits in the Top Five every year from 1951 through 1954. During those four calendar years her tunes spent a collective thirty-seven weeks at #1.

Brown spent years out of the public eye serving as a mother and housewife, but at the urging of comedian Redd Foxx she returned to her singing profession in 1975. She subsequently embarked on an acting career, first on television and then on Broadway. She earned a Tony Award in 1989 for "Best Actress in a Musical" for her performance in *Black and Blue.* She also won a Grammy in 1990 for the related *Blues on Broadway* for "Best Jazz Vocal Performance, Female."

Ms. Brown also spearheaded a fight seeking to obtain royalties to underpaid rhythm and blues artists. Her old boss at Atlantic, Ahmet Ertegun, contributed $1.5 million to help establish the Rhythm and Blues Foundation in 1988. (Earlier in the decade, Ertegun had been one of the co-founders of the Rock and Roll Hall of Fame, eventually located in Cleveland in a building designed by I.M. Pei, the designer of the National Gallery of Art's East Building and of the Bank of China Tower in Hong Kong.)

Ruth Brown's synthesis and accessible mastery of vocal genres ranging from gospel to jump blues and jazz produced an engaging pattern for other female R&B vocalists to follow into the popular market.

Prominent Number One R&B

"Teardrops from My Eyes" 1950
"5-10-15 Hours" 1952
"Mama, He Treats Your Daughter Mean" 1953
"Oh, What a Dream" (with the Drifters) 1954

Jerry Butler (1939–present)

"The Iceman" (or "The Ice Man")
Rhythm and Blues Foundation 1994

Raised in the Cabrini-Green projects of Chicago's Near North Side; check. "Traveling Souls Spiritual Church" choir member; check. Northern Jubilee Gospel Singers vocalist; check. Baritone street-corner doo-wopper; check. Form singing group with Curtis Mayfield; check. Composed and sang "For Your Precious Love" (#3 R&B; #11 U.S.); check.

Okay, Jerry Butler clearly had the credentials to become "the Ice Man" of soul music.

Misunderstandings and some bickering over Vee-Jay Records's labeling of the group as "Jerry Butler and the Impressions" made for a short tenure for Butler with the band. He and Curtis Mayfield, however, continued on good terms musically and professionally. (See separate article on the Impressions.)

Branching out into a solo career, Butler popped a #1 R&B (#7 U.S.) in 1960 with "He Will Break Your Heart" (covered in 1975 by Tony Orlando as "He Don't Love You").

His late 1960s collaborations with Kenny Gamble and Leon Huff at Mercury Records ushered in the "Ice" age. In 1968 and 1969 Butler had four hits that were in the Top Ten R&B and also in the Top Twenty U.S.: "Never (Gonna) Give You Up"; "Hey, Western Union Man"; "Only the Strong Survive"; and "What's the Use of Breaking Up." Butler recorded a total of fifteen Top Ten R&B offerings.

Since 1985 Butler has served on the Cook County (Chicago) Board of Commissioners. He has served as Chairman of the Board of the Rhythm and Blues Foundation. He and the rest of the original Impressions were inducted into the Rock and Roll Hall of Fame in 1991.

Number One R&B

"He Will Break Your Heart" 1960
"Hey, Western Union Man" 1968
"Only the Strong Survive" 1969

The Cadillacs

Rhythm and Blues Foundation 1996

"Well, they often call me Speedoo, but my real name is Mr. Earl." Remember that song lyric?

Earl "Speedoo" Carroll was the lead vocalist of the Cadillacs at their zenith—1953–1957 (and every once in a while after that). Their appeal was comprised of their excellent vocals, often zany characters, natural dancing abilities, and a tough yet hip New York City persona.

Their first big record, "Gloria," was a version of a song often recorded, but theretofore with but modest sales. (A later cover of the song, performed by the Manhattan Transfer, was influential in the revival of 1940s style vocal harmonies featured in much of a cappella music today.)

The fast-steppin', fancy-dressin' Cadillacs' hit, "Speedoo" (#3 R&B; #17 U.S.), made a dent in the heavily white Pop market of 1955 that included insipid songs by Mitch Miller, the McGuire Sisters, and three different versions of "The Ballad of Davy Crockett" in the Top 25.

It's a head-scratcher why the Cadillacs' subsequent recordings rarely broke high onto the charts. Their live concerts, however, continued to be the stuff of legend among fans of doo wop and set the performance bar for future rhythm and blues singing groups.

Ray Charles (1930-2004)

"The Genius"
Rock and Roll Hall of Fame 1986*
Rhythm and Blues Foundation 1990/1
Rolling Stone's 100 Greatest Singers #2

Ray Charles (Robinson) suffered a complete loss of sight at age seven. That misfortune led him to the Florida School for the Deaf and Blind, where from 1937–1945 he formally studied classical piano but privately gravitated to jazz, blues, and popular stylings.

After scuffling for a time here and there in Florida, he moved to Seattle where he befriended the three-years-younger Quincy Jones. In 1949 Charles registered his first R&B hit, "Confession Blues," the first of over sixty Top Ten R&B. One no less than Frank Sinatra dubbed Ray Charles "the only true genius in show business."

In 1955 "I Got a Woman" became his first of twelve #1 R&B hits. "What'd I Say" was his first major crossover hit as a #6 on the U.S. Top Ten in 1959. The following year "Georgia On My Mind" became his first U.S. #1. Then in 1961 "Hit the Road, Jack" became #1 U.S. and R&B. Charles' genius became even more evident when his album "Modern Sounds in Country and Western Music" went to #1 U.S.

In 1979 his version of "Georgia on My Mind" was proclaimed the state song of Georgia. He performed for Ronald Reagan's second Inauguration in 1985, the same year his duet with Willie Nelson of "Seven Spanish Angels" went to #1 U.S. Country.

The "You Got the Right One, Baby!" commercials of 1990–1993 for Diet Pepsi kept him before the public eye, as did his performance for President Clinton's first Inauguration in 1993. In 2001 Charles performed his classic rendition of "America the Beautiful" at Super Bowl XXXV.

Ray Charles died in 2004, but he wasn't finished! His 2005 album "Genius Loves Company" (including duets with a number of his admirers) became the #1 album U.S., won eight Grammys, and sold three million copies.

Ray Charles's songs "Hallelujah I Just Love Her So" and "I Can't Stop Loving You" showcased his talent for blending idioms in ways that smacked of genius. Illustration by Beth Meier.

Prominent Number One R&B
"I Got a Woman" 1955
"What'd I Say" 1959
"Hit the Road Jack" 1961
"I Can't Stop Loving You" 1962
"Let's Go Get Stoned" 1966
"I'll Be Good to You" (with Quincy Jones and Chaka Khan) 1990

Chubby Checker (1941-present)
Rhythm and Blues Foundation 2006

Talk about being in the right place at the right time—Chubby Checker can "Amen" that!

Born Ernest Evans, he grew up with his family in the South Philly projects. His singing ability coupled with his good-natured joking led to his delighting of schoolmates by doing vocal impressions of various pop singers. Friends arranged for young Ernest to do a private recording for a youthful looking fellow who happened to host a local television show: Dick Clark.

On one occasion Clark's wife asked Evans his name. He replied that his friends called him "Chubby." As he had just completed his mimicking of Fats Domino, Clark's wife added the "Checker" part, and it stuck.

Meanwhile, legendary Baltimore DJ and television host Buddy Dean recommended to Clark a song that had been recorded as the B-side of a Hank Ballard and the Midnighters single. Clark wanted to book Ballard's band for his "American Bandstand" in order to showcase the song, but they were unavail-

America's chiropractors received a bonanza as Chubby Checker had America twisting the night away and ducking under the limbo pole in the early 1960s. Illustration by Beth Meier.

able. Clark remembered Checker and arranged for him to record a cover of the song, "The Twist."

"Twist" as a dance term had been around for over a century, but apparently it was Chubby himself who in preparation for his "American Bandstand" appearance gave the dance the look we know today. Exposure on "Bandstand" propelled the song to #1 Pop (#2 R&B) in the summer of 1960. America's teens were twistin' the night away. The adults caught on later.

In late 1961 adults in high society dressed in suits and fur coats were sighted waiting in long lines in the cold outside the Peppermint Lounge in Manhattan to belatedly get in on the dance craze they had earlier missed. "The Twist" rocketed back to #1 (#4 R&B) in early 1962 and became, along with Bing Crosby's all-time bestseller "White Christmas," the only song to chart #1 on entirely separate runs.

Number One U.S. Pop
"The Twist" 1960
"Pony Time" 1961
"The Twist" 1962
"Limbo Rock" 1962 (#1 Cash Box; #2 Hot 100)

Claudine Clark (1941–present)

Claudine Clark received formal musical training at Philadelphia's Combs College, whose alumni include saxophonist John Coltrane and whose faculty once featured the innovative classical pianist and composer Leopold Godowski. Miss Clark had her "fifteen minutes of fame" in the summer of 1962 when her composition "Party Lights" rose to #5 on the Hot 100.

The song was written from the perspective of a teenage girl who was grounded and confined to quarters, but who could see through her window the multi-colored lights in the house across the street where her friends were dancing the latest dances.

"Party Lights" finished 1962 as *Billboard* magazine's 35th biggest hit. Toward the end of that record's run, Claudine Clark appeared at John Brown's Farm as part of the undercard for Clyde McPhatter on Labor Day of 1962.

The Coasters

Rock and Roll Hall of Fame 1987
Rhythm and Blues Foundation 1994

Two Jewish songwriters plus a fun-loving black vocal group equals a crossover hit-making machine when the talents on tap are Jerry Leiber, Mike Stoller, and the Coasters.

The Coasters evolved out of the Robins, an L.A.-based vocal group discovered by the legendary musician and talent scout Johnny Otis. The Robins scored several hits with the Leiber-Stoller songwriting duo, including "Riot in Cell Block #9" in 1954 and "Smoky Joe's Cafe" in 1955.

The Coasters were a quartet of musically talented class clowns who collaborated with songwriters Leiber and Stoller to entertain America in the late 1950s.
Illustration by Beth Meier.

Those collaborative successes led to Ahmet Ertugun's Atlantic Records offering Leiber and Stoller an independent production deal that included the Robins. However, the deal meant everybody moving from the West Coast to the East Coast.

After some personnel re-shuffling, the group solidified under the new name, the Coasters. The classic group includes original "Robin" Carl Gardner, plus Billy Guy, Cornell Hunter, and bassist Will "Dub" Jones. The group dominated the upper echelons of the R&B and Pop charts in the closing years of the 1950s. In addition to the #1s listed below, you also may remember "Along Came Jones" (#14 R&B and #9 Pop) and "Charlie Brown" (#2 R&B and Pop).

Their infectious style was described by Leiber as "a white kid's view of a black person's conception of white society." Illustrating how thin was the line between rhythm & blues and rock & roll, Leiber described the Coasters' songs as "R&B hits that white kids were attracted to, and if (white kids) bought it, it became rock and roll."

Number One R&B
"Young Blood" 1957
"Searchin'" 1957
"Yakety Yak" 1958 (also #1 U.S.)
"Poison Ivy" 1959

The Crystals

The Crystals was one of the early "girl groups" of rhythm and blues as the music made its way into mainstream pop. The original Crystals quintet scored early successes with Barbara Alston on lead vocal for the 1961 hit (#20 U.S.) "There's No Other (Like My Baby)" and in early 1962 with the Barry Mann and Cynthia Weill composition "Uptown" (#13 U.S.).

Producer Phil Spector, sensing that a certain Gene Pitney composition was going to be a hit for somebody, rushed Darlene Love and the Blossoms into the studio in L.A. to record that song under the Crystals banner. As shady as that move might have been, Spector's intuition was right about Pitney's song. "He's a Rebel" was a smash and climbed to the summit of the Hot 100.

The ruse worked well enough that Spector used Love and the Blossoms again as if they were the Crystals to record "He's Sure the Boy I Love," which narrowly missed the Top Ten (#11).

Perhaps in part because of a contractual dispute between Spector and Love, the "real" Crystals returned, but with Barbara Alston stepping down from the lead role (because of increasing shyness bordering on stage fright) in favor of Dolores "La La" Brooks.

If you listen closely, perhaps you can hear a young Cher Sarkisian (Bono) among the layered background vocalists of the Crystal's 1963 #3 hit "Da Doo Run Run." Later that same year "Then He Kissed Me" gave the Crystals their sixth and last Top Twenty song of their meteoric career as their popularity plummeted amidst the arrival of husbands, babies, and the Beatles.

Number One U.S. Pop
"He's a Rebel" 1962

Bo Diddley (1928-2008)

"The Originator"
Rock and Roll Hall of Fame 1987
Rhythm and Blues Foundation 1996

Bo Diddley's (born Ellas Otha Bates) influenced rhythm and blues to take on a rockier edge. His songs were covered passionately in the 1960s by the Rolling Stones ("You Can't Judge a Book by the Cover"), the Doors ("Who Do You Love"), and the Yardbirds ("I'm a Man").

Perhaps his work appealed to young musicians because of its simple chord structures, the heavily syncopated "Bo Diddley" drum beat (see Buddy Holly's "Not Fade Away" and the Who's "Magic Bus"), and his manly stage presence. Whatever the precise allure, his music provided a key transition from blues to rock 'n' roll.

His eponymous composition "Bo Diddley" rode the elevator all the way to the top floor of the R&B chart in 1955. "Pretty Thing" in 1955 and "Say Man" in 1959 were also Top Five R&B.

Number One R&B
"Bo Diddley" 1955

Bo Diddley was an innovator who stretched rhythm and blues toward rock 'n' roll as he gained an appreciative following on both sides of the Atlantic. Illustration by Beth Meier.

Fats Domino (1928–present)

Rock and Roll Hall of Fame 1986*
Rhythm and Blues Foundation 1995

New Orleans's Antoine Dominique (Fats) Domino, Jr. was arguably the most popular rhythm and blues performer of the 1950s. During that decade he produced nine #1s and eight #2s. During his career, he has earned forty Top Tens R&B and eleven Top Tens on the U.S. Hot 100.

Twenty-three of his songs were million sellers, including his first record, "The Fat Man" (#2 R&B). That 1949 offering featured Domino's vocal and rollicking piano while seminal drummer Earl Palmer supplied the constant back beat—you can't lose it.

"Blueberry Hill" was Fats's highest charter on the Hot 100 at #2. Ron Howard, playing Richie Cunningham on television's retro-hit "Happy Days," characteristically chirped that song when an attractive teenage girl caught his attention.

Among Domino's gigantic successes were "I'm Walkin'" (#4 Pop for Ricky Nelson's cover in 1957) and "Ain't That a Shame," which Pat Boone covered to a #1 Hot 100.

That Fats Domino, an established mega-star, would perform at John Brown's Farm underscores the venue's significance as a premier mid-sized stop on the Chitlin' Circuit.

Prominent Number One R&B

"Goin' Home" 1952
"Ain't That a Shame" 1955
"Blueberry Hill" 1956
"I'm Walkin'" 1957
"I Want to Walk You Home" 1959

Lee Dorsey (1924–1986)

He never did work in a coal mine, but Lee Dorsey was no stranger to hard work. After serving in the Navy and spending some time as a light heavyweight boxer, Dorsey returned to his New Orleans birthplace and settled into working in an auto body shop.

Dorsey cut a few obscure and unsuccessful singles before meeting his long-time collaborator, Allen Toussaint, another "Big Easy" product. Dorsey's "Ya Ya" went to #7 on the Billboard Hot 100 in 1961, and it reached #1 R&B for a week in November (between Ray Charles's "Hit the Road Jack" and "Please Mr. Postman" by the Marvelettes).

Other memorable tunes by Dorsey included "Ride Your Pony" and (just try and stop your body from rocking on this one!) "Yes We Can" (later covered as "Yes We Can Can" by the Pointer Sisters).

Dorsey is perhaps best known for his 1966 "Working in the Coal Mine," which eventually peaked at #5 R&B, #8 Hot 100. That song became a hit shortly after the dances at John Brown's Farm had come to an end. Although the patrons there would have enjoyed the song immensely, they would have vigorously disagreed with its Allen Toussaint lyric that lamented, "When Saturday rolls around, I'm too tired for havin' fun."

Number One R&B
"Ya Ya" 1961

Jimmy Dotson (?–1991)

This Baltimore product (not Jimmy "Louisiana" Dotson) was managed for a time by Rufus Mitchell, hence the connection to John Brown's Farm. Dotson's commercial success was limited (and most of that came after the JBF era), but his fine, soulful tenor made him one of the most memorable of the area talents to grace the Farm.

Dotson cut records with major labels Volt and Mercury, as well as Mitchell's Ru-Jac nameplate. Give Dotson's "Turn Your Head" a listen on YouTube whenever you are in the mood for a little "beach music" and dancing the "Carolina Shag."

The Drifters

Rock and Roll Hall of Fame 1988

The Drifters were a perfect example of what a New York City vocal group could offer. Great voices, imperious management, brilliant songwriting, and arrangements featuring uptown strings and Latin rhythms enabled the constantly revolving door that was the Drifters to keep spinning out those classic hits—twenty Top Ten R&B in all.

"The Drifters" is an apt name for a group that eventually would have more than sixty different members, including its various splinter groups. The principal reason for the high turnover is that their manager, George Treadwell, the husband of Sarah Vaughn, essentially owned the Drifters brand. (Those interested in following the group's entire tortuous history may elect to consult the pertinent Wikipedia article.)

Ahmet Ertugun, Atlantic Records founder, was enamored with the vocal talent of Clyde McPhatter. Ertugun encouraged McPhatter, recently estranged from his previous group, to pull together a collection of singers that would become the Drifters.

Personnel turmoil commenced almost immediately, but the group squirted out several Top Five R&B hits including "Money Honey" that was king of the R&B hill for eleven weeks in late 1953. McPhatter departed for a solo career in 1955.

As Johnny Moore was brought in to take over the bulk of the lead singing responsibilities, the group continued to chart highly, including "Ruby Baby" which was later covered in 1962 by Dion (DiMucci) to a #2 in the Hot 100.

Fresh squabbles resulted in manager George Treadwell sacking the entire group and re-forming the "New Drifters" that produced the golden, though again brief, era of the group. Ben E. King was the lead voice of such memorable hits as Leiber and Stoller's Latin-rhythmed compositions "There Goes My Baby," "This Magic Moment," and the only Drifters song to go to #1 on both charts, "Save the Last Dance for Me" in 1960.

More squabbles led to King leaving the Drifters in May of 1960 and someone (usually Charlie Thomas) lip-synching King's already-recorded vocals for various television performances. Rudy Lewis then was brought in to share lead vocals with Thomas.

Lewis was the featured vocalist on the 1963 hits "Up On the Roof" by Goffin-King and "On Broadway" by the songwriting husband and wife team of Barry Mann and Cynthia Weil, with an assist by Leiber-Stoller. By 1964, after a stint in the Army and a shot at a solo career, Johnny Moore was back in the group and at the helm as the lead singer for "Under the Boardwalk" (#4 Pop).

Because the John Brown's Farm patrons so distinctly remembered Charlie Thomas as the front man, the most likely date of the Drifters' appearance would seem to be the summer of 1960.

Prominent Number One R&B

"Money Honey" 1953
"There Goes My Baby" 1959
"Save the Last Dance for Me" 1960

The Esquires

The Esquires (known at times also as "Fabulous Ray Johnson and the Esquires") was a four-piece (sometimes five-piece) band that had the privilege of opening at various venues for Otis Redding, as well as Smokey Robinson and the Miracles. Jazz guitarist Mike Jackson was a prominent member of that group. Jackson related that the band played "many, many times" at John Brown's Farm. Jackson said of JBF and places like it on the Chitlin' Circuit, "Those were some soulful joints, let me tell you!"

In addition to being a featured act at the Farm, the Esquires also served as frequent backup band there. Mike Jackson reminisced, "We played with everybody." Those "everybodies" included Billy Stewart, Baby Washington, and Marvin Gaye.

The Esquires are considered to be, along with Chuck Brown and the Soul Searchers, pioneers of a sub-genre of funk that has become known as Go-Go. The Esquires played at the African-American Cultural and Heritage Festival in Charles Town, West Virginia, in 2004.

Sammy Fitzhugh and the Moroccos

Sammy Fitzhugh (?–2005) was a flamboyant performer whose "Linda Baby," a Little Richard-type rocker, still gets some radio airplay. From nearby Washington, D.C., he was a frequent and much-appreciated performer at JBF. Little Bobby Parker said of Fitzhugh that he "gigged with him all the time" and that he was "very talented—a good, a great singer."

Piedmont blues-style guitarist Warner Williams, Winfield Parker (playing saxophone), and Chico Vega were among the dozens of musicians who at one time or another played in the Moroccos. John Bishop signed the group to Atco Records in 1961. They backed Maxine Brown, Chuck Jackson, and other performers at John Brown's Farm.

Summer after summer, Sammy Fitzhugh, a flashy dresser and ostentatious performer, was a fan favorite at John Brown's Farm. *Photos courtesy of LaVerne Bishop.*

The Five Du-Tones

The Five Du-Tones recorded the original hit version of "Shake a Tail Feather," which peaked at #28 R&B chart (#51 Hot 100). The song was famously covered by James & Bobby Purify, as well as by Ike and Tina Turner, and the Blues Brothers.

Its flip side was the humorous "Divorce Court." That song included an over-the-top courtroom scene presided over by "Judge Frank Chillipepper" and the divorcing couple, John and Dulamae Heissenberger. The group often acted out this song in costume, backed by their touring band, the Exciters.

The Five Keys

Rhythm and Blues Foundation 1990-1991

Originally a gospel quartet called the Sentimental Four, the group won several talent competitions in the Tidewater area of Virginia during the late 1940s. Styling themselves after the Ink Spots and the Mills Brothers, their local successes won for them the chance to appear at one of the renowned amateur nights at the Apollo Theatre in 1949, this one hosted by Billie Holiday.

They received a standing ovation and the first place prize that included being booked for a week at the Apollo Theater and another week at Baltimore's Royal Theatre as a featured vocal group with Count Basie. A subsequent record deal with Aladdin records and having their own radio show readied them for their next "lucky" breaks.

The theme song for their radio show was an old standard, Benny Goodman's 1936 hit record "The Glory of Love." Its recording by the Five Keys in 1951 propelled it to both a gold record and #1 on the R&B chart.

In 1954 Alan Freed hosted his "Moondog's Birthday" show in Akron, Ohio. The Five Keys appeared with Big Joe Turner, Faye Adams, and others to a sold-out audience, one-third of which was white—a fact not unnoticed by radio station WINS in New York, which was considering hiring Freed away to that larger market.

In November of 1955, the Five Keys, along with LaVern Baker and Bo Diddley, appeared as part of a rhythm and blues segment for the Ed Sullivan Show on CBS television.

Record companies pushed the Five Keys to sand down the rougher and jazzier elements of their earlier presentations. The group responded with a professional pliability, and their revamped sound proved to be an important and influential musical link between post-World War II popular music and rhythm and blues.

Number One R&B

"The Glory of Love" 1951

The Flamingos

Rock and Roll Hall of Fame 2001
Rhythm and Blues Foundation 1996

We know them best as the group that performed "I Only Have Eyes for You." In that classic hit (#3 R&B; #11 U.S.), we hear the essential elements of what made them popular: an elegant lead vocal, carefully blended harmony, and soaring falsetto counterpoint. But their distinctive sound explains only half the story of their popularity and incredible influence on such artists as the Temptations.

The other half is the visual half. Locate their "Jump Children" on the Internet and you will see handsome faces, sharply tailored suits, pert choreography, and athleticism that could be matched only by the likes of Jackie Wilson, James Brown, and Michael Jackson.

Although they charted only five times in the Top 25 R&B, their influence on the tone colorings of doo wop is legendary. They frequently added suspensions and other "color tones" to their basic triads. Their individual voices were of such quality that members Terry Johnson, Paul Wilson, Tommy Hunt, and Nate Nelson all could and did sing lead on various songs.

Because several patrons specifically remembered Tommy Hunt being with the Flamingos at the time, their appearance at John Brown's Farm was therefore somewhere between late 1956 and 1960.

Inez and Charlie Foxx

Rhythm and Blues Foundation 1995

The sister and brother team Inez (1942–present) and Charlie (1939–1998) Foxx had a successful career and one gigantic hit. "Mockingbird" was one of those perfect songs—the harmonic mesh that can only come from family, a classic call and response, lyrics based on "Hush, Little Baby" (a lullaby from the mists of Americana), and underpinned by that cha-cha beat.

"Mockingbird," written by the Foxxes, soared to #7 on the Pop Chart and #2 on the Top Black Singles chart in late 1963. (Perhaps because of genre confusion as rhythm and blues worked its way into mainstream music, there were no Billboard R&B singles charts from November 30, 1963, to January 23, 1965.)

The good-looking and talented siblings were far from one-hit wonders. "Hurt by Love" and "Ask Me" were notable offerings reaching the Hot 100. Additionally, their touring in Europe contributed significantly to the development of the Northern Soul—a music, dance, and fashion movement that arose from the British Mod scene.

Aretha Franklin (1942–present)

"The Queen of Soul"
Rock and Roll Hall of Fame 1987
Rhythm and Blues Foundation 1992
Rolling Stone's 100 Greatest Singers #1

If God has a fireplace, he surely has a picture of Aretha Franklin over the mantle.

In her girlhood Aretha regularly sang solos in Detroit's New Bethel Baptist Church, where her father, C. L. Franklin, was pastor. She had several R&B hit singles by the time she was nineteen, but it took a few more years before record producers fully comprehended what was necessary to cultivate the gospel roots in the future "Queen of Soul." Once that happened at Atlantic Records, we all have been blessed.

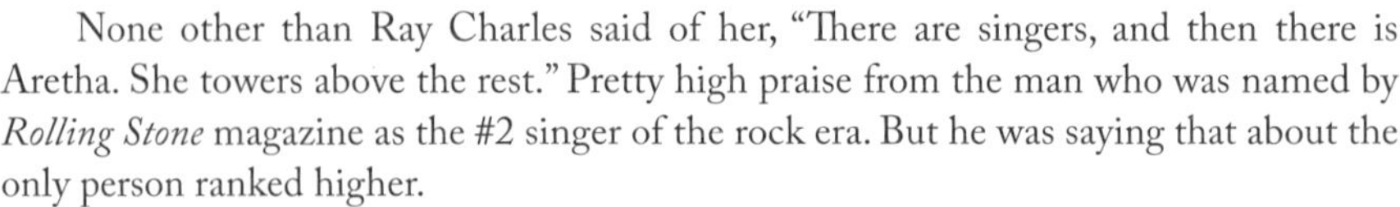

None other than Ray Charles said of her, "There are singers, and then there is Aretha. She towers above the rest." Pretty high praise from the man who was named by *Rolling Stone* magazine as the #2 singer of the rock era. But he was saying that about the only person ranked higher.

What about Aretha Franklin brings forth such brimming tributes from people? As multiple Grammy Award-winning vocalist Mary J. Blige puts it, "Aretha is a gift from God. She has everything—the power, the technique. She is honest with everything she (sings)... I think her gospel base brings that confidence."

Franklin's soulful ballads "I Never Loved a Man (The Way I Love You)" and "(You Make Me Feel Like) A Natural Woman" arise from that same earnest place in the heart as her 1972 Double Platinum offering, *Amazing Grace,* which remains the top selling Gospel album in history.

Now nearing the end of her illustrious career, Ms. Franklin has become a virtual institution. She sang "The Star-Spangled Banner" at the 2006 Super Bowl, performed "America" at Barack Obama's 2009 presidential Inauguration, and sang "Precious Lord (Take My Hand)" at the 2011 dedication ceremony of the Dr. Martin Luther King, Jr. Memorial in Washington, D.C.

Still active, Aretha thus far has notched seventeen Top Ten U.S. singles and fifty-two Top 10 R&B singles. She was awarded the Grammy for the "Best Female Vocal R&B

Aretha Franklin parlayed her gospel foundation, nearly four-octave vocal range, and supreme emotive power into becoming America's beloved "Queen of Soul." Illustration by Beth Meier.

Performance" every year for the first eight years of its existence (1968–1975). In 1968 she became just the second black woman (after actress Dorothy Dandridge in 1954) to appear on the cover of *TIME* magazine.

In 1987 she became the first woman inducted into the Rock and Roll Hall of Fame.

Prominent Number One R&B
"I Never Loved a Man (The Way I Love You)" 1967
"Respect" 1967
"Baby I Love You" 1967
"Chain of Fools" 1967
"Think" 1968

Marvin Gaye (1939–1984)

"The Prince of Soul"
Rock and Roll Hall of Fame 1987
Rhythm and Blues Foundation 2000
Rolling Stone's 100 Greatest Singers #6

Marvin Gaye's voice was a splendid blend of the honey of Sam Cooke and the grit of David Ruffin. An early apprenticeship with Harvey (Fuqua) and the Moonglows eventually gave Marvin Gaye entrance into Berry Gordy's burgeoning "Hitsville U.S.A." and the chance to sing background vocals for the likes of Etta James and Chuck Berry.

Marvin Gaye channeled his frequent bouts with depression into the poignant singing and song-writing that led to his being esteemed as "the Prince of Soul." Illustration by Beth Meier.

His own first hit, "Stubborn Kind of Fellow" (backed by the Vandellas), reached #8 R&B. It was reported that when producer Phil Spector first heard the song, he lost control of his car.

Gaye crescendoed in popularity with "How Sweet It Is (to be Loved by You)" and the Smokey Robinson-penned "I'll Be Doggone," Gaye's first #1 R&B and first million-seller. A succession of memorable duets with Tammi Terrell followed. Their "Ain't No Mountain High Enough," "Your Precious Love," and "If I Could Build My Whole World Around You" were perfect anthems for 1967's "Summer of Love."

Gaye then recorded a Whitfield-Strong tune that reached #1 R&B for seven weeks over the 1968–1969 holiday season. "I Heard It Through the Grapevine" sold four million copies and became Motown's biggest-selling hit to date.

A major life heartache, however, was in full attack mode. His musical and personal relationship with Tammi Terrell was a brother-sister love that stood in stark contrast to the tempestuous violence allegedly perpetrated upon Terrell by first James Brown and then David Ruffin of the Temptations.

Terrell, long a victim of intense migraines, famously collapsed into Gaye's arms during a stage performance in the fall of 1967. Soon thereafter she was diagnosed with a malignant tumor from which she died in March of 1970. Her illness and death was devastating to Gaye. As he began to recover from severe depression, a profound turn in his music became evident.

His landmark album "What's Going On" produced three #1 singles R&B that also charted in the Top Ten U.S; "What's Going On," "Mercy Mercy Me," and "Inner City Blues (Make Me Wanna Holler)" were each million sellers. Their successes led that socially conscious concept album to sales of over two million—double platinum.

It is difficult to begrudge Carole King winning the 1972 Grammy for Album of the Year for her magnificent "Tapestry," but how is it that Gaye's "What's Going On" was not even nominated? Makes you want to know what's goin' on. Makes you wanna holler.

By the time of his tragic death on the eve of his forty-fifth birthday by a bullet from the hand of his violence-prone father, Gaye's career had produced forty-one Top Ten R&B (18 U.S.) and thirteen #1 R&B (three U.S.).

Gaye appeared at John Brown's Farm as a member of Harvey and the Moonglows in either 1957 or 1958. He also performed there as a headliner in the early 1960s.

Prominent Number One R&B

"Ain't That Peculiar" 1965
"Ain't Nothing Like the Real Thing" (with Tammi Terrell) 1968
"I Heard It Through the Grapevine" 1968
"What's Goin' On" 1971
"Inner City Blues (Makes Me Wanna Holler)" 1971

Kenny Hamber (1943–present)

Also performed as "Kenny Hamber and the Hitchhikers"

Kenny Hamber is a product and shining example of the Baltimore rhythm and blues scene. He cut his musical teeth as a soloist at the Weldon Baptist Church. As he immersed himself in the sounds of such local and legendary doo-woppers as the Orioles and the Clovers, his voice matured into one similar to those of Luther Vandross and Teddy Pendergrass.

Hamber, a great natural networker, parlayed his relationship with several Baltimore-area deejays into a recording session at one of the radio station studios. The recording quality was predictably sub-standard, but led to a re-recording of the song "Tears in My Eyes" in New York.

The improved version of the song produced enough buzz that Hamber was able to gain entry into performing at the Black Jack, a prestigious hot spot near Penn Station north of downtown Baltimore. Among the many stars that played that venue were the Temptations and Marvin Gaye. Hamber opened for many such acts and also was the headliner there on several occasions.

At other points in his career, Hamber shared the stage with the Four Tops, James Brown, and Dionne Warwick. Periodic regional hits such as "Show Me Your Monkey" (distributed by Atlantic Records) kept Hamber's name in circulation and his performances in demand.

He came to know JBF through promoter Rufus Mitchell, the principal booking agent for Carr's Beach in nearby Annapolis, Maryland. The relatively short distance of seventy miles between Baltimore and JBF enabled Hamber to perform there repeatedly.

He still performs on the R&B circuit, as well as singing gospel music. As one of his latest album titles indicates, Kenny Hamber is a man "Truly Blessed."

Kenny Hamber was a frequent headliner at JBF and a primary source of information about promoter Rufus Mitchell of Carr's Beach. Photo courtesy of Kenny Hamber.

The Impressions

Rock and Roll Hall of Fame 1991
Rhythm and Blues Foundation 2000
Rolling Stone's 100 Greatest Singers (Curtis Mayfield) #40

Heavenly sounds were bound to happen when Jerry Butler and Curtis Mayfield met in a Chicago church choir. The two drew musical and spiritual inspiration from the Soul Stirrers and the Five Blind Boys of Mississippi. Butler and Mayfield grew that soulful foundation into first several gospel groups and then into their early forays into rhythm and blues.

A secular group called the Roosters, comprised of Chattanooga natives Sam Gooden and brothers Richard and Arthur Brooks, moved to Chicago and picked up Butler and Mayfield. As a record deal was being finalized, the group became Jerry Butler & the Impressions.

The Butler-penned "For Your Precious Love" rose to #3 R&B in 1958, the first of sixteen Top Tens R&B for the Impressions. The sudden departure of Butler for a solo career and the exit of the Brooks brothers led to a re-shuffling, though one that did little to harm either Butler's or Mayfield's careers. The two remained close with Mayfield often accompanying Butler on guitar and helping to write several of his early hits, including "He Will Break Your Heart."

The new line-up (sans Butler) had the 1961 #2 hit "Gypsy Woman." In 1963 "It's All Right" rang up a #1 R&B and #4 U.S., the group's highest Hot 100 ranking ever.

Mayfield increasingly incorporated into his lyrics a black church sensibility that said, "Let's look toward heaven, but let's make thing right down here too." Three of his compositions struck a deep-rooted chord with an America that was seeking to re-establish its religious roots. (Clergymen were at the forefront of the Civil Rights movement; just around the corner was the worldwide charismatic renewal that brought hundreds of millions of people to faith in Christ.)

"Keep On Pushing" and "Amen" (featured in the Sidney Poitier movie "Lilies of the Field") were both #1 R&B and in the Top Ten U.S. "People Get Ready" had a lovingly prophetic quality to it. Mayfield said, "That was taken from my church or from the upbringing of messages from the church... I must have been in a very deep mood of that type of religious inspiration when I wrote that song." "People Get Ready" has been covered by more than one hundred other artists.

Much in the spirit of Dr. Martin Luther King, Jr., Mayfield continued to write songs that called for persistent courage in the face of entrenched injustice. In 1967 "We're a Winner" became a virtual anthem for the Civil Rights movement, including lyrics such as "Keep on pushin' like your leaders tell you to." Similarly, Mayfield's 1969 composition "Choice of Colors" called for love, respect, education, and common patriotism in a season when division and even hatred threatened to overwhelm American society.

The Impressions, more clearly than any other musical group, projected through their songs John Brown's hopes for spiritual and political liberty for all people.

Prominent Number One R&B
"It's All Right" 1963
"Keep On Pushing" 1964
"We're a Winner" 1967
"Choice of Colors" 1969

The Isley Brothers

Rock and Roll Hall of Fame 1992
Rhythm and Blues Foundation 1996

What's your guess as to how high the Isley Brothers' million-seller 1959 release "Shout" charted on the Hot 100? If you guessed (as I did) somewhere in the Top Ten, you weren't that close. Try forty-seventh. Although "Shout" is an iconic song, its initial lack of recognition is emblematic of the plight of the early Isley Brothers.

The Isley Brothers started out in their boyhood in Cincinnati as a gospel quartet comprised of Kelly, Rudy, Ronnie, and Vernon, who died upon being struck by a car while riding his bicycle in 1955. After some time away from singing because of their grieving, they re-grouped and journeyed to New York where they quickly landed a record deal.

Although the initial record flopped, several subsequent regional hits gave them encouragement to keep going. A fan base built largely upon their energetic stage performances led to their opening for Jackie Wilson. Apparently, while riffing on the closing chords to Wilson's "Lonely Teardrop," they spontaneously inserted the now-famous line, "You know you make me want to shout," which prompted an immediate gleeful reaction from the audience.

The Isleys later expanded the riff into the song we know today. It endured a protracted accumulation of sales, and their version of "Shout" eventually did become a million-seller.

With "Twist and Shout" in 1962, the Isley Brothers gained more deserved recognition as that classic went to #2 R&B (#17 U.S.). Surely more success was now at their doorstep. Nope. Success was still far down the block–maybe over in the next neighborhood. Eventually it did come, however.

"This Old Heart of Mine" was a hit during their Tamla/Motown years in the late 1960s. Their obvious talent, coupled with persistence and flexibility finally paid off big-time in the late 1960s and beyond. The group earned its first (and only) Grammy with the 1969 monster hit "It's Your Thing."

Moving forward, they added their younger brothers, Ernie and Marvin Isley, as well as Rudy's brother-in-law Chris Jasper. The results were spectacular. Ernie's soaring guitar solos on "That Lady" in 1973 and their cover of Seals and Croft's "Summer Breeze" in 1974 pointed the ever-flexible Isleys in yet another new direction.

The group charted Top Ten R&B hits in six (!) consecutive decades for a total of twenty-eight.

The patrons of John Brown's Farm got to experience them early on and thoroughly appreciated the Isley Brothers' own delight in facilitating a party atmosphere whenever they performed.

Number One R&B

"It's Your Thing" 1969
"Fight the Power" 1975
"Don't Say Good-night (It's Time for Love)" 1980
"Down Low (Nobody Has to Know)" (with R. Kelly) 1996

"Bull Moose" Jackson (1919–1989)

Benjamin Clarence Jackson could cruise from a ballad to the blues. In the mid-1940s this versatile musician was a featured saxophonist with Lucky Millinder's orchestra, whose members gave him the nickname "Bull Moose" for his strapping facial features.

Jackson's singing career took a giant step forward when Millinder designated him as the stand-in for vocal soloist Wynonie Harris, who was unable to make a show in Texas. Jackson subsequently was recruited to King Records to play rhythm and blues. His big band ballad "I Love You, Yes I Do" made it to #1 (#24 Pop) and is often purported to be the first R&B gold record.

Jackson's recordings with his Buffalo Bearcats ranged from soulful crooners to bawdy bouncers. His two-sided 1948 hit displayed both elements in the ballad "All My Love Belongs to You" backed by the risqué "I Want a Bowlegged Woman."

Jackson's longest run at #1 was "I Can't Go On Without You" which perched atop the R&B chart in 1948 for eight weeks. Big band blues numbers such as "Big Ten Inch Record" and "Nosey Joe" (by Leiber and Stoller) marked Jackson's foray into the 1950s. For a fun listen, try Jackson's big band bopper "Big Fat Mamas Are Back in Style."

As the public's musical tastes changed, Jackson alternated working for a catering firm in Washington, D.C., and continuing to perform at relatively nearby places like John Brown's Farm, where he was always anticipated and experienced with delight.

Number One R&B

"I Love You, Yes I Do" 1947
"I Can't Go On Without You" 1948

Chuck Jackson (1937–present)

Rhythm and Blues Foundation 1992

Chuck Jackson's stylish look was matched by versatile vocal styling the ranged from sensuous to soaring. Photo from the author's private collection.

Chuck Jackson took a spin through the revolving door that was the Del-Vikings following their 1957 hit "Come Go With Me." Soon after going solo he opened for Jackie Wilson at the Apollo Theater, which led to a recording contract with Scepter Records. Jackson's debut single "I Don't Want to Cry" charted well on the Pop chart and zoomed to #5 R&B.

Burt Bacharach's composition "Any Day Now" became Jackson's signature piece and charted at #23 in U.S. Pop and #2 in R&B in 1962. (Ronnie Millsap's 1982 rendition of the song made it to #1 Country and #14 U.S.)

Partially on the strength of Jackson's notching a nifty twenty-three entries on Billboard's Hot One Hundred, he was honored with the Pioneer Award of the Rhythm and Blues Foundation in 1992, the same year as the transcendent Aretha Franklin.

Walter Jackson (1938–1983)

"Sir Walter Jackson"

The voice of Walter Jackson epitomizes the Chicago Soul sound of the early 1960s—urban, uptown, polished, restrained. Chicagoans Jerry Butler, Curtis Mayfield, Major Lance, and Gene Chandler all dished up a mélange of those same ingredients.

Jackson was stricken with poliomyelitis in his childhood and used crutches for the rest of his life. Polio did not affect his vocal cords, although his experience in dealing with the consequences of the disease may well have contributed to the depth of his vocal expressiveness. (If you haven't heard Walter Jackson's voice, think somewhere in the Teddy Pendergrass, Barry White, Billy Paul orbit.)

Jackson's string of successful mid-1960s Top Twenty R&B songs, many of them ballads, included "Suddenly I'm All Alone," "Welcome Home," and "It's An Uphill Climb To the Bottom." In the mid-70s, he again reached the Top Twenty on the R&B Chart with soulful covers of Morris Albert's "Feelings" and Peter Frampton's "Baby, I Love Your Way."

Jackson died of a cerebral hemorrhage at age forty-five. You will do your ears a favor to listen to his regal voice on his biggest pop hit (1964), the Curtis Mayfield-penned "It's All Over."

Etta James (1938-2012)

Rock and Roll Hall of Fame 1993
Rhythm and Blues Foundation 1989*
Rolling Stone's 100 Greatest Singers #22

Born Jamesetta Hawkins, the future Etta James was a gospel child prodigy featured with the St. Paul Baptist church choir and on the radio in Los Angeles at the age of five.

A decade later she found her way to the attention of legendary musician and talent scout Johnny Otis. Otis gave James her stage name and recorded her lead vocal (purportedly on the first take) for "The Wallflower (Dance with Me Henry)" in late 1954. (Nearly sixty years later, in January of 2012, Miss James would die just three days after Johnny Otis.)

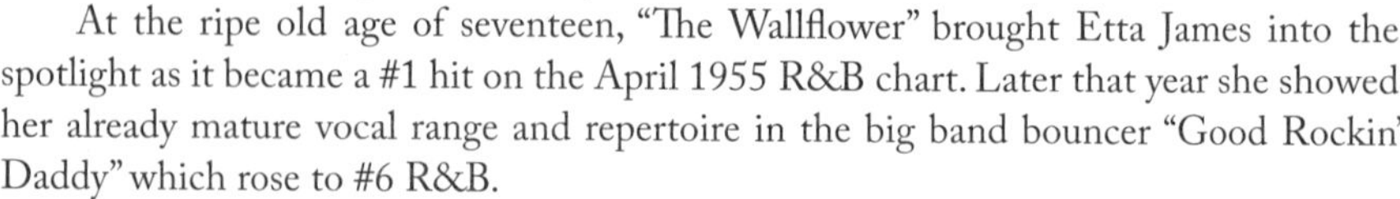

At the ripe old age of seventeen, "The Wallflower" brought Etta James into the spotlight as it became a #1 hit on the April 1955 R&B chart. Later that year she showed her already mature vocal range and repertoire in the big band bouncer "Good Rockin' Daddy" which rose to #6 R&B.

Upon signing with Chess Records in 1960, James charted again via two duets with Harvey Fuqua: "If I Can't Have You" and Willie Dixon's "Spoonful." Her first solo hit with that label was the moan of a jilted lover in "All I Could Do Is Cry" (# R&B) which showcased her ability to emote in ways unsurpassed.

Chess's choice to back "At Last" (#2 R&B) with a lush arrangement evoked genius in James, and it eventuated in one of the all-time best rhythm and blues ballads. (That song made it to only #47 U.S. Somebody should research whether the majority of the American public went temporarily deaf in 1961.)

Her lushly-produced debut album (similarly titled *At Last!*) was released that same year and included standards such as "Stormy Weather" and "A Sunday Kind of Love." She sang those torch songs with enough romantic energy to make a confirmed bachelor grab a woman and head to the nearest chapel!

Miss James charted regularly throughout the 1960s, registering eleven times in the Top Ten R&B. By mid-decade, however, she was battling (and often completely

Female patrons of John Brown's Farm recalled being stimulated to rapturous screaming in showing appreciation for Etta James's heavenly voice. Illustration by Beth Meier.

surrendering to) an addiction to heroin. She emerged temporarily to record her last Top Ten hit (of thirteen), the fervent and funky "Tell Mama." Flip over that single and you'll find another James classic, her love lament "I'd Rather Go Blind."

Already the recipient of four Grammy Awards, in 2003 James was honored with the Grammy Lifetime Achievement Award.

Number One R&B
"The Wallflower (Dance with Me, Henry)" 1955

Little Willie John (1937–1968)

"The Prince of the Blues"
Rock and Roll Hall of Fame 1996

William Edward John was an important R&B figure who remains somewhat obscure to the wider culture. Known as "the Prince of the Blues," John's biggest Hot 100 hit, "Sleep," made it just to #13. John's influence in the R&B community, however, was rousing.

Considered a pioneer of "soul music," you can hear echoes of John's voice, vocal styling, and choice of material in Sam Cooke ("Talk to Me"), Jackie Wilson ("Heartbreak"), and early James Brown ("Need Your Love So Bad"). Stevie Wonder gave John's induction speech into the Rock and Roll Hall of Fame and noted with admiration, "As a little boy I grew up listening to the music of Little Willie John."

At just seventeen years old in 1955, John charted a #5 R&B with "All Around the World." He averaged two Top Fifteen R&B hits per year over the next six years, including the original version of "Fever," a million-seller that reached #1 R&B in 1956. ("Fever" was covered by Peggy Lee in 1958, becoming her signature song and reaching #8 Pop.)

In the heat of an altercation following a show in Seattle, John stabbed a man to death. He died subsequently under mysterious circumstances at a penitentiary hospital at just thirty years of age. His funeral service was conducted at New Bethel Baptist Church in Detroit by Aretha Franklin's father, Rev. C. L. Franklin. Among the three thousand mourners were pall-bearers Sam and Dave, Joe Tex, and Johnny Taylor.

Number One R&B
"Fever" 1956

B. B. King (1925–2015)

Rock and Roll Hall of Fame 1987
Rolling Stone's 100 Greatest Singers #96
Rolling Stone's 100 Greatest Guitarists #6

Riley B. King came a long way from the cotton flatlands of western Mississippi and the little cabin where he was born. Allegedly, he got his first acoustic guitar in his early teens and liked picking it a lot better than he liked picking cotton.

Making his way up to West Memphis, Arkansas, he eventually traveled east to the "good side" of the river. There he heard T-Bone Walker doing special things on an electric guitar. King made up his mind to get himself one. He basically skipped that whole "chord thing" and proceeded directly to improvising on lead guitar and trading licks with his own voice.

Along with Bobby "Blue" Bland, Junior Parker, and Johnny Ace, King became part of the "Beale Streeters," a loosely confederated group of Memphis musicians. Such men were staples on the Chitlin' Circuit (really there were several main loops of it) throughout the South.

According to the legend, in 1949 King was gigging at a dance hall that caught on fire as a result of a brawl over a woman named Lucille. King fled outdoors with the rest of the crowd before realizing that he had left his beloved Gibson semi-hollow electric guitar inside. Rushing back into that treacherous conflagration led him to make two lifetime resolutions: (1) never run into a burning building and (2) never get involved in fights over women. To memorialize those intentions, he began to call that and every subsequent guitar "Lucille."

Back in 1952 when "rhythm and blues" and "the blues" were harder to distinguish, King had his first hit with "3 O'Clock

The King of the Blues, B. B. King, with his constant instrumental companion "Lucille," performed 15,000 live performances spanning six decades.
Illustration by Beth Meier.

Blues," which spent five weeks atop the chart. Almost half (ten) of King's eventually twenty-one Top Ten R&B hits occurred prior to the end of 1956.

"The Thrill Is Gone" became in 1970 King's highest charter U.S. at #15 (#3 R&B). In addition to the Grammy Lifetime Achievement Award conferred on him in 1987, he earned fifteen Grammys. Records sales, however, were not the major component of his legacy. Rather, it was his more than 15,000 live performances, at least one of which was at John Brown's Farm.

Number One R&B

"3 O'Clock Blues" 1951
"You Know I Love You" 1952
"Please Love Me" 1953
"You Upset Me Baby" 1954

Ben E. King (1938-2015)

Rock and Roll Hall of Fame (as member of the Drifters) 1988

One of the great voices of rhythm and blues, Ben E. King performed the lead vocal for the Drifters on their mega-hits "There Goes My Baby," "This Magic Moment," and "Save the Last Dance for Me."

Upon being spun out of the Drifters' incessantly revolving door, King recovered his professional equilibrium to embark on a solo career that spawned an illustrious discography and spanned an additional half-century, during which he scored more than two dozen Top 40 hits.

"Stand By Me" was a #1 R&B (#4 U.S.) for King in 1961. He backed it up the following year with the #2 "Don't Play That Song." Demonstrating his staying power, King climbed back to the top in 1975 to record his final Number One, #1 "Supernatural Thing, Part 1."

Number One R&B (solo)

"Stand By Me" 1961
"Supernatural Thing, Part 1" 1975

Eartha Kitt (1927–2008)

The life of Eartha Kitt is one of the great and literal "rags to riches" stories in American history. Abandoned by her father in infancy and her mother in toddlerhood, Kitt was left in the care (if that word can rightly be used) of a neighbor who compelled her to cook, clean, and pick cotton among the many chores required for her to cover her keep.

A well-meaning but difficult "aunt" (perhaps Kitt's birth mother) called for her to come to New York City when she was eight. At times government-supplied apples comprised the entirety of their Depression-era diet. Her aunt recognized and encouraged a musical aptitude and perhaps an artistic temperament in her niece.

Kitt eventually attended the Mayor Fiorello LaGuardia-founded "High School of Music & Art" in Upper Manhattan. A downturn in her relationship with her aunt led to Kitt's dropping out of school and spending some time working in a factory and on a farm.

A chance conversation on the street led to the now sixteen-year-old Kitt's winning a scholarship to the prestigious Katherine Dunham Dance School. As a member of the school's traveling troupe, Kitt toured several countries in Latin America and Europe. The indomitable Kitt became fluent in at least four languages and could sing convincingly in ten.

She elected to stay in France and began to hone her dancing, singing, and acting skills toward what would one day become her inimitable show business persona: "a glamorous, calculating international gold digger enslaving rich men with exaggerated feline wiles, then treating them like cat toys" (Steven Holder of the New York Times).

In 1950 she acted the part of Helen of Troy in *Time Runs,* produced for the stage by Orson Welles, who notably described Kitt as "the most exciting woman in the world." She also was a headliner in the 1952 Broadway musical *New Faces of 1952.*

The height of her popularity as a recording artist followed. Her 1953 "C'est Si Bon" (with flip-side "African Lullaby") reached the Top Ten U.S. Her masterly and masterful treatment of "Santa Baby" that same year continued to build her legend and to expand her repertoire.

In the latter half of the 1950s and into the 1960s, Kitt was in heavy demand for film, nightclubs, Broadway, and television, where she famously played Catwoman in the Batman series. A younger generation appreciated her work as the voice of Yzma in Disney's animated feature "The Emperor's New Groove." Kitt's prolific body of work includes more than thirty movies, ten Broadway plays, countless appearances on television, and more than two dozen albums.

As the revelations continued to unfold concerning what artists played at John Brown's Farm, perhaps chief among the surprises was the multi-talented international superstar, Eartha Kitt.

Patti LaBelle and the (Her) Blue Belles

Rhythm and Blues Foundation 1999 (as "LaBelle")
Rolling Stone's 100 Greatest Singers (Patti LaBelle) #95

Patti LaBelle and the Blue Belles (and its various spellings) was formed out of two rival Philadelphia girl groups. Patricia Louise Holte (Patti LaBelle) and Cindy Birdsong from the Ordettes merged their vocal talents with Nona Hendryx and Sarah Dash from the Del Capris.

Patti LaBelle and the Blue Belles at the height of their popularity: (clockwise from right) Cindy Birdsong, Nona Hendryx, Patti LaBelle, and Sarah Dash (top) who became a dear friend of JBF promoter John Bishop. Illustration by Beth Meier.

Amidst a controversy that has never been entirely sorted out, the Blue Belles were credited with being (but perhaps were not) the vocalists on "I Sold My Heart to the Junkman," which became in 1962 a #15 hit on the Hot 100. The quartet's 1963 "Down the Aisle (The Wedding Song)" reached #14 R&B and got a lot of national play at #37 on Billboard's Hot 100.

In subsequent recording sessions, Patti LaBelle began incorporating a trademark high note finale, often accompanied by the angelic soprano harmony of her Blue Belles including the 1962 "You'll Never Walk Alone" and 1964's "Danny Boy" (#4 R&B and Pop). The recording of their live performance of "Over the Rainbow" in 1966 showcases the power and clarity of the quartet at its finest.

Cindy Birdsong's departure to join the Supremes in the late 1960s prompted the remaining members of the Blue Belles to ponder a new direction. The result was Labelle. Although the new group's success was not immediate, eventually it was stratospheric.

They debuted their new flamboyant look while on tour serving as an opening for British rock legends, The Who. LaBelle's brew of glam rock and high-powered soul was epitomized in the smash hit "Lady Marmalade" that let you know that you could "gitchi gitchi ya ya here." That Allen Toussaint production garnered a #1 on both the R&B and Hot 100 charts for LaBelle in 1974.

Labelle broke up in 1977, but LaBelle, Hendryx, and Dash have reunited from time to time for several different projects. Sarah Dash became lifelong friends with John Bishop, attending a tribute to him a few months prior to his death in 2006.

Number One R&B and U.S.
"Lady Marmalade" (as LaBelle) 1974

Little Anthony and the Imperials

Rock and Roll Hall of Fame 2009
Rhythm and Blues Foundation 1993

The Imperials was one of those groups that, like the Drifters, somehow just sounded like they were from New York City—a combination of street smarts and theatrical sparkle perhaps. The vocalists deftly polished their street-corner doo wop into something more urbane and ethereal.

The group was fronted by Anthony Gourdine with his soulful childlike tenor from that special vocal heaven inhabited by Smokey Robinson and Michael Jackson. With Gourdine's innocent lead vocal tucked in by highly tone-colored background harmonies, "Tears on My Pillow" in 1958 brought the group to national attention with a #2 Pop matched by a #2 R&B. "Shimmy-Shimmy Ko-Ko-Bop" got a lot of airplay in 1959, although reaching just #14 R&B and #24 Pop.

The group's fortunes dwindled thereafter, and "Little Anthony" took the opportunity to try a solo career. Recognizing that the grass on the original side of the fence was pretty green after all, the group reformed in 1963 into the group's classic lineup of Gourdine, Clarence Collins, Sammy Strain, and Ernest Wright.

Childhood friend Tony Randazzo brought them several of his cultured compositions, creating a niche for the group in what someone described as "dramatic pop-soul." Their two gleaming signature tunes of 1966 were "Goin' Out of My Head" (#6 on both charts) and "Hurt So Bad" (#3 R&B; #10 Pop). Both showcased the singers' strengths and gave them entrance to multiple television performances, including the Ed Sullivan Show, Shindig!, Hullabaloo, American Bandstand, and the Tonight Show.

The ages of the many people who remembered them at John Brown's Farm indicates that they appeared there during their second incarnation—between their re-forming in 1963 and late summer of 1965.

Little Eva (Boyd) (1943-2003)

If you are an aspiring singer, you could do worse for a day job than babysitting for the Goffin family. Eva Narcissus Boyd, still a teenager at nineteen, was just a year younger than Gerry Goffin's new wife, Carole King, the mother of toddling Louise born in 1960.

The newlyweds had been aware that Eva was a singer, and they certainly could hear that for themselves around the house. After their composition "Will You Love Me Tomorrow" went to #1 for the Shirelles on Billboard's Hot 100 in early 1961, Goffin and King gave Boyd the opportunity to record a song they originally intended for Dee Dee Sharp. By August of 1962 the whole country was doing "The Loco-Motion" along with Little Eva as the million-seller skied to #1 on Billboard's Hot 100.

Despite the obvious public success, tragedy lurked in Eva Boyd's private life; she was being beaten by her boyfriend on a regular basis. As Goffin and King quizzed her as to why she allowed the abuse to continue, they were stunned by her earnest explanation that her boyfriend's actions were motivated by, and even proof of, his love for her. Boyd's all-too-common rationalization led the songwriting duo to pen "He Hit Me (It Felt Like a Kiss)" which was produced in correspondingly raw fashion by Phil Spector as recorded by the Crystals.

Eva recorded "Keep Your Hands Off My Baby" (#12) and several more Top Twenty hits, mostly of the "dance craze" genre, before retiring from the music business. The popularity of Kylie Minogue's cover titled "The Locomotion" in the late 1980s propelled Little Eva out of retirement and into a nice run on the Oldies circuit.

Little Richard (1932–present)

"The Architect of Rock and Roll"
Rock and Roll Hall of Fame 1986*
Rhythm and Blues Foundation 1994
Rolling Stone's 100 Greatest Singers #12

If you spanked the newborn "Rock & Roll" on its bottom, out would come the cry "A-wop bop-a loo-mop, a-lop bam-boom!" From the time he was born, Little Richard Penniman was just not going to be one of those shrinking violets. Born into a family of vocalists, his raucous singing voice as a child earned him the nickname "The War Hawk."

The Pentecostal Church appealed equally to the spiritual and physical sides of his rambunctious personality. Faith healers and singing evangelists particularly enthralled him, and as a child Penniman did an effective turn at both.

Billy Wright, a slightly older, gospel-oriented, jump blues shouter, influenced Little Richard in his personal appearance and stage presence. Wright also ushered him into relationships that led to a recording contract. Early recording attempts had no sizzle, so the easily bored Penniman turned his attention toward forming a hot R&B band, the Upsetters, to accompany him on the road.

A return to the studio led to the collective realization that trying to make Little

In the mid-1950s, flamboyant personality Little Richard marshaled his talents to combine boogie woogie with R&B and to become "The Architect of Rock and Roll." Illustration by Beth Meier.

Richard "the next somebody else" was going to be a waste. "Take five," suggested somebody. During the break Little Richard let out his nervous energy by laying down a boogie woogie piano riff and wailing out a song of his that he had been using in his stage act for years. Ah, here is what we've been waiting for!

The song's bawdy lyrics needed some substantial scrubbing up, but it was definitely a hit in the making. Penniman, who later claimed to be "the architect of rock and roll," had just laid a big foundation stone. "Tutti Frutti" became a smash at #2 R&B (#17 Pop).

As the calendar turned to 1956, Little Richard bawled seven songs into the Top Ten R&B, two #1s with "Long Tall Sally" (#6 Pop) and "Rip It Up," and 1957 continued the streak. Among the five songs in the Top Ten R&B were "Lucille," "Jenny, Jenny," and "Keep-A-Knockin'." In less than three years, Penniman had cranked out hits at the rate of one every seven weeks, for a total of fourteen Top Ten R&B.

In October of 1957, at the height of popularity, Little Richard had a life-transforming experience with Jesus Christ. He made an abrupt exit from the secular music business and presently entered Bible college with the goal of becoming a minister of the gospel. As often happens when a newly saved musical star begins to contemplate his or her new life in Christ, there is a period of confusion over how now to view one's previous life and career. Little Richard wobbled awkwardly for decades between the two worlds before coming to a resolution that satisfied his conscience. He sings many, though not all, of his old songs and preaches with fervor.

He is today loved and revered around the world. Among the many stars who idolized him and who credited him with being an impelling influence on their musical lives are Paul McCartney, Mick Jagger, Bob Dylan, Jimi Hendrix, Prince, Freddie Mercury, and Michael Jackson.

Number One R&B

"Long Tall Sally" 1956
"Rip It up" 1956
"Lucille" 1957

Frankie Lymon and the Teenagers

Rock and Roll Hall of Fame 1993

Nowadays we have become used to hearing teenagers singing to teenagers—the Jonas Brothers, Miley Cyrus, Justin Bieber. It wasn't always that way. The trend pretty much started with Frankie Lymon and the Teenagers.

One of the early ethnically integrated groups, the Teenagers was a Washington Heights (Manhattan) quintet, consisting of two Puerto Ricans (Herman Santiago and Joe Negroni) and three blacks (Jimmy Merchant, Sherman Garnes, and lead singer Frankie Lymon).

Lymon, the youngest member, was 14 years old when "Why Do Fools Fall in Love" soared to #1 R&B (#6 U.S.). The rest of the group was sixteen and under, including that marvelous bass, Sherman Garnes.

"Why Do Fools" sat atop the R&B chart for five weeks in early 1956 and boosted the group into international stardom, including a tour of Europe and many television appearances. They followed up with the #3 R&B "I Want You to Be My Girl," another song anchored by a Garnes bass intro and unleashed by Lymon's pre-pubescent tenor. "Goody Goody" became a #20 Pop hit in 1957.

On stage they presented a clean-cut, energetic image complemented by the choreography of Cholly Atkins, later of Motown fame. They were among the groups that appeared in July of 1956 at racially segregated Carr's Beach in Annapolis before a crowd of 15,000. Other artists at that event included Chuck Berry, Shirley & Lee, and Della Reese. It is possible that their appearance at JBF, less than one hundred miles away, occurred on that same weekend.

The group charted several more times, but predictable juvenile squabbles arose. External manipulation and internal immaturity doomed the group to a quick and irreversible exit through the popularity turnstile and into the land of "whatever happened to?" Tragically, Lymon died at twenty-five due to a heroin overdose, and two of the other four died of natural causes in their thirties.

Number One R&B

"Why Do Fools Fall in Love" 1956

Gene McDaniels (1935–2011)

Gene McDaniels had two huge hits in 1961: "A Hundred Pounds of Clay" and "Tower of Strength" were both Top Five on the Hot One Hundred. The following year he just missed the Top Twenty with Goffin-King's "Point of No Return," in which he jubilantly warbled, "I'm at the point of no return a-a-a-a-a-nd for me there'll be no turning back."

The assassination of Dr. Martin Luther King, Jr. in 1968, however, provoked McDaniel into a depressive sabbatical in Denmark and Sweden and into song-writing in the black consciousness genre. An excellent example is his composition recorded by Les McCann and Eddie Harris, "Compared to What."

Upon returning to America, the now "Eugene" McDaniels wrote Roberta Flack's Grammy-nominated single "Feel Like Makin' Love" (#1 R&B, Pop, and Easy Listening in 1974), which has been recorded on over 400 albums. That album also featured "Mister Magic" (later covered by Grover Washington, Jr. and becoming a jazz-funk classic).

Later in life, the multi-talented McDaniels wrote and recorded jazz albums, acted in short films, and voiced the character "Nasus" in the popular online video game "League of Legends."

ADVANCE SALE TICKET
John Brown's Farm
LABOR DAY DANCE
Sept. 3, 1962
Clyde McPhatter and Trio
"CLAUDINE CLARK"
"THE ESQUIRES"
$2.00 "ADVANCE" $2.00

One of the precious few surviving memorabilia from the dances at JBF was this advance sale ticket featuring Clyde McPhatter.

Clyde McPhatter (1937–1972)

Rock and Roll Hall of Fame 1987

At five years old, young Clyde, along with six siblings, began to sing in his father's Durham, North Carolina, church choir. By age ten he was the boy soprano soloist. In his early teens, his father moved the family north—first to New Jersey and then to New York City.

McPhatter worked his way through a gospel group (the Mount Lebanon Singers), to winning an "Amateur Night" at Harlem's Apollo Theater, and into the already popular singing group, the Dominoes. To that ensemble, McPhatter brought a vocal approach steeped in the gospel tradition of a soulful delivery aimed at evoking a visceral response.

The handsome tenor became widely imitated and was a formative influence on other doo-wop and R&B vocalists, including Ben E. King, Smokey Robinson, and (surprisingly perhaps) country legend Patsy Cline.

Wanting to make a name for himself, McPhatter gave notice to the Dominoes of his intended exit. That professional courtesy gave the group time to groom Jackie Wilson as his understudy and replacement. Atlantic Records' Ahmet Ertegun signed him to a record deal with the stipulation that he form a group to back him. That unit became the Drifters.

With McPhatter headlining, between 1953 and 1955 the Drifters struck two #1s R&B with "Money Honey" and "Honey Love" as well as two #2s, "Such a Night" and "Whatcha Gonna Do."

McPhatter had been drafted into the Army in late 1954, but his stateside assignment allowed him to keep recording with the Drifters. Once his tour of duty was finished, however, McPhatter went AWOL from the Drifters to launch a solo career. He produced the duet "Love Has Joined Us Together" (as he had earlier produced a child) with Ruth Brown. A string of Top Ten R&B hits followed.

The tune most commonly associated with McPhatter's name is "A Lover's Question." That pleasant pop number with the snappy bass vocal intro and prominent finger-popping rose to #1 R&B and #6 Pop. The re-release of "Lover Please" in 1962 became his last Hot 100 hit at #7.

As music styles changed, and with an escalating drinking problem clouding his judgment, McPhatter did not handle his slipping popularity well. Still revered in the United Kingdom, however, he moved there in the late 1960s before returning in 1970 to America with the hope of revitalizing his career. That comeback hope was forever squelched in 1972 when the increasingly embittered man died in his sleep from complications of alcoholism at the age of 39.

Number One R&B

"Money Honey" (with the Drifters) 1953
"Honey Love" (with the Drifters) 1954
"Treasure of Love" 1956
"Long Lonely Nights" 1957
"A Lover's Question" 1958

The Moonglows

(aka "Harvey and the Moonglows")
Rock and Roll Hall of Fame 2000
Rhythm and Blues Foundation 1995

Harvey Fuqua (1929-2010), nephew of the Ink Spots' Charlie Fuqua, helped found the vocal group the Crazy Sounds in Louisville, Kentucky, in 1951. Upon moving north to Cleveland, Ohio, the group was re-named the Moonglows by local disc jockey Alan "Moondog" Freed who is widely saluted as "The Father of Rock and Roll."

The Moonglows recorded initially with Freed's "Champagne" label. They later signed with Chess Records in 1954 where they recorded their six Top Ten R&B hits. The doo-wop 6/8 stroller "Sincerely" reached #1 on the Billboard R&B chart and crossed over to score as high as #20 U.S.

In 1957 Fuqua dismissed the original members and replaced them wholesale with the members of the Marquees, including their young lead vocalist, Marvin Gaye. Now billed as Harvey and the Moonglows, the group had a crossover hit with "Ten Commandments of Love" prior to Fuqua's exit in 1958.

In 1959–1960 while with Argo Records (U.S.), a Chess Records subsidiary, Fuqua recorded several spectacular duets with Etta James, including "If I Can't Have You" and Willie Dixon's "Spoonful," wherein Fuqua's cool baritone smacks palms with Etta's hot alto in a horn-bolstered bounce arrangement.

At the recommendation of Leonard Chess, Fuqua moved to Detroit in 1960, began working at Anna Records with Anna Gordy, Berry Gordy's sister, and soon married their sister Gwen. During this phase of his career, particularly while at Motown Records, Fuqua is credited with either discovering or promoting to prominence the Spinners, Junior Walker, Tammi Terrell and Marvin Gaye (whom Fuqua helped pair), and David Ruffin, eventually of the Temptations.

The incarnation of the Moonglows with both Fuqua and Gaye was together for only parts of 1957 into 1958, so their appearance at JBF necessarily occurred during that time frame.

Number One R&B
"Sincerely" 1955

Johnny Moore (1934-1998)

Rock and Roll Hall of Fame (as member of the Drifters)
Rhythm and Blues Foundation (as soloist) 1999

Johnny Moore achieved his greatest fame as the once and future lead singer of the Drifters. In between (sometime in the early 1960s), he performed at John Brown's

Farm as a soloist. Here's how his career unfolded.

When Clyde McPhatter, the original lead singer of the Drifters, left for greener financial pastures in 1955, Moore was brought in to replace him. He fronted their 1955 #1 R&B hit "Adorable." He also sang lead on "Ruby Baby" (#10), later covered by Dion (DiMucci), and the boogie-woogie "Fools Fall in Love" (#10).

Moore was drafted in 1957 and spent several years in the U.S. Army. While Moore was in the Army, the ever-changing personnel of the Drifters employed a rotation of lead singers that included Ben E. King and Rudy Lewis (see article on the Drifters for further detail).

Upon his return to the States, Moore recorded for a time as "Johnny Darrow." Following Rudy Lewis's death, Moore returned to an all-new ensemble of the Drifters in 1964, just in time to be appointed to the lead vocal for "Under the Boardwalk" (#4 U.S.). Johnny Moore's voice was also featured in "Saturday Night at the Movies" (#18 U.S.) and the Drifters' final Top Ten R&B song—the 1965 cha-cha, "At the Club."

During the 1970s, the Moore-fronted version of the Drifters scored a number of Top Ten Hits in the U.K. That run qualified him to become the longest-serving member of the more than two dozen vocalists who sang for the (official) Drifters.

Aaron Neville (1941–present)

"The touch, the feel of cotton; the fabric of our lives." That voice? Aaron Neville.

Despite several earlier recordings on Minit records, "Over You" in 1960 was the first opportunity America had to hear "that voice." Not sure why it took six more years before another Aaron Neville tune charted, but charted it did. "Tell It Like It Is" reached #1 R&B (#2 Pop) in 1966. Slow forward another twenty years.

Linda Ronstadt's 1989 album *Cry Like a Windstorm, Howl Like the Wind* included four duets with Neville. Three of those elegant pairings made it into the Top Five in Adult Contemporary: "Don't Know Much" (#1), "All My Life" (#1), and "When Something Is Wrong with My Baby." Additionally, Neville's cover of "Everybody Plays the Fool" (originally by the Main Ingredient featuring Cuba Gooding, Sr.) reached #1 Adult Contemporary in 1991.

Neville and Ronstadt's skin-thrilling performance of Mann and Weil's "Don't Know Much" at the 1990 Grammys was one of those experiences where you could think, "This would be a good time to go deaf, because I will never hear anything more beautiful."

The Creole Crooner's version of "Cotton," introduced during the 1992 Summer Olympics, reinforced the fact that Aaron Neville and his voice have been woven into the fabric of our lives.

Number One R&B
"Tell It Like It is" 1966

The Orioles

Rock and Roll Hall of Fame 1995, ("Early Influences" Category)

The Orioles of Baltimore were the classic street corner cats—singing in the alley after everyone else had gone to bed. They are frequently credited with being the first rhythm and blues vocal group. The prominent bass voice, harmonic voicings ranging from gospel to jazz, a moving falsetto tenor in the background, and the plaintive tones of lead singer Sonny Til (1928–1981) established the basic pattern for future doo-woppers to follow.

After performing well at a 1948 radio appearance on Arthur Godfrey's talent show, the group secured a record deal and recorded "It's Too Soon to Know." That song made a brief appearance at the top of the R&B chart and crossed over to a high ranking (#13) on the pop chart—one of the first "race records" to do so. "Tell Me So" charted to #1 R&B in early 1949, the first of six by this group in a row to make it into the top dozen.

At that phase of their career, during their performances the Orioles provoked a nearly hysterical reaction among the girls in the audience, similar to that experienced earlier by Frank Sinatra and later by Elvis Presley and the Beatles.

Beginning in late 1950 an unfortunate string of car accidents and personal problems inaugurated a turnover in the group's make-up that marked the group henceforth—more than thirty vocalists have been Orioles at one time or another. The group persevered for a few years to moderate success before hitting a home run in 1953 with "Crying in the Chapel," which had a splendid run of five weeks at #1 R&B while reaching #11 Pop.

Number One R&B
"It's Too Soon to Know" 1948
"Tell Me So" 1949
"Crying in the Chapel" 1953

Bobby Parker (1937-2013)

"Little Bobby Parker"

Many rock music fans have noticed the similarity in the guitar licks between Led Zeppelin's "Moby Dick" and the Beatles' "I Feel Fine." Did one "borrow" from the other? No, both bands freely admit that they adapted them from the same source—Bobby Parker's 1961 hit "Watch Your Step." In that song Parker's fine voice, accompanied by his famous guitar motif and a "What'd I Say" groove, makes for a "Yeah, man!" listening experience.

Louisiana-born Parker got his first big break by winning a West Coast talent contest sponsored by Johnny Otis. Parker then worked with the likes of LaVern Baker, Chuck Berry, Sam Cooke, Bo Diddley (on the "Ed Sullivan Show"), the Everly Brothers, Jackie

Wilson, and Little Richard. He was touring with Buddy Holly on "the day the music died."

Though "Watch Your Step" received comparatively little airplay nationally in the U.S., the Beatles routinely had "Watch Your Step" on their set list during their grueling stint in Germany preparatory to their impending intercontinental fame. Parker's thoughtful yet dynamic style influenced no less than Carlos Santana who says of Parker, "He inspired me to play guitar."

Little Bobby Parker was a first-order musician who toured with Sam Cooke and Jackie Wilson and who inspired Carlos Santana to take up the guitar.
Illustration by Beth Meier.

Junior Parker (1932-1971)

While still in his teens, Herman Parker, Jr. immersed himself in the Memphis Beale Street scene. He was schooled on harmonica by Sonny Boy Williamson, gigged with Howlin' Wolf, hung out with B. B. King and Bobby "Blue" Bland, and was recruited into the studio by Ike Turner.

Little Junior Parker made his debut hit single on Sam Phillips's Sun Records in 1953 with "Feelin' Good," one of those rock-a-boogie tunes that makes you imagine Chuck Berry cruising past with the top down. That record made it to #5 on the R&B chart, the first of many hits for the velvety vocalist.

After moving over to Don Robey's Duke Records in late 1953, it took a few years for Parker to get his musical feet firmly under himself. Upon hitting his stride again in 1957, he had seven hits in the R&B top fifteen from 1957-1963. "Sweet Home Chicago" and "Driving Wheel" were typical of Parker's offerings, featuring a big band blues style with a prominent horn section. The Paul Butterfield Blues Band later recorded many of those same songs with a similar instrumentation and feel.

Parker died at age 39 during surgery for a brain tumor. He was inducted posthumously into the Blues Hall of Fame.

Winfield Parker (1942–present)

Winfield Parker was arguably the most frequent entertainer at JBF and a principal authenticator of other musicians who performed there. *Photo courtesy Winfield Parker.*

Winfield Parker performed at John Brown's Farm more than any other artist. His various groups would sometimes play there as frequently as once a month, functioning as a virtual house band.

In 1960 the Cooksville, Maryland, native was recruited into the band Sammy Fitzhugh & the Moroccos based near Washington, D.C. Winfield played sax on the recording of their biggest hit, "Linda Baby." When Little Richard returned in 1962 from his famous hiatus into Christian ministry, Parker was invited to tour with him as the youngest member of the band.

When Little Richard later traveled to Europe where he retained a popularity that largely had slipped away in the United States, Parker stayed in the U.S. and formed his own group, the Imperial Thrillers. For the first time, he was the vocalist and front man.

He came to the notice of Rufus Mitchell, the owner of Ru-Jac Records and Ace Booking Agency that placed scores of top R&B acts into Carr's Beach in Annapolis, Maryland. Parker rose to becoming a headliner at that fabulous vacation venue. One of his opening acts was Arthur Conley.

When Otis Redding came to Baltimore in 1965, Parker's band backed him up. Because Redding's hit "I've Been Loving You Too Long" suddenly was getting considerable recognition, he needed his own band in a hurry in order to tour. Parker and Redding had become friends, so, as Parker described it, "I gave him half my band."

Rufus Mitchell asked Redding to consider producing first Winfield Parker, and then Arthur Conley. Mitchell consequently sent Parker to Redding in Cincinnati to record "Sweet Soul Music." The problem was that Redding was down in Muscle Shoals, Alabama, not in Cincinnati, and so was Arthur Conley.

Those two put the finishing touches on the composition, and Conley recorded it. The 1967 song reached the #2 spot on both R&B and Hot 100. As Parker reflects on the mix-up, "I felt hurt, but there was nothing I could do about it." (Talk about the one that got away!)

A few years later Parker did get a hit, though admittedly not as major. His 1971 version of Edwin Starr's earlier "S.O.S. (Stop Her on Sight)" made it to Billboard's R&B chart at #48.

At various times from the mid-1960s into the early 1970s, Parker opened for the Four Tops, the Shirelles, and the Temptations. Parker recalled pleasantly, "I was a hard act to follow!" In addition to his contemporary Gospel career, Parker remains popular in Europe as a veteran voice in what is known as Northern Soul.

Wilson Pickett (1941-2006)

Rock and Roll Hall of Fame 1991
Rhythm and Blues Foundation 1993
Rolling Stone's Top 100 Singers #68

Roy Orbison had a big hit with "Mean Woman Blues." In it he sang of a woman "mean as she could be." Wilson Pickett had a similar woman in his life. Too bad it was his mother.

When Pickett was a child, his mother would smack him with the handiest thing she could grab, including a skillet or stove wood. As an adult he divulged, "I get scared of her now." How does that affect a young man? It may have contributed to his becoming one of the great soul singers of all time. Perhaps it also contributed to his tendency for reckless behavior.

In his early teens Pickett had been part of a gospel group that toured with such legends as the Soul Stirrers and the Swan Silvertones. In his late teens he switched over to the secular field and joined the Falcons, whose members included Eddie Floyd ("Knock on Wood") and Mack Rice (composer of soul classics "Mustang Sally" and "Respect Yourself"). With Pickett on lead, the Falcons in 1962 scored a #6 R&B hit with "I Found a Love."

Two special sessions in 1965 at the Stax recording studio in Memphis ignited Pickett's solo career. The house band at the time included keyboardist Isaac Hayes and guitarist Steve Cropper, with whom Pickett wrote "In the Midnight Hour." That oft-covered song became a million-seller.

Switching over to Fame Studios in nearby Muscle Shoals, and making use of the renowned "Muscle Shoals Rhythm Section," Pickett recorded some of his biggest hits: "Land of 1000 Dances," "Mustang Sally," and his remake of "Funky Broadway," recorded originally by Dyke and the Blazers.

As hinted at in the opening paragraph, Pickett harbored an anger problem that frequently boiled over. With drugs, alcohol, and his preoccupation with firearms frequently in the mix, a lethal cocktail was fermenting. Jail time followed. To his credit, upon his release he returned to the studio and earned a Grammy Award nomination in 1999.

In his early sixties, Pickett began to encounter increasingly serious health problems. During one stay in the hospital he confided to his sister that he was being drawn back to his spiritual roots and wanted to record a gospel album. He was unable to fulfill that desire before succumbing to a fatal heart attack in early 2006.

Number One R&B

"In the Midnight Hour" 1965
"634-5789" 1966
"Land of 1000 Dances" 1966
"Funky Broadway" 1967
"Don't Knock My Love" 1971

The Platters

Rock and Roll Hall of Fame 1990

If you can detect the New York City glitz in the Drifters, you probably have no trouble spotting the Los Angeles glamour in the Platters.

The Platters were already a thriving touring act, but having little success in the studio until they came under the patronage of veteran song-writer and talent scout Samuel "Buck" Ram, who secured for the group a recording contract with Mercury Records.

Ram also orchestrated a line-up shuffle that eventuated in their adding Paul Robi, alto Zola Taylor, and a new lead singer: the silky and soaring tenor, Tony Williams. Teamed now with existing members David Lynch and basso profundo Herb Reed, the Platters became an elegant quintet more than able to carry off the "four tuxedos and a gown" image that became their trademark.

The Platters became a golden crossover bridge between Tin Pan Alley and an increasingly youth-oriented market. The result was a string of hits during which the Platters not infrequently charted higher on the Pop charts than they did the R&B.

The Ram-penned "Only You (And You Alone)" zoomed to the top of the R&B chart and remained there for seven weeks in the fall of 1955. As the calendar turned to 1956, the Platters topped both charts (for eleven weeks on the R&B side) with another Ram composition, "The Great Pretender."

The Platters' appeal to both black and white audiences continued throughout 1956 and into 1957 with several more offerings, including "My Prayer," a song which earlier had charted highly for (get this!) both Glenn Miller (#2) and for the Ink Spots (#3) back in 1939.

In the spring of 1958 the Platters scored again with their third hit song, "Twilight Time," which rose to #1 in both charts and was nearly matched (#3 R&B; #1 Pop) the following year by their signature offering, the Jerome Kern classic "Smoke Gets In Your Eyes."

The group was rocked by scandal in 1960, when the four male members were arrested in Cincinnati and charged with having sexual relations with four (three of them white) female minors. Though acquitted of the charges, it was a career-damaging incident in the racially divided atmosphere. As a result, their songs were yanked from the playlists of many American radio stations.

The resulting chaos led to multiple splinterings of the personnel and decades of competitive bickering over the lucrative "Platters" brand. In the pantheon of soulful singing groups, however, the place of the five members from the late 1950s glory years has been assured.

Number One R&B

"Only You (And You Alone)" 1955
"The Great Pretender" 1955
"Twilight Time" 1958

Lloyd Price (1933–present)

Rock and Roll Hall of Fame 1998
Rhythm and Blues Foundation 1993

Take a kid from New Orleans, have him sing in church, get him some music lessons, let him help out at his mother's soul food restaurant, get him discovered by legendary composer and arranger Dave Bartholomew, and have his first record start out with a piano riff by a young Fats Domino. Stir all that together, bake, and what do you have? You have Lloyd Price and his "Lawdy Miss Clawdy."

That million-seller sat atop the R&B chart for seven weeks in 1952 and stayed on it for six months total. Price charted four more hits in the Top Ten before being drafted into the army and spending time in Korea. While Price was away on duty, Little Richard ratcheted things up a few notches with songs such as "Tutti Frutti," "Long Tall Sally," and "Lucille."

Price returned to civilian life, and by 1959 it was clear that he had gotten the new hang of things. "Stagger Lee" found a home at #1 R&B for a full month while also climbing to #1 on the Hot 100. That effort soon was followed by Price's signature song "Personality" (#1 R&B, #2 Pop) and a fourth smash hit "I'm Gonna Get Married," which was not only #1 R&B (#3 Pop) but also gave Price his third gold record in his golden year of 1959.

Price scored his fourteenth Top Ten R&B in 1960 and continued to chart, but his interest increasingly was drawn into other entrepreneurial directions. After founding the record label ("Double L") that first recorded Wilson Pickett, Price opened a Manhattan restaurant/nightclub, promoted boxing with Don King, and built dozens of townhouses in the Bronx.

Seemingly come full circle from his mother's culinary roots, Price has become active in managing Icon Food Brands, including his "Lawdy Miss Clawdy" and "Lloyd Price" lines of food products.

In 2005 he toured with legendary soul singers Jerry Butler, Gene Chandler, and Ben E. King as "the Four Kings of Rhythm and Blues."

Number One R&B

"Lawdy Miss Clawdy" 1952
"Stagger Lee" 1958
"Personality" 1959
"I'm Gonna Get Married" 1959

Lou Rawls (1933-2006)

Lou Rawls was born on the south side of Chicago in, yes, the baddest part of town—or not far from it. He was raised by his grandmother in the Ida B. Wells projects. As a child, he sang in the Greater Mount Olive Baptist Church choir. In his teens, he sang with Sam Cooke. As a young adult, he sang with the gospel innovators, the Pilgrim Travelers.

Rawls survived a stint in the Army as a paratrooper and a car crash that left him pronounced "dead on arrival" at the hospital. Following five days in a coma and nearly a year of recuperation, Rawls returned to live performance and then to a recording contract with Capitol Records in 1962. (That same year Sam Cooke recorded "Bring It On Home to Me." Listen to that cut, and take a moment to recognize that other voice!)

Rawls's first album release was a compilation of blues and jazz standards that included a noteworthy rendition of "I'd Rather Drink Muddy Water" with Les McCann providing a rockin' jazz organ. The 1963 album title cut "Tobacco Road" also received wide notice. At one point, Frank Sinatra is reputed to have ascribed to Rawls "the classiest singing and silkiest chops in the singing game."

"Love Is a Hurtin' Thing" achieved #1 R&B in 1966. The following year "Dead End Street" won the Grammy for best R&B vocal. Later in his career, Rawls added his elegant touch to mid-1970s Disco with "You'll Never Find Another Love Like Mine" and "Lady Love."

In 2004 he recorded a gospel album entitled *Amen.* From beginning to end, Lou Rawls was a soul man.

Number One R&B
"Love Is a Hurtin' Thing" 1966
"You'll Never Find Another Love Like Mine" 1976

Otis Redding (1941-1967)

"The King of Soul"
Rock and Roll Hall of Fame 1989
Rhythm and Blues Foundation 2006
Rolling Stone's 100 Greatest Singers #8

It remains almost unfathomable that Otis Redding was barely 26 years old when he died.

Redding had to leave school at age fifteen to help support his family when his father was stricken with tuberculosis. Young Otis dug wells, pumped gas, and made a weekly habit of winning the $5 prize at a local talent show. An opportunity at the end of a friend's recording session led to Redding being able to demonstrate a song that he had written. The studio was impressed, and Redding was signed to a contract with Stax. The song he had demoed, "These Arms of Mine," made it to #20 R&B.

The majority of his subsequent releases had a slow tempo accompanied by Redding's plaintive lyrics and almost preacher-style vocals. Disc jockeys began to introduce his records as sung by "Mr. Pitiful." Not to be discouraged, Redding and guitarist Steve Cropper wrote a song by that name, which Redding released to a #10 R&B in 1965, his fourth Top Ten R&B song.

In preparation for an LP (*Otis Blue: Otis Redding Sings Soul*) that would eventually become a #1 R&B album, Redding co-wrote with Jerry Butler the ballad, "I've Been Loving You Too Long." That Redding offering rose to #2 R&B and attracted national attention at #21 Pop.

Another Redding composition on that album was released as a single. Maybe you've heard of it: "Respect" climbed to #4 R&B and the notice of Aretha Franklin whose version added her famous spelling out of the word and the "sock it to me" background vocals.

In 1965 and 1966, Redding kept the momentum going with "I Can't Turn You Loose," his cover of the Rolling Stones' "Satisfaction," and his own "Fa-Fa-Fa-Fa-Fa (Sad Song)."

Redding's duets with Carla Thomas on their 1967 "King and Queen" album included "Knock On Wood" (#8 R&B) and "Tramp" (#2 R&B), where her intended insult "You're straight from the Georgia wood" is answered by the Georgia-born Redding with the simple protest, "That's good!"

As 1967 drew to a close, Redding returned to the studio hoping to branch out musically. He recorded a whimsical slow song that a lot of people in and around the studio weren't all that crazy about. They liked it even less when Redding stuck on some whistling at the end.

Just three days hence, on December 10, Redding died in a small aircraft accident near Madison, Wisconsin. A month later that little ditty with that whistling at the end was released and went on to sell some four million copies worldwide. "(Sittin' On) The Dock of the Bay" became Redding's only #1 single on the Billboard's Hot 100 and the first posthumous #1 single in U.S. chart history.

So, when did Otis Redding perform at John Brown's Farm? It would appear that he played there at least twice. A number of people mentioned remembering an early performance (perhaps with either the Shooters or the Pinetoppers) when his style was as unpolished as his shoes. A later performance by Redding as the impeccably-dressed headliner was remembered in vivid detail by a multitude of attendees.

A CONTROVERSY

Winfield Parker, one of our top authorities and a personal friend of Otis Redding, is adamant that Redding did not play the Farm. Others were equally adamant that they did see him there, with several citing vivid memories of the experience. It leads me to wonder if Redding, like more than a few others, simply did not know where he was when he was out at John Brown's Farm. Thus, he may not have thought to have mentioned in the mid-1960s to his new friend Parker that he had performed there.

Number One R&B

"(Sittin' On) The Dock of the Bay" 1967 (also #1 U.S.)

The Shirelles

Rock and Roll Hall of Fame 1996
Rhythm and Blues Foundation 1994

Passaic, New Jersey, is a city with character–and some real characters. Now 60% Hispanic, Passaic has long been home to a rich and churning ethnic mix including Jews (writer Mitch Albom and Steely Dan's Donald Fagen), Italians (sportscaster Dick Vitale and comedian Joe Piscopo), and blacks (football's Craig "Ironhead" Heyward and a group of girls that redefined a genre, the Shirelles).

The Shirelles (Shirley Owens, Doris Coley, Addie Harris, and Beverly Lee) formed on a whim for a talent show at their integrated high school where they performed a song they had written. A Jewish classmate, Mary Jane Greenberg, was impressed and referred the group to her mother, Florence, a suburban housewife just beginning to dabble in the music business.

The Shirelles were the quintessential "girls group." This photo was a promotional piece that Leonard Cooper purchased at John Brown's Farm the night the Shirelles appeared there in the 1960s.

Perhaps to everyone's amazement, the resulting record ("I Met Him On a Sunday") on Mrs. Greenberg's start-up label made a buzz first locally and then nationally as it reached #50 on the Hot 100 in 1958. Greenberg retained the management rights to the Shirelles but sold her little label to Decca. With that $4,000 she started another label, Scepter Records, eventually regained the recording rights to the girls, and began to network like crazy for them.

In preparation for a 1960 recording session with established writer-producer Luther Dixon, Mrs. Greenberg informed the girls that they would need one more song. "When do we need it?" the quartet asked. Greenberg declared, "Tonight!" Shirley Owens shrugged her shoulders and acquiesced, "Well, I guess tonight's the night." Owens (later Alston-Reeves) and Dixon went to work and quickly came up with what became "Tonight's the Night."

The song did well enough (#14 R&B; #39 Pop) to attract the interest of producer-promoter Don Kirshner, "The Man with the Golden Ear." Kirshner had under contract a new husband and wife songwriting team, Gerry Goffin and Carole King. They had written a song that the Shirelles might be able to use.

"Will You Love Me Tomorrow" rocketed the Shirelles, Goffin-King, and girl groups generally into national prominence. Having gained national name recognition, the Shirelles re-released their earlier "Dedicated to the One I Love," which began a string of Top Five hits including "Baby It's You," an early Burt Bacharach composition. In May of 1962, the Shirelles' blockbuster "Soldier Boy" topped the Hot 100 for three weeks.

As the girls (finally!) began to turn twenty-one, several of them looked toward a supposed (but actually non-existent) Scepter Records trust fund, hoping they might take a break from touring in order to start families. Coming to realize that that cupboard was bare was not only a blow, but a betrayal.

Legal wrangling coupled with the competition of other girl groups (often similarly taken advantage of) and the British Invasion contributed to the demise of the Shirelles. Their place in pop music history is assured, however, and perhaps, in their minds, their greatest honor was the renaming by their home town of the street section in front of Passaic High School as "Shirelles Boulevard."

Number One U.S. Pop
"Will You Love Me Tomorrow" 1960
"Soldier Boy" 1962

Shirley and Lee

"The Sweethearts of the Blues"

Early in their careers, New Orleans high school friends Shirley Goodman (1936–2005) and Leonard Lee (1935–1976) were marketed as if they were a romantic couple and were dubbed "the Sweethearts of the Blues." Goodman's girlish soprano was a tough duet even for Lee's capable tenor voice, so the duo's initial approach tended to be one of alternated melodies. Their first single was "I'm Gone," a 6/8 New Orleans stroller that crested at #2 R&B in 1952.

By the mid-1950s, the duo had changed its style and scored a brief but spectacular run of hits on the R&B charts. Their #2 "Feel So Good" (later recorded by Johnny Preston in 1960 as "Feel So Fine") and #3 "I Feel Good" sandwiched their million seller "Let the Good Times Roll." That oft-covered classic topped the chart for three weeks in September of 1956 and crossed over to #20 on the Hot One Hundred. Subsequent releases fared less well, and the two had parted ways by early 1963.

Based upon the high percentage of various-aged attendees that mentioned having seen Shirley and Lee, it may be that they played JBF several times.

Number One R&B
"Let the Good Times Roll" 1956

Billy Stewart (1937-1970)

His fresh vocal stylings and general zest for life made Billy Stewart a fan favorite at John Brown's Farm. As a youth, he sang with his brothers on Sundays for five years on the radio in Washington, D.C. He also won a local talent show singing a certain George Gershwin classic. In that rich Capital music scene, Stewart met locals Don Covay and Marvin Gaye, and the touring Bo Diddley who conscripted Stewart as his piano player and sometime vocalist.

Encouraged by Chess Records A&R man Billy Davis, in 1962 Stewart penned and recorded "Fat Man" (#18 R&B). That song portended Stewart's future success, but, sadly, also his future struggles with his weight and, ultimately, diabetes. Among Stewart's six Top 25 R&B hits were the future Carolina Beach Music classics "I Do Love You" (#6) and "Sitting in the Park" (#4).

His signature song was a thrilling rendition of the Gershwin tune that Stewart had used to win the talent contest as a teen: "Summertime" (#7 R&B; #10 Pop). His opening trill is joined by the drum fill of Maurice White, the erstwhile Chess session drummer and future cofounder of Earth, Wind & Fire. The three minutes of ear candy that follows is emblematic of the joyous treatment Stewart could give to any song, and it is surely one of the most unforgettable vocal performances of all time.

Billy Stewart's voice and personality captured not only the hearts of the JBF faithful, but also of no less than Duke Ellington, who hoped to produce an album featuring Stewart. Shortly before that was to happen, however, Stewart (age thirty-two) along with several bandmates died in a tragic car accident. A void remains. The trill is gone.

Barrett Strong (1941-present)

Barrett Strong appeared at John Brown's Farm on the basis of his one hit song, "Money (That's What I Want" (#2 R&B). His one hit song as a vocalist, that is.

By the mid-1960s, Strong had become a staff lyricist at Motown, teaming with producer Norman Whitfield to pen a string of R&B classics. Perhaps you remember seeing "N. Whitfield—B. Strong" as the composers of such songs as Marvin Gaye's triplet of hits "I Heard it Through the Grapevine," "Too Busy Thinking About My Baby," and "That's the Way Love Is."

If you had a romantic streak, you might have related better to their compositions for the Temptations in a mellower mood with "I Wish It Would Rain" and "Just My Imagination (Running Away with Me)."

If you preferred songs with a social conscience, then you probably appreciated these classics: "War" by Edwin Starr, "Smiling Faces Sometimes" by the Undisputed Truth, or any of these Temptations contributions to Psychedelic Soul: "Cloud Nine, " "I Can't Get Next to You," "Psychedelic Shack," "Ball of Confusion," and "Papa Was a Rolling Stone."

Barrett Strong supplied Motown (Anna Records) with its first hit in "Money," its first monster seller with Gladys Knight and the Pips' version of "I Heard It Through the Grapevine," and its first Grammy for "Papa Was a Rolling Stone." As of publication, the "Money" man is still making records and going strong.

The Swallows

In Baltimore in the late 1940s there was a singing group on virtually every street corner, particularly among the black population that comprised a quarter of the city. The root of that phenomenon was the success of the Orioles–the singing group, that is. The baseball team, the former St. Louis Browns, didn't move to Baltimore until the 1954 season.

In one neighborhood, the Oakeleers occupied one side of the street while the Shields held sway on the other. The two groups eventually joined forces to become a sextet with a few of the fellows playing whatever instruments they could scrounge up.

A local businessman landed them a record contract with the King label. Now billed as the Swallows, their debut single was their own composition, "Will You Be Mine" (#9 R&B). Tenor Eddie Rich and bass "Bunky" Mack shared the vocals on that 1951 song, which is regarded as one of the music industry's earliest doo-wop hits.

Their material included the occasional good-time roller such as "It Ain't the Meat (It's the Motion)." The core of their repertoire, however, was slow honky-tonk ballads like their 1952 release, "Beside You," which became their second national hit (#10 R&B).

They played the major stops on the Chitlin' Circuit including the Apollo, Howard, and Royal theaters, and shared the stage with Count Basie, Sarah Vaughan, and Pearl Bailey. Confided Rich, "We were glad to get out there and make some money."

In contrast to the often crooked shenanigans foisted upon them by producers and agents, John Bishop's upright dealings enabled the Swallows to "make some money" when they motored west out of Baltimore to John Brown's Farm.

The Swallows would appear to have been one of the earliest groups to play JBF, perhaps as early as 1952. Eddie Rich's biographical account of the band's breaking up in nearby West Virginia in 1956 may hint that the Farm also hosted one of the original lineup's final gigs.

Joe Tex (1933–1981)

His birth certificate reads Joseph Arrington; his death certificate reads Yusuf Hazziez. In between he was Joe Tex, the man who didn't "want no woman with no skinny legs."

In his first ten years in the recording business, beginning in 1955, Tex released some thirty singles on King, Ace, and Anna Records without once charting. Beginning in the mid-1960s, however, Joe Tex found his niche under Billy Killen's guidance at Dial Records, and three Tex hits quickly soared to #1 R&B (see below). "Skinny Legs and All" with its chicken-scratchin' guitar lick had enough crossover appeal to make it to #10 Pop in 1967.

Tex, a man who made a living with his mouth, may have opened it one too many times. His verbal swipes at James Brown in the aftermath of Brown's making off with Tex's wife reportedly led to Brown's spraying bullets in his direction in a nightclub, injuring several patrons in the process. Tex survived that incident and continued to be successful throughout the 1970s.

Number One R&B
"Hold What You've Got" 1964
"I Want To (Do Everything for You)" 1965
"A Sweet Woman Like You" 1965
"I Gotcha" 1972

Ike and Tina Turner

Rock and Roll Hall of Fame 1991
Rolling Stone's 100 Greatest Singers (Tina Turner) #17

Early in his musical career, Ike Turner (1931–2007) was more victim than perpetrator. Stiffed out of money and recognition on multiple occasions, he came to the realization that the individual musician is the nail, while the promoter or producer is the hammer.

By the time he was in his early twenties, Ike had served apprenticeships as a deejay, sideman, studio musician, and talent scout. He put a lot of money in other people's pockets.

Thinking he was taking the bull by the horns, Turner brought a group together to record a collaboration, "Rocket 88." That song, along with Fats Domino's "The Fat Man," is often cited as the first true rock and roll song.

"Rocket 88" sold nearly half a million copies. For all his efforts, Turner reaped a nice fat twenty dollar bill. After spending another five years learning that hammer-nail lesson, Turner got good and fed up with being knocked in the head, and a control freak was born.

Moving his band, Kings of Rhythm, to St. Louis, Turner exercised strict control over its members, allegedly fining, firing, or fisting them as he felt was needed. He controlled the arrangements, the uniforms, the schedule, the finances, whatever. For those who stayed in line, the money was good and the popularity increasing.

In the late 1950s one young girl became a regular at Club Manhattan where Turner was the house band. Anna Mae Bullock, a transplant from Nut Bush, Tennessee, climbed the musical ladder from groupie through backup singer to occasional lead vocalist and eventually to the spotlight of his soul review.

An opportunity arose for Ike to record his danceable composition, "A Fool in Love." He permitted Bullock to record the lead demo vocal for a male vocalist to cover later. The execs at Sun Records liked the way the girl did it—"nice and rough" would be a good description. Sun offered an advance of $25,000 for it. The public liked it, too, to the tune of #2 R&B and #27 U.S. Ike changed the name of the band and the name of the girl. May we introduce you to the Ike and Tina Turner Review?

Now a headliner, Tina Turner (1939–present) poured her soul into the funky "I Idolize You" (#5 R&B) in 1961 in a ground-breaking way. People just didn't sing like that in 1961. Maybe James Brown. No one else. Certainly no women.

Ike and Tina cutesied it up for "It's Gonna Work Out Fine," which scored a #2 R&B, became their first crossover hit at #14, and earned them a Grammy nomination. They followed with several substantial R&B hits before Ike began shuffling the act around to some ten different labels between 1964 and 1969, always looking for a better deal.

During that same time period, "The Ike and Tina Turner Review" became legendary both for its grueling schedule and for its consistent top-quality and high-energy performances. To Ike's credit, unlike many R&B veterans, he was able to continually guide the band in new directions. Groups like Tower of Power, Sly and the Family Stone, and James Brown were propelling soul music into an increasingly high-powered groove. Ike and Tina contributed to the genre with a cover of "I Want to Take You Higher" and with their Grammy Award-winning re-working of Creedence Clearwater Revival's "Proud Mary" (#5 R&B; #4 U.S.).

Ike and Tina Turner papered over their own tempestuous relationship for decades while providing fans with memorable high-energy performances. Illustration by Beth Meier.

From that lofty pinnacle, their career and marriage became a death spiral. Ike's addictions and violence begat a terrified Tina on the run with thirty-six cents in her purse. Eventually, she was able to resurrect her career, but Ike was not. He was too busy getting hammered.

The duo was elected to the Rock and Roll Hall of Fame in 1991. Tina chose not to attend the ceremony. Ike could not attend the ceremony. He was in jail at the time.

Jr. Walker and the All Stars

Rhythm and Blues Foundation 2002 (Junior Walker)

Junior Walker (1931–1995) and his various band mates recorded thirteen Top Ten R&B songs. Among them were Number Ones "Shotgun" and "What Does it Take." An additional offering that still receives significant airplay on oldies stations is the jubilant "(I'm a) Roadrunner" (#4) recorded in 1966.

The band played at John Brown's Farm in the summer of 1965.

Number One R&B

"Shotgun" 1965
"What Does It Take (To Win Your Love)" 1969

Dionne Warwick (1940–present)

Rhythm and Blues Foundation 2003

If Aretha Franklin is the "Queen of Soul," then what do we call Dionne Warwick? It has to be something good, and one feels a bit sheepish comparing the incomparable Dionne Warwick with anyone. Then again, she's probably used to it. In fact, she has some serious competition in being considered the best vocalist within her own family.

Her mother and aunts were members of the renowned gospel group, the Drinkard Singers. A maternal cousin is legendary opera diva, Leontyne Price. Dionne's sister is Dee Dee Warwick, who had several Top Ten R&B hits. One of her aunts is Cissy Houston, a member of the celebrated studio backup group the Sweet Inspirations. And Aunt Cissy's daughter is cousin Whitney Houston. So, yeah. There's some vocal competition in that family.

As far as hit songs go, though, Dionne Warwick's fifty-six Hot 100 singles take a back seat only to Aretha's crazy seventy-three among female soloists all-time. Here's how she did it.

While studying music in college, Warwick was part of a gospel performance group that was also in demand at New York City studios. During one session backing the Drifters, the song's composer noticed her elegant voice. He asked if she would be interested in making demo recordings of his compositions that he could use to pitch the songs to record labels. She was interested.

One of those demos caught the attention of Florence Greenberg, the manager of the Shirelles and president of Scepter Records. Greenberg told the young composer, Burt Bacharach, "Forget the song; get the girl!" A remarkable pairing was born. These and other songs by Bacharach and David were brought to perfection by Dionne Warwick: "Walk on By, " "I Say a Little Prayer," "Do You Know the Way to San Jose," and "I'll Never Fall in Love Again."

Artists who lined up to partner with her included the Spinners for "Then Came You" (#1 Pop in 1974), the Bee Gees "Heartbreaker" in 1982, and Luther Vandross for 1983's "How Many times Can We Say Goodbye."

Miss Warwick also sang duets on television with the likes of Barry White, Smokey Robinson, Frank Sinatra, and Ray Charles. Among the most memorable has to be one she shared with Aretha Franklin doing the song with which they each had a Top Five hit.

As the pair sits together singing "I Say a Little Prayer," you do not have so much the feeling of watching "The Queen" and "The Princess" (or some other title) in a competitive sing-off. What you see are two sisters and two of the greatest voices ever to grace the Farm's or any other stage.

Number One R&B
"Walk On By" 1964
"Reach Out for Me" 1964
"That's What Friends Are For" (with Elton John, Gladys Knight, and Stevie Wonder) 1986

Dinah Washington (1924–1963)

"Queen of the Blues"
Rock and Roll Hall of Fame 1993

During her twenty-year singing career, Dinah Washington had thirty-four Top Ten hits on the R&B chart. So why hasn't she received the Pioneer Award from the Rhythm and Blues Foundation? Perhaps it's because she didn't sing rhythm and blues. She sang songs.

She sang hot swingin' jazz. She sang ballads. She sang gospel. She sang pop. Heck, she had a huge hit with a country song ("Cold, Cold Heart"). And, yeah, she could sing the blues—well enough to be known in her day as the "Queen of the Blues."

Born Ruth Lee Jones in Tuscaloosa, Alabama, her family migrated to Chicago. Cutting her musical teeth in church, she went on to win an amateur contest at the Regal

Theater, then progressed to nightclubs, including the Downbeat Room of the Sherman Hotel where she sang with the prodigious pianist Fats Waller.

Lionel Hampton heard her singing in 1943 at the Garrick Theater Lounge where she and Billie Holiday had house gigs in separate rooms. That meeting with Hampton led to her name change, a two-year stint as chanteuse for his band, and her first recording opportunity.

Hampton's band backed Washington on her initial offering, "Evil Gal Blues" written by Leonard Feather, the future legendary jazz critic and chronicler. Her relentless string of Top Twenty R&B hits from 1944–1961 included #1s "Am I Asking Too Much" in 1948 and "Baby Get Lost" in 1949.

Her knack for drawing talented accompanists reached perhaps its high-water mark in the late 1950s when she scored her first Top Ten Pop hit "What a Difference a Day Made." For that 1959 recording she used her touring band comprised in part by guitarist Kenny Burrell, pianist Joe Zawinul (future leader of pioneering jazz fusion band Weather Report), and drummer Panama Francis, whose lengthy career spanned performances with Lucky Millinder's Orchestra to his ear-catching studio work on the earliest hits by the Four Seasons.

Cognizant of how the music industry limited the venues and thus the earning power of black artists, in 1959 Washington and Ruth Bowen founded the booking agency, Queen Artists. Bowen would subsequently grow that enterprise into Queen Booking Corporation, which by 1969 had become the largest black-owned entertainment agency in the world.

In the early 1960s Washington teamed with Brooke Benton to record consecutive #1 R&B hits (see below). She followed up those duets with her solo "This Bitter Earth," the fifth and last of her #1s on the R&B chart. (Did you catch that, Rhythm and Blues Foundation—the R&B chart!)

Miss Washington's often tumultuous marital life culminated in her eighth marriage, to Dick "Night Train" Lane, the former NFL cornerback who still holds the record for most interceptions in a single season. Perhaps trying to manage her weight, she died of an overdose of barbiturates while only thirty-nine years old.

Prominent Number One R&B

"Am I Asking Too Much" 1948

"Baby You've Got What It Takes" (with Brook Benton) 1960

"A Rockin' Good Way (To Mess Around and Fall in Love)" (with Brook Benton) 1960

Justine Washington (1940-present)

"Baby Washington"
Rhythm and Blues Foundation 1995

Justine "Baby" Washington (sometimes confused with Jeanette Washington of the funk band Parliament) had a string of some sixteen charted Rhythm and Blues singles, several in the Top 30, primarily in the late 1950s and early 1960s. British songstress Dusty Springfield cited Baby Washington as her all-time favorite vocalist.

Baby Washington's biggest hit on Billboard's Hot 100 (#40; #10 R&B) was the elegant "That's How Heartaches Are Made," covered later by Springfield, Jerry Butler, and Bette Midler. As of publication, Washington is still active and performing, primarily on the East Coast.

Mary Wells (1943-1992)

"The Queen of Motown"
Rhythm and Blues Foundation 1989*

Mary Wells was trying to contact fellow Detroiter Jackie Wilson in the hope that he might consider recording a song she had written. Robert Bateman, an associate of Berry Gordy, intercepted Wells and her song. She was ushered into the studio to record it herself. "Bye Bye Baby" scored a #8 on the R&B chart and propelled Miss Wells into recognition as "The Queen of Motown."

Her subsequent collaboration with Smokey Robinson coincided with softening her vocal style from a blues-oriented sound toward a more pop orientation. Three smash hits resulted. In 1962 Wells strung together "The One Who Really Loves You" (#2 R&B; #8 U.S.), the calypso-oriented "You Beat Me to the Punch" (#1 R&B; #8 U.S.), and the two-sided gold record "Two Lovers"/"Operator" (#1 R&B; #7 U.S.).

Still just twenty years old, Wells followed with three more Top Ten R&B songs in 1963. Those successes proved to be merely preparation for the song that propelled her not only to the pinnacle of the Motown pantheon, but to international notice.

In the midst of the Beatles onslaught on the Pop Charts, Wells's "My Guy" battled to #1 on both the R&B and the Hot 100 charts. A #5 in the United Kingdom brought her fully to the attention of the Beatles, with whom she toured the U.K. in the fall of 1964, and with whom she became personal friends.

Miss Wells became disenchanted with the relative lack of remuneration she had received, and she desperately wanted to be able to provide financial relief for her mother from the hard life of domestic labor. The doubly-motivated Wells sued for and was awarded a release from Motown, but ensuing artistic mismatches with a series of record labels led to only a few subsequent successes.

After many years out of the music business, she had a surprising comeback with the disco hit "Gigolo" in 1982. Her equally surprising popularity with the Cholo subculture of the Mexican-American southwest provided some of the last highlights of Mary Wells's career. Smokey Robinson gave the eulogy at her funeral following her protracted bout with cancer.

Number One R&B
"You Beat Me to the Punch" 1962
"Two Lovers/Operator" 1962
"My Guy" 1964

Warner Williams (1930–present)

Warner Williams is a living legend representing the Piedmont blues style of guitar playing. In later life he became a headliner, but as a young man he appeared at JBF as a side man for Stan "the Man" Jackson and the Famous Moroccos, featuring Sammy Fitzhugh.

The liner notes of Williams's album *Blues Highway* (with harmonica player Jay Summerour) includes these words:

"Warner Williams is one of the greatest unsung heroes of the Piedmont blues—an Eastern seaboard style that incorporates fiddle tunes, ballads, country and popular songs, ragtime, and gospel. With a jaunty rhythmic finger-picked guitar style and an eclectic repertoire that ranges from blues to honky-tonk, (he) is an old-style community entertainer of national significance."

Larry Williams (1935–1980)

As a musician, Larry Williams was enthralling. As a person, he was appalling.

As a person, he was a thug, a drug dealer, plausibly a pimp, and the person who put the fear of God back into Little Richard. As a musician, he gave to the world such early rock and roll classics as "Bony Moronie," "Slow Down," and "Dizzy Miss Lizzy."

While on a visit back to his hometown of New Orleans in 1954, Williams, a competent pianist, found employment with Lloyd Price as a "valet" (bodyguard?) and then as a band member. During this time, Little Richard Penniman came to New Orleans to record at Cosimo Matassa's studio for Specialty Records. That session ultimately produced "Tutti Frutti'" and propelled Little Richard to stardom.

Penniman and Williams developed a friendship, which then led to a record contract for the latter. When Little Richard took his famous hiatus from rock 'n' roll in 1957,

Williams quickly was groomed to become his heir apparent at Specialty.

Williams often evoked Little Richard's frenzied style in his burst of releases. "Short Fat Fannie" (#5 U.S.) was a Williams original that in 1957 sold a million copies nationwide. Williams's handlers went for a slow song as his follow-up. "High School Dance" (#5 U.S.) was a Fats Domino-style stroller. co-written by Sonny Bono, who at that time was on the production team at Specialty Records. The next release was a Williams composition, "Bony Moronie" (#14 U.S.), another million seller.

Subsequent releases were not quite as successful commercially but became rock and roll classics as several reached the ears of other musicians, both in the United States and Europe. Williams's two biggest songs of 1958 were "Slow Down" (later covered by the Beatles and the Young Rascals) and "Dizzy Miss Lizzy" (covered by the Beatles).

As to that reference of Williams putting the fear of God back into Little Richard, that allegedly had to do with one cocaine-addled brother stiffing another. The furious Williams chased down Little Richard, pulled a gun on him, and appeared for all the world that he was going to blow his brains out. Apparently God spoke to Little Richard right then and there, as he quickly returned to church and the ministry.

Larry Williams's appearance at John Brown's Farm would appear to have been between the onset of his stardom in late 1957 and his 1960 incarceration for dealing narcotics. In 1980 he was found dead of a gunshot to the head. It might have been suicide, but given his long-standing underworld connections, that's just a guess.

Number One R&B
"Walk On By" 1964
"Reach Out for Me" 1964

Jackie Wilson (1934–1984)

"Mr. Excitement"
Rock and Roll Hall of Fame 1987
Rhythm and Blues Foundation 2002
Rolling Stone's 100 Greatest Singers #26

Jackie Wilson was a knockout artist, in both senses of the term. Elvis Presley and Michael Jackson are among the many admiring artists who were knocked out by his talent. And who knows how many hecklers were knocked out by the former Golden Glove boxer's fists?

Wilson generally channeled his passion into music, however. Whether the musical vehicle was a dramatic ballad or a kickin' rhumba, his brilliant tenor and athletic showmanship filled the platform.

Wilson grew up in depression-era Detroit, the product of a troubled father and a churched mother. He wobbled back and forth between those two sets of genes throughout his life. He wound his way through a gospel group, two stints in the juvenile justice system (where he learned to box), into fatherhood, and on to secular music.

In 1953, while still in his teens, Wilson was recruited by the Dominoes to fill the spot of the popular Clyde McPhatter, who was leaving to form his own group, the Drifters. During Wilson's tenure with the Dominoes, their biggest hit was the schmaltzy ballad "St. Therese of the Roses."

Wilson next was signed as a solo act at Decca Records subsidiary, Brunswick. His first release was "Reet Petite," a perfect showcase for Wilson's strengths, but stalling in its climb up the Hot 100 at #62. (Twenty-nine years later, based on the strength of a charming BBC claymation accompaniment, "Reet Petite" shot to #1 in the U.K. in 1986, two years after Wilson's death.)

That song soon was followed up by "Lonely Teardrops." Treat yourself sometime to the video of Wilson performing that chart-topping song on Dick Clark's "American Bandstand." Wilson's already-blazing magnetism flares up several notches when on the second chorus he drops from the staircase to the floor below onto his knees.

In 1961 Wilson had a career setback, to say the least, when someone (depending on which story you believe, possibly a jealous girlfriend) shot him twice. One bullet lodged inoperably near his spine, and the other took out a kidney. In 1963 the miraculously-mended Wilson took the big band twister "Baby Workout" to another #1 R&B (#5 Hot 100).

After a brief lull in popularity, Wilson recorded the 1967 song about which one person remarked, "Don't play this around the Statue of Liberty; she might start dancing." That song, "Higher and Higher," became one of Wilson's 46 R&B and 24 U.S. Top Forty hits.

Wilson died in 1984 after spending nine years in a coma as a result of an onstage heart attack. Later that year, with Quincy Jones standing at his side, Michael Jackson dedicated his "Album of the Year" Grammy for *Thriller* to Jackie Wilson.

Number One R&B
"Lonely Teardrops" 1958
"Baby Workout" 1963
"Higher and Higher" 1967

The Winstons

At the time the Winstons played JBF in the early 1960s, they were just a local band from nearby Washington, D.C. Their two primary achievements came later: one active, one passive.

First, a few years after the JBF venue closed, the Winstons' lone hit, 1969's "Color Him Father" (#2 R&B; #7 U.S.), won the Grammy Award in 1970 for its composer Richard Spencer as "Best Rhythm and Blues Song."

Second, through a remarkable series of events a four-measure (5.2 seconds) drum break from the flip side of "Color Him Father" has become what chronicler Nate Harrison described as "a six second clip that spawned several entire subcultures."

The B-side of "Color Him Father" is "Amen, Brother," an up-tempo instrumental version of "Amen" from the movie "Lilies of the Field." Halfway through there is a short drum break by percussionist G. C. Coleman. As "sampler" technology came into being, an enterprising fellow known as "Breakbeat Lenny" included the "Amen break" in a 1986 bootleg series for DJs called "Ultimate Breaks and Beats."

As a result, that four measure clip found its way into hip-hop and from there into the European dance music scenes. As those genres branched out, the "Amen break" became the rhythmic signature of such genres as big beat, breakbeat hardcore, drum and bass, industrial, and electronica. As a result "Amen, Brother," albeit just four measures of it, has become perhaps the most widely sampled record in history.

Arthur Conley

In 1967, when the members of our soul band first heard "Sweet Soul Music" by Arthur Conley (1946–2003), we knew immediately that we would add it to our repertoire. With its striking opening horn line, catchy melody, and harmonized backup vocals, it was right up our alley. Funny thing though, the song sounded familiar. Turns out we weren't the only ones to think so. So did Sam Cooke's lawyers.

Have a listen to Cooke's song "Yeah Man," then listen to "Sweet Soul Music." Oops. Too similar. The ensuing legal settlement required, among other stipulations, that Cooke was to be credited as a co-writer. (Apparently, no one was similarly provoked that the opening horn line also was "borrowed" from Elmer Bernstein's film score for the 1960 western movie "The Magnificent Seven.")

Wherever all the component parts of "Sweet Soul Music" came from, America wanted to hear it. Here's how that gold record transpired.

Arthur Conley had recorded a song, "I'm a Lonely Stranger," on Rufus Mitchell's Baltimore-based Ru-Jac Records. Otis Redding heard the jam, liked Conley's vocal, and eventually met Conley in early 1967. The two collaborated on reworking the thinly veiled cover of Cooke's song, and recorded it at FAME studios in Muscle Shoals, Alabama.

Upon its quick release, "Sweet Soul Music" scurried up the charts to a #2 spot in both the Pop and R&B charts. Redding's untimely death in December put an early end to what had promised to be a successful partnership. Conley soldiered on for a time, but the loss of his friend and mentor became increasingly evident. He did, however, manage to chart several more times, the most notable of which was "Funky Street" that reached #5 R&B in 1968.

AFTERWORD

Well, there you have it: the story of one little piece of property employed by America's premier abolitionist, developed by a prominent black fraternal organization, the IBPOEW, and embellished by rhythm and blues in its march toward becoming America's music.

John Brown's encompassing motivation was not merely to hasten the end of race-based slavery in America. At his mystical best, Brown foresaw and represented racial equality and fraternity. His principled integrity, in turn, galvanized the IBPOEW. Its primary goal for John Brown's Farm was that it become an educational site, one that would bring honor to Brown and foster impetus toward the shared dream of full societal integration.

Serendipitously, the IBPOEW's willingness to host dances on the property contributed to the broadening appeal of what once had been narrowly termed "race music." A common infatuation with rhythm and blues among America's youth cultivated relationships, touched hearts, and dismantled social barriers in ways that laws often do not—and perhaps cannot.

The ideals incorporated into our U.S. Constitution are yet to be fulfilled. Our long national march toward racial harmony remains stubbornly waylaid. But the hope lives on that we could learn not only to tolerate, but even to celebrate, our cultural differences. How awful it seems to me that our nation might press for a coercive one-size-fits-all societal homogenization that would deprive us of the precious and distinctive virtues of black culture.

Consequently, John Brown, the IBPOEW, and those early practitioners of R&B are to me heroes in our collective trek toward the full liberty that John Brown championed and that so many black people experienced at the dances and other family-oriented events at John Brown's Farm.

Perhaps you are ready, as I clearly have become, to cast your heart's ballot for John Brown's Farm as being America's foremost civil rights location. My hope is that you have at least caught such a fondness for the place that it might draw you there in the near future.

Toward that end I have a favor to ask, but not for myself. Please consider becoming involved in helping to make John Brown's Farm become a more widely-appreciated historical site. I have three prospects especially in mind.

First, perhaps you or someone you know attended those dances or the family-style holiday events. We would love to hear from you. Visit our interactive website at www.johnbrownsfarm.com and tell us your stories.

Additionally, although we have been able to uncover a few precious artifacts from the dances, it would be thrilling to learn that more still exist out there somewhere. Do you know of any posters, photographs, tickets, or other memorabilia from John Brown's Farm? If so, please contact us.

Second, we understand that several professional athletes and media talents are interested in filming black history documentaries. Well-qualified persons who are intrigued by this project are encouraged to contact us regarding the potential use of the videotaped interviews, photographs, documents, memorabilia, local re-enactors, and insights that we have gathered along the way.

Third, some readers may have the financial means or benevolent networks to help restore the dance hall to its former glory. If that describes you, those of us who already love this venue would have a ball working with you to make it everything that it could be.

Today, the old dance hall is in dilapidated condition, awaiting a historical rescue akin to that of the old farmhouse. The current owners are entirely on board toward that goal. The possibilities for decorating the auditorium with the accoutrements of rhythm and blues lie open to our collective imagination. For instance, South T. Lynn hopes to install a mannequin of Ray Charles at an upright piano, and one of James Brown doing the splits onstage. I can certainly imagine a vintage jukebox gracing the corner of the old dance floor or a reproduction of the ornate bar that once stood along the back interior wall.

Were such goals to be accomplished, how wonderful it would be to see busloads of school children come out on field trips. How exciting to have thousands of visitors to nearby Harpers Ferry and the Antietam Battlefield make the short swing over to John Brown's Farm.

How marvelous it would be to experience a repaired and restored auditorium where once upon a time, summer after summer, the auditorium's block walls and tiled floor witnessed the wiles of Eartha Kitt, the clowning of the

Coasters, and the drops of sweat falling from the brow of James Brown.

If you find such a vision dancing in your imagination, then let us hear from you. Let's make some more history—together.

BIBLIOGRAPHY

Cooke, George Willis, *Ralph Waldo Emerson: His Life Writings, and Philosophy.* Boston: J. R. Osgood and Company, 1882

Du Bois, W. E. B., *John Brown.* Philadelphia: G. W. Jacobs & company, 1909.

Larson, Kate Clifford, *Bound For the Promised Land.* New York: Random House Publishing Group, 2004.

Newton, John, *Captain John Brown of Harper's Ferry.* New York: A. Wessels company, 1902.

Oates, Stephen B., *The Approaching Fury.* New York: HarperCollins, 1997.

ENDNOTES

1. W. E. B. Du Bois, *John Brown* (Philadelphia: G. W. Jacobs & company, 1909), Kindle edition, 667.
2. Ibid., 608.
3. Ibid., 596.
4. Stephen B. Oates, *The Approaching Fury* (New York: HarperCollins, 1997), 172.
5. Du Bois, John Brown, 725.
6. Ibid., 715.
7. Ibid., 1386.
8. Ibid., 1387.
9. Ibid., 1409.
10. Ibid., 1279.
11. Ibid., 1285.
12. Ibid., 1327.
13. Ibid., 1435.
14. Ibid., 1111.
15. Ibid., 3103.
16. Ibid., 1157.
17. Ibid., 1163.
18. Ibid., 1171.
19. Ibid., 1504.
20. Ibid., 1821.
21. Ibid., 1830.
22. Ibid., 2088.
23. Ibid., 2097.
24. Ibid., 2653.
25. Ibid., 2656.
26. Ibid., 3144.
27. Kate Clifford Larson, *Bound For the Promised Land* (New York: Random House Publishing Group, 2004).
28. Du Bois, John Brown, 3133.
29. Ibid., 3139.
30. Ibid., 3210.

31. Ibid., 3279.
32. Ibid., 3637.
33. Ibid., 3445.
34. Ibid., 3459.
35. Ibid., 3469.
36. Ibid., 3467.
37. Ibid., 3656.
38. Ibid., 3703.
39. Ibid., 3448.
40. Ibid., 3594.
41. Ibid., 3713.
42. Ibid., 3720.
43. Ibid., 3742.
44. Ibid., 3717.
45. Ibid., 3727.
46. Ibid., 3746.
47. Ibid., 3750.
48. Ibid., 3794.
49. Ibid., 3805.
50. Ibid., 3810.
51. Ibid., 3856.
52. Ibid., 3891.
53. Ibid., 3907.
54. Ibid., 3920.
55. Ibid., 4134.
56. Ibid., 4175.
57. Ibid., 4176.
58. Ibid., 4357.
59. Ibid., 4356.
60. Ibid., 4221.
61. Ibid., 4496.
62. George Willis Cooke, *Ralph Waldo Emerson: His Life Writings, and Philosophy* (Boston: J. R. Osgood and Company, 1882), 140.
63. Du Bois, *John Brown,* 3133.
64. John Newton, *Captain John Brown of Harper's Ferry* (New York: A Wessels company, 1902), 271.
65. *Sun* (North Canton, OH), October 12, 1938.
66. In accepting the award, Marshall "expressed appreciation for the check of $2,000, which the Grand Lodge had given to him through (Robert) Johnson and Hobson Reynolds to support the costs of the various court cases." Marshall later became, in 1967, the first African-American Supreme Court Justice.

ACKNOWLEDGMENTS

A project of this scope and duration requires the help of so very many others to bring it to fruition. Since its inception more than eight years ago, one of the sad realities is that scores of delightful people who contributed to this book and who looked forward to reading it are no longer with us. Accordingly, I have often wished that I had discovered this historical gem a decade or more earlier in my life, but that was probably impossible. And I must grant that I am simultaneously, perhaps paradoxically, grateful that its comprehensive telling seemingly was conserved for me.

The liveliest bits of this story, though, were neither mine to witness nor essentially to tell. That privilege rightly belongs to those who participated in this "secret garden" where liberty has been so readily embraced over the course of more than one hundred and fifty years. That is to say, the best, and my favorite, parts of this book are the quotes from the now senior citizens who fifty plus years ago in their youth experienced the special joy that was John Brown's Farm.

Thus, my opening expression of gratitude goes out to the nearly two hundred such people, all strangers at first, who took the initial risk and often extensive time to tell me their stories. Without your first-hand accounts, this book would have been little more than a re-shuffling of a few, often inaccurate, newspaper articles. With your accounts, however, we have a precious primary source window into a truly remarkable time and place. Thank you, thank you, thank you.

That being said and deeply felt, there are a dozen or so people who blessed me extraordinarily, either by momentous revelations or continued kindnesses or both. I begin chronologically to the story and conclude with those putting the finishing touches on the book.

My beloved and beautiful wife, Judi Maliskas, deserves to go first. She has been a constant and encouraging suitable helper. More specifically, she has enabled me in this pursuit by trundling off to work on hundreds of weekday mornings while I sat home at the computer in my pajamas.

On many a weekend she enthusiastically accompanied me on a trip to interview someone or to visit some little black history museum. I do believe that if even now I said to her, "Honey, quick, I need to do an interview at the bottom of a fifty foot well," she would spring to her feet and grab an extension ladder and a flashlight.

But I had said that these expressions of thanks would be chronological. And they are. In a very real sense, Judi got this adventure started by choosing to shop for clothing at Hagerstown's L & L Classic Clothing, the consignment store where seven years ago we met…

Thanks, Wendell!

Wendell Greene. It was Wendell's original reference to John Brown's Farm that got me hooked and eventually obsessed. Wendell, you serve as a wonderful example to everyone out there that sharing our little stories with an interested listener can be literally life-changing. I appreciate that you have resisted giving me the "Yeah, right" look as I shared with you repeatedly and gullibly over the last five years, "The book is almost finished."

Reginald Keyes is the on-site manager for IBPOEW Lodge #278 in Hagerstown. I am grateful to him for providing years of congenial and ongoing help, and for entrusting precious family photographs to my care.

Leonard Harris, the sometime business associate of John Bishop, gave me invaluable help early in the process by verifying that John Brown's Farm wasn't just some dance hall that booked local bands. It was a major stop on the Chitlin' Circuit featuring the giants of rhythm and blues. Mr. Harris, I appreciate your gracious nature and continuous encouragement.

Leonard Cooper was one of my first interviewees and one of the best storytellers. He has become a dear friend through the course of lively interviews (some of them waaaay off topic!) and evenings of perusing his photo albums from back in the day.

"Captain" South T. Lynn, the long-time owner of the farmhouse and now the dance hall as well, opened his property to me, as well as his heart, when he gave to me the combination to the lock on the Kennedy Farm gate. He paid me the ultimate compliment in calling me, as he also calls himself, "a history nut." Thank you for honoring and preserving those two eminent buildings—the farmhouse and the dance hall. No one wants to see that property achieve its deserved recognition as a major American historical landmark more than you do.

The world's hardest-working octogenarian, Bo Morgan, bought the property from the IBPOEW. On those occasions when I can get him to put down some power tool and pick up the phone, he has been a delightful source of anecdotes, insight, and homespun wisdom. I am grateful that he protected the two historic buildings during his tenure and that he bequeathed to me several of the few remaining artifacts of the dances. I am even more grateful that there is always a smile in his voice when he talks to me about John Brown's Farm and about life.

George Rutherford, a patriarchal figure in the civil rights movement if there ever was one, repeatedly opened his home to me. He richly blessed me on one of those occasions by his inviting me to rummage around in old boxes and bags of memorabilia under his care. He also was entirely instrumental in staging a lovely event in Charles Town's Fisherman's Hall where we were able to video-record the testimonies of a number of former attendees of the dances at JBF.

LaVerne Bishop, the daughter of entrepreneur John Bishop and a staunch defender of his legacy, also has become a dear friend. She was gracious to entrust me with hundreds of photos and mementos from her father's various enterprises and to share prayer concerns and times of fellowship with Judi and me.

Winfield Parker has been a congenial fountain of knowledge about the typical activities on dance nights at the Farm, as well as being one of our resident experts concerning which artists performed there. He repeatedly made time for me, sometimes when not feeling well. We'll get that reunion concert scheduled yet, Winfield.

Gerald Barnett was kind to open his home to me unannounced on a day when I had been knocking on virtually every door in the neighborhood, trying to locate him. I particularly appreciate his painstakingly searching and reconstructing his early childhood memories of living with his Aunt Mame and Uncle Maynard on John Brown's Farm.

It has been an honor to get to know Dr. Peggy Coplin, a chief historian of the IBPOEW. I was initially impressed by her pluckiness to meet two strangers (my wife and me) in downtown Philadelphia. I was perhaps doubly impressed that at first she obviously was keeping her history of the organization tucked under her arm and away from my prying eyes. Once she deemed that I was trustworthy, from that day forward she has been a solid supporter of the project.

Thanks and kudos to Winston Pitman, not only for his fine original photography, but also for spending his cherished and rare free time cooped up for hours on end in a car with an extrovert.

Abigail Yeager is the world's finest proof-reader—in her price-range. Her remuneration consisted primarily of a free lifetime pass to all of America's Interstate Highway Rest Areas (I know, but please don't tell her; she thinks it's a heckuva good deal). All kidding aside, I love her like a daughter and was blessed to benefit from her expertise in this collaborative process.

Will Carpenter, whom I love like a son, graciously ventured outside his professional comfort zone of stylized suburban landscapes to do the painting for the book cover. As Professor of Art at Indiana Wesleyan University, his job description does not include reading other people's minds, as he often had to do in this case. Thanks, Will, for your artistic and personal sensitivity throughout the process.

Bethany Meier's illustrations added welcome zing to the book's visual appeal. I especially thank her for being willing to burn the midnight oil to get them all finished ahead of schedule.

Dr. Claudia Springer cleared her busy calendar to do the final editing of the manuscript in layout form. Thanks for your keen eye and longstanding friendship.

Kate Rader's professional editing and interpersonal expertise has been invaluable. Thank you for making all those tough calls, including pressing the need to reorganize some of the material; I realize that at such times I displayed all the cheeriness of a lion toward its tamer (growling included). Finally, thanks for staying excited about the revision process when sometimes I just wanted to be done with it already. The book wouldn't have been half as good without you.

A COMPANION VOLUME

One of my major "rabbit trails" in writing this book was an inquiry into how the music itself got to John Brown's Farm. That research led to a 25,000 word excursion into the history of American popular music leading up to rhythm and blues. We decided not to include that digression in "John Brown to James Brown." But be on the lookout for a forthcoming companion volume, a history of American popular music leading up to rhythm and blues entitled "The Music of John Brown's Farm."

Please contact the author at:
www.johnbrownsfarm.com